D0836386

BASIC INTERVIEWING
A Practical Guide
for Counselors and Clinicians

Edited by

Michel Hersen
Pacific University

Vincent B. Van Hasselt
Nova Southeastern University

LEA LAWRENCE ERLBAUM ASSOCIATES, PUBLISHERS
1998   Mahwah, New Jersey   London

Lawrence Erlbaum Associates, Inc., Publishers
10 Industrial Avenue
Mahwah, New Jersey 07430

Cover Design by Kathryn Houghtaling Lacey

Library of Congress Cataloging-in-Publication-Data

Basic interviewing : a practical guide for counselors and
clinicians / edited by Michel Hersen, Vincent B. Van Hasselt.
      p. cm.
   Includes bibliographical references and indexes.
   ISBN 0-8058-2369-7 (pbk. : alk. paper)
   1. Interviewing in psychiatry. I. Hersen, Michel. II.
Van Hasselt, Vincent B.
   [DNLM: 1. Interview, Psychological—methods. 2.
Psychology, Clinical—methods. WM 141 B311 1997]
   RC480.7.B37 1997
  616.89—dc21
  DNLM/DLC
  for Library of Congress   97-30349
                                  CIP

Printed in the United States of America
10 9 8 7 6 5 4 3 2 1

Contents

Preface

Basic Interviewing: A Practical Guide for Counselors and Clinicians is a reflection of the old adage that necessity is the mother of invention. For many years, the editors of this text have taught beginning level clinicians at the master's and doctoral levels. However, no extant text has proven to be satisfactory, including a number edited by ourselves. Some were too difficult; some were too doctrinaire; others were too simplistic; still others had missing elements. Therefore, in consultation with a number of our colleagues and friends in the field, we developed the present format.

Basic Interviewing is designed to answer some of the questions posed most frequently by graduate students who are beginning to learn how to talk to clients and extract critical data from them. Written in a direct, how-to style, it has no references in the bodies of the chapters, but suggested readings do appear at the conclusion of each chapter for students or instructors who wish to pursue questions further. After the initial overview chapter, there are 12 chapters that deal with the nuts-and-bolts issues faced by all clinicians that can be particularly vexing for the neophyte.

We expect that students and trainees in counseling psychology, clinical psychology, mental health counseling, social work, psychiatry, and other allied mental health fields will find this text helpful. Throughout, rich clinical examples facilitate pragmatic application of fundamental principles.

ACKNOWLEDGMENTS

Many people have contributed to the fruition of this book. First, we thank our contributors for sharing their clinical expertise with us. Second, we thank our assistants, Burt G. Bolton, Maura Sullivan, and Sue Warshal, for providing their technical expertise. And third, we thank Larry Erlbaum and his excellent editorial staff, who understood the importance of this project.

Michel Hersen
Vincent B. Van Hasselt

1

General Issues

Jan Faust
Nova Southeastern University

The clinical interview is the foundation for all aspects of the practice of psychology. It is the primary mechanism by which psychological services are formulated and delivered. While most novice therapists believe the purpose of the clinical interview is exclusively for diagnosing, it is much more encompassing than mere classification of symptoms. The interview is the initial contact between therapist and client and sets the tone for many facets of therapist–client interaction. It is this early contact that will dictate the quality of the therapist–client relationship including the level of patient commitment to evaluation and treatment.

An effective interview is similar to a tightly choreographed dance in that the therapist must help set the tempo and tone of initial session(s) and guide the interviewee through a series of intricate steps. These steps weave together communication of empathy, validation, and understanding while simultaneously extricating information pertinent to the task at hand. The purpose of the latter, information gathering, is to develop a basic coherent conceptualization, a clinical frame of reference by which to understand the symptoms presented. In order to achieve the goals of the interview, practice is crucial for the novice therapist. The interview experience, first through role play and then through direct client contact, facilitates integration of information gathering skills with therapy relationship building skills. Ultimately such integration enhances assessment and treatment planning. In fact, the majority of surveyed graduate students endorsed critiqued role-playing as the most important didactic for honing their interviewing skills and improving their clinical performance.

It is evident then that the goal of the clinical interview is multifaceted including, but not limited to, the detective work in establishing the parameters of the presenting problem and problem conceptualization. Other goals include developing a working relationship with the patient and setting the foundation for therapy. This chapter identifies those factors and issues that are critical to the goals of the diagnostic interview. They include basic skills such as knowledge, therapist communication ability, and people/social skills, and more advanced skills which include integrating the specific parts of the clinical interview (e.g., mental status exam, medical interview, social history, etc.). Finally, critical issues which significantly impact the clinical interview are discussed. These include referral source, interview setting, confidentiality, client diversity, and issues specific to novices.

GETTING STARTED/THE BASICS

Knowledge

Requisite tools of the interviewer include a comprehensive foundation in psychopathology and diagnostic classification. Additionally, the interviewer should be knowledgeable about the impact life events and experiences have on people, in general, and specifically with respect to their psychopathology. Therapists need to consider the influence of culture and ethnicity on symptom manifestation and attitudes toward treatment. As society becomes a more diverse amalgamation of cultures, ethnic heritages, and subcultural blends, the complexity of symptoms increases. The role of client diversity in interviewing is covered in greater depth later in this chapter.

Empathy/People Skills

Finally "people skills" frequently are deemed to be the most important aspect of the interview and client contact. These behaviors are commonly referred to as non-specifics of therapy: appropriate social skills, ability to relate effectively and comfortably with people, and ability to empathize and convey such empathy through validation and understanding of others' positions and plights. Empathy is derived from the Greek word *empatheia* which means *passion*. Passion, in this context, refers to the intensity of feeling one experiences in understanding another's feelings and cognitions. In fact, a literal dictionary definition states, "Understanding so intimate that the feelings, thoughts, motives of one are readily comprehended by another" (*American Heritage*, 1983, p. 428). The therapist needs to understand the client to this depth and then be able to convey such understanding to that client. Hence, there is an experiential aspect to empathy such that, in our field, empathy is the ability to perceive and understand a person's feelings "as if" the therapist were experiencing them and convey such experience to the client. The interviewer needs to listen to all client communications in order to understand the client. This includes not only words but body language, tone of voice, cadence of speech, and other non-verbal behaviors. Other non-specific behaviors such as timeliness to sessions and approach to the interviewer and staff are also important.

The interviewer's ability to empathize with the client's dilemma and associative experiences increases client trust. The client first experiences the therapist as an attentive listener and perceives the therapist as caring and concerned. Then the interviewee realizes that the therapist has the capacity to understand; hence, the interviewee is likely to perceive the therapist as competent and able to help. Finally, with the client's realization that the therapist understands, he or she experiences hope for symptom/problem resolution. It is also probable that through the interviewer's empathy and experiencing the problem "as if" he or she were in the client's predicament, the therapist's own comprehension of the problem increases.

The use of empathy and validation of the client's emotional and other experiences is a critical tool. Once the client trusts the interviewer, the latter is often able to extract information that has never been disclosed previously. Such information may be embarrassing or frightening to the client. Interviewers need to cautiously approach such topics so as not to divulge, verbally or behaviorally, their own fear, shock, or embarrassment.

There are many ways to convey empathy which affords interviewers the opportunity to select a style that is comfortable for them. Some interviewers rely more heavily on paralinguistic validation, such as facial expressions and body gestures, than on verbalizations. Other interviewers are more comfortable with linguistics than non-verbal modes of communication. However, most clinicians utilize some combination of both. Other validation strategies include tone of voice, timing and rate of comments and questions, and area of questioning. Although these latter strategies appear to be trivial, they may be critical in the communication of empathy. For example, a trainee was treating a very bright schizophrenic man in his early 40s. His only mode of transportation to therapy was the city bus. On one particular session day, it was raining relentlessly. The patient was determined, despite the rain, to attend therapy despite the fact that he would have to take the bus, transfer buses twice in the process, and walk four blocks to the psychology office. He arrived at the office, drenched and refused the offer by his therapist to dry off in the bathroom. It was evident that this client had some important work to do in session that day. However, instead of empathizing with the urgency by which the patient needed to see the therapist, the therapist could only focus on his wet state, encouraging him to dry off and assessing, periodically throughout the session, whether he was cold. Finally, after 30 minutes she terminated the session suggesting he go home because she was sure he had to be cold. So after taking three buses and walking several blocks in the pouring rain, which took him approximately 2½ hours, she sent the client home prematurely. Prior to this session, the client had good session attendance; however, after this session he missed the subsequent one.

For almost all beginning practitioners, the acquisition of diagnostic and nosology information is easily attainable. It is somewhat more difficult to learn the nuances of such classification schemes and to attain an understanding of symptoms as they are influenced by individual differences. These unique differences include the person's ethnic background, primary culture, and subcultures (e.g., drug culture). But through exposure and practice, eventually most clinicians-in-training can demonstrate competency in these areas. However, the educability of clinicians in people skills remains in question. The feasibility of "teaching" empathy has been extensively debated. Some professionals believe that empathy cannot be learned. Others disagree with this premise, professing that empathy skills can be acquired through instruction. Still others offer an alternative axiom between the two preceding premises. These individuals believe that some empathy skills can be taught while others remain partially innate. Irrespective of the theoretical position, if the novice therapist is having difficulty empathizing and conveying care and validation, measures need to determine wherein the problems lie. The burden is on the supervisor or professor to help the novice interviewer elucidate those issues and conflicts that hinder the caring response.

In addition to empathy, validation, and the caring response, there are other therapist "non-specific" variables that may contribute to the success of the interview. These include therapist's language, use of therapist's personality and experience, and therapist's ability to set limits/assertiveness.

Therapist Language

The quality of communication between interviewer and interviewee is an integral part to the success of the interview. In order to obtain a lucid diagnostic picture, it is important for the client to understand what is being asked of him or her. The clarity and comprehensibility of interviewer's questions will render accurate and pertinent information while facilitating a positive working relationship between interviewer and interviewee. Two linguistic problems of novice interviewers include use of jargon and non-familiar vocabulary. With respect to the former, novice therapists attempt to communicate with vocabulary heavily embedded with psychological mumbo-jumbo. For example, a graduate student asked her new potentially depressed client, "Are you experiencing any vegetative signs of depression?" Now the graduate student risked her client believing that he is either a vegetable or that the therapist is oddly concerned about his vegetarian dietary habits. In two other examples of the use of clinical jargon, novice therapists asked interviewees about a specific behavior, requesting a "functional analysis" of such behavior from one client, and the other therapist asked specifically about the patient's smoking and overeating habits with respect to Freudian oral stage development. The use of clinical jargon is a method by which the interviewer distances the interviewee from the real issues at hand. The interviewer may or may not do this intentionally. He or she may be uncomfortable with the material being discussed or with the new situation of therapy. Or the use of jargon may be the product of therapist naivete. In any event, most people will not understand the message/request being transmitted, but even if they do, the terms are often abstract rendering many different correct meanings. Finally, the client may become so focused on the sterile clinical term that the psychologically/affectual meaning of the term is lost. At best, the interviewer will spend an inordinate amount of interview time defining jargon for the client.

Similar risks are evident with respect to unfamiliar language. In speaking with clients, the therapist must account for their education level, intelligence, life experiences, and geographic locale. Vocabulary spoken by the therapist should match on these preceding variables. In fact, professionals have found that clients respond favorably to therapists use of clients' language. Limited swearing would be such an example. There are many terms and phrases specific to various geographic locales and subcultures. For example, in one part of the country the sentence "Momma is going to fix my bottom" means a spanking. But it is always useful to check the meaning of slang or cultural idioms even if the words are germane to the locale. A child from part of the country wherein "fix your bottom" means a spanking, utilized such a phrase in session. Inadvertently (and perhaps a bit serendipitously) in exploring further, the child was actually making reference to an incident of sexual abuse. Another example of geographic or culture-specific language includes the phrase "nervous breakdown." Most seasoned therapists have heard this term applied to every possible psychological problem (e.g., psychosis, depression, agoraphobia, fatigue). Practitioners not only need to exercise caution in their use of language but need to guide clients in specificity and clarity of their responses to prevent miscommunication.

The sensitivity of language does not suggest the client be "talked down to." The therapist needs to be respectful of the client. In one glaring example a graduate student said she knew a particular foreign language and could help another student therapist with her case, wherein the client's mother spoke limited English. The former's knowledge of the foreign language was actually limited to a few words interspersed with loudly and slowly spoken English. The client, in this case, was not deaf, nor intellectually impaired;

she was just not well versed in English. Hence, the therapist needs to monitor the tone, pitch, and volume of voice as well as the speed of delivery and the words chosen so as not to offend clients by "talking down to them."

Use of Therapist's Personality and Experience

Our profession has failed to reach a consensus as to the benefits of therapist self-disclosure. For many decades traditional professionals pontificated that therapist self-disclosure should not be used under any circumstances. Others believe there may be a limited use for self-disclosure. But in any situation wherein self-disclosure is advocated by professionals, all believe it should be used sparingly lest the client feel excluded and not understood or, worse yet, the client's therapy becomes the therapist's. Although this writer utilizes self-disclosure very sparingly, she has found that once disclosed the communication does not add or elicit new information to the interview nor does it enhance the relationship even when the client presses for disclosure. With respect to the latter, clients will often prod therapists for self-disclosure in an attempt to test the limits of the therapist or therapy (e.g., testing if therapy relationship vs. friendship). Amazingly, often when disclosures are made, the client will continue as if no response were given. There are rare occasions when it appears to add to the process such as therapist credibility (e.g., client is referred for a child problem and they are comforted to know that therapist has own children) or due to very noticeable physical changes in the therapist, such as pregnancy or illness/disability.

Pregnancy can raise a variety of issues for the client including those emanating from their own childhood as well as those that evolve directly from current treatment (i.e., loss of therapist to maternity leave). Personally, this writer is hesitant to suggest the use of self-disclosure to novice therapists as there is a tendency for new therapists to overuse the process. Overuse generally occurs when the therapist is lacking direction (i.e., is lost in session), knowledge, or self-confidence. These three variables are often operative for new clinicians, hence their propensity for self-disclosure when not necessary.

BEYOND THE BASICS

Once the therapist-in-training has attained proficiency in the basics, then the instruction of more advanced skills can be implemented. These include specific techniques focusing on structuring and beginning the interview; building rapport, empathy, and reflection; understanding the presenting complaints; obtaining a social history; extricating a medical history; conducting a mental status exam; writing the intake interview; addressing defensiveness; addressing the over-talkative client; ending the interview; knowing when to refer;

and identifying targets for treatment. There are variations in the use of interview components, and this list is not necessarily exhaustive. The way these components are integrated into the interview, and its disposition, will vary by individual client and by interviewer. In the beginning, novice therapists appear disjointed in their attempt to rigidly address all the components. They follow an information gathering formula instead of following the client. Students are so intent on the parts of the interview, that they overlook important information as well as critical aspects of the client–therapist relationship. With practice, many novice therapists are able to integrate the components of the interview without sacrificing the therapeutic relationship. Timing of questions improves such that novice therapists are able to ask questions at the relevant time and to follow-up on a particular of line of questioning in a timely manner.

All of these 12 areas can be covered in an hour to an hour and a half. The progression through the topics will depend on the type of client and his/her responsiveness/resistance to the interview. The amount of structure and type of questions will depend on the client's style. If the client is not very forthcoming in information, open-ended questions that require patient elaboration are a better choice than closed-ended questions that merely require a yes or no response. However, with individuals who are very talkative and tangential, direct and specific questions including a fair number of closed-ended questions are important in maintaining the structure of the interview. This strategy also enables the interviewer to obtain sufficient information within a reasonable amount of time.

Resistant and defensive patients may perceive frequent use of closed-ended questions as an interrogation, and their defensiveness will increase. Children and adolescents often become more resistant when therapists frequently ask closed-ended questions because it reminds them of their parent or teacher.

CRITICAL ISSUES AND THE INTERVIEW

Referral Source/Referral Questions

The interview is frequently guided by the referral source or referral questions. If a client is referred for treatment or evaluation by a specific person, it is important to determine the role the person has in the client's life and purpose for referral. The purpose for referral may be very general or the referral source will request specific information of the therapist. For example, the referral may be made by the person's employer either directly or indirectly by the client. As example, a general referral complaint includes determining problems impacting job performance. A more specific referral question might include determining factors impacting client's ability to cooperate with co-workers.

Irrespective of referral source, the therapist must clarify as specifically as possible the referral question or problem. In considering our previous example, once the therapist obtains appropriate consent to contact the employer, the therapist gathers as much information about the presenting problem from the employer as possible. It is important for the employer to specifically describe the problematic or concerning behaviors. The interviewer encourages the employer to be concrete and behaviorally descriptive. The interviewer attempts to solicit the frequency, duration, and components of the targeted behavior from the employer. It is helpful if the employer identifies antecedents (e.g., triggers) of the behavior as well as the consequences (others' reactions). For our example, the therapist has the employer behaviorally define and make operative the terms "problems," "job performance," and "cooperation." In addition, the therapist assesses when and where the behaviors occur, who was present, what did he or she do (consequences for the behavior), and the client's response to the consequences or responses of coworkers. In addition, the employer is asked to describe previous actions implemented to rectify/remedy the problems, etc.

Although referral sources are limitless, frequently identified sources include physicians/medical personnel, clergy, teachers/professors, employers, extended family members, judicial/law enforcement personnel, and other mental health professionals.

A pivotal caution must be heeded when working with referral sources. Indeed, at times, it is difficult to determine the consumer's or client's identity. Is it the person requesting the consultation (making the referral) or is it the targeted person (client)? At first glance, one would expect the client to be the consumer but, once services are implemented the referral sources often project an aura of entitlement given the fact that they made the referral, and the referral impacts them in some way directly (e.g., company productivity in the case of an employer referral, medical treatment in the case of physician referral). However, in almost all cases, it is incumbent on the therapist to secure permission from the individual who directly receives the service prior to releasing any information to the referral source. Confidentiality issues are discussed in more depth next.

Interview Setting/Environment. The setting in which the clinical interview is conducted will also often dictate how the client is approached. The setting, in part, helps determine the types of questions asked and the client's expectancy set. The latter refers to the client's expectations of the interview and of their own role in the process. One would expect very different interviewing behavior from an accused felon undergoing an involuntary court-ordered evaluation than from a clinic-referred mother distressed in response to the suicide of her teenager. In the first case, the client may either be very hostile and defensive due to the allegations or very compliant in an attempt to prove his or her innocence (whether innocent or not). Even in cases with similar settings, the interviewer can expect differences in the client's approach to the interviewing session. For example, within the same medical setting, the level of cooperation and the types of questions asked of the client can vary significantly if interviewing a patient from a psychiatric unit than one from a general nonpsychiatric medical unit. The degree of privacy can also differ with respect to setting thereby influencing both the interviewer and interviewee's behavior. For example, an at-home interview is also at-risk for a breach of privacy such that the threat of a family member inadvertently entering the private therapy setting is ever-present. Hence, the interviewer may feel restrained from asking specific family questions and the interviewee may be reserved in responding to the queries.

The type of setting dictates the variety of questions selected, the expectancies of the interviewee, and their responses: emergency medical care and crisis settings, outpatient medical or psychological offices, private consultation facilities, public mental health services (e.g., community mental health), inpatient nonpsychiatric medical, inpatient psychiatric, university/school counseling, prisons, and courthouses.

Emergent Care/Crisis Setting. This setting includes a variety of venues such as inpatient medical, nonpsychiatric emergency rooms, inpatient psychiatric facilities, crisis centers (walk-in and crisis phoneline), and jails. These clients are often brought to the center via a third party: relatives, friends, law enforcement personnel, emergency medical technicians (EMTs), individuals involved in involuntary commitment proceedings, the judiciary, and individuals involved in volatile or potentially volatile situations (e.g., hostages). Extreme or crisis behaviors expressed by individuals requiring emergent care include psychoses; organic brain syndromes, such as substance abuse, head injury, and neurological diseases; psychological disorders with a physical expression, such as panic disorder, disorders with vegetative symptoms including suicidal ideation, and medical diagnosis which create stress for the patient (terminally ill patients' attempts to gain control over their own death). An example of the latter includes an 18-year-old patient who had been diagnosed with a progressive invasive cancer of the bone. Odds of surviving this painful malignancy were extremely slim for the population as a whole and nonexistent for this patient given that he refused treatment. In a frantic attempt to obtain control over his own life, the patient reported that he would suicide via street drugs at the concert of his favorite musician. Although the moral obligation to intervene was murky at best (i.e., to "save" a young man from taking his own life knowing the cancer would painfully kill him in a few months), the legal obligation to involuntary commit to a crisis facility was indisputable. Police were contacted and involuntary admitted him to a facility for evaluation; he was enraged at nearly missing the concert. The interviewer at the hospital and this author worked together to diffuse the situation and enhance treatment.

Because the interview in this setting occurs under emergent conditions, the interviewer needs to be prepared to alter the content and style of the interview. First, patients in crisis settings often exhibit extremes in emotion and may be either quite agitated or depressed. One goal is to establish an adequate working relationship with these individuals to gain requisite information for diagnosing and emergent treatment planning. Hence, extensive histories of the patient's problem and early development are not the immediate goals. In fact, considerable time may be spent addressing emotional lability or volatile behavior of the client and engendering enough trust to gather pertinent information to render a temporary disposition. Clients with psychosis are usually terrified and confused by their symptoms and are in significant emotional distress. Many novice therapists believe that people with psychosis are "out of touch with reality" and impervious to pain. In actuality the opposite is quite true. Consequently, due to the clients' emotional functioning and time and space constraints of the emergency setting, a mental status examination to determine the clients' orientation to reality and their relevant thought processes may only be possible. In addition to the mental status exam, other information that is most accessible to the interviewer (and maybe the most important information) includes information from other individuals who are in close contact with the interviewee and behavioral observations of the client both before and during the interview. Hence, the goals of the interview change within these settings and may be limited to the determination of inpatient hospitalization.

Issues clinicians need to address include not only the client's cognitive (disorientation, disorganization) and emotional state, but also time constraints due to crisis environments or involuntary commitment laws, pressure from other medical personnel, and resistance due to many cases of involuntary commitment.

Psychiatric and Nonpsychiatric Medical Inpatient Settings. Interviews conducted within hospitals present their own special interviewing conditions. First, privacy may be hampered, especially in nonpsychiatric medical facilities. Often there are an insufficient number of interview rooms on medical wards, and the interview is forced to occur within the patient's hospital room. Depending on how mobile the patient is, one could potentially move to a less public environment, such as another part of the unit or an outside patio. If the patient is not mobile, then the interviewer is often forced to establish a working relationship and gather information within an extremely disruptive environment. It is not unusual for the interview to be interrupted by lab technicians drawing blood samples, nurses obtaining vitals, and physicians conducting rounds. Even housekeeping and kitchen personnel enter a patient's room several times a day, as well as visitors, hospital clergy, occupational therapists, physical therapists, and radiology. In addition, the interviewer may be confronted with a patient who is on medication with side effects (e.g., drowsy) or who is disoriented due to medical illness or by being in the hospital environment. In fact, professionals have developed diagnostic nosology to describe psychological disorientation as a result of hospital exposure (e.g., ICU Psychosis).

Other problems include patient confusion as to the interviewer's role in their treatment. Typically, the physician makes the referral, and the patient is unaware as to the reason for the mental health practitioner's intervention. The client assumes he/she is in the hospital for medical purposes and may not be sophisticated enough to understand the impact of the mind on body and the reverse. As a result, the client may be extremely resistant to engaging in the interview process. It is useful for the interviewee to introduce him/herself, explain the general nature of the consultation, identify the referral source, and indicate the interviewer's role in the patient's treatment. Due to resistance, it is imperative to acknowledge the client's medical condition and pain. Even if there is no known organic basis to the patient's medical symptoms, his/her subjective experience includes pain or other physical symptoms. This subjective experience needs to be validated, if not, the patient is likely to assume the interviewer believes the medical problem is "all in his/her head." It is best to approach the consultation for information gathering purposes without acknowledging the psychological issue. Several visits, if time allows, can reduce resistance and foster the client–interviewer relationship.

Determining the identity of the consumer is another difficulty on medical units. As previously described, the referral often originates with a primary physician treating the patient. His/her expectations for the patient's behavior or reaction may be incongruent with the client's expectations or psychological state. For example, a little girl with severe burns on her body was having a difficult time adjusting to extremely painful debridement treatments. Her surgeon requested a consult to assist her in adaptation and coping, because her behavior was interfering with treatment (e.g., flailing, screaming, etc.). Intervention helped her compliance with medical treatment and allowed her opportunity to express her feelings through crying and self-statements. Her ability to express emotions about her burns and treatment was an integral part of her coping; however, the surgeon, who wanted a compliant patient, unrealistically perceived any negative expression of feeling to be inadequate coping. The psychologist's dilemma was then to determine the consumer of services: Was it the little girl who was appropriately expressing affect and coping or the referring physician who was not obtaining the outcome, a quiet motionless child, he desired? Morally, for this author, there was no question as to the consumer's identity and because costs of psychological services are borne by patients, legally the little girl and her family were the consumers. This becomes a tricky balance in providing services on medical units between the many personnel involved and patient considerations which are often in conflict. At the same time, the interviewer does not wish to alienate the source from which the referral is made. Good skills in diplomacy are necessary on these units.

Finally, with respect to both nonpsychiatric and psychiatric inpatient units, time is a limited commodity. Often the patient is in the hospital for a short time, thereby restricting the amount of time available to assess and render decisions/recommendations. It is not unusual for patients to be imminently discharged and to have a medical professional request a "last-minute" assessment. A psychologist-psychiatrist team requested a discharge evaluation for an adolescent patient whom they were uncomfortable releasing from the hospital. The therapist was given an hour to complete an evaluation and render an opinion. Unfortunately the adolescent was extremely resistant to a formal interview. Because the adolescent prided herself on her artistic and creative ability, the therapist administered the Thematic Apperception Test. This instrument requires the client to create a story from a series of pictures. The clients' stories contained themes of death, suicide, hopelessness, and unavailable support (absent family members). As the client warmed up to the process, she was better able to tolerate the interviewer's queries and admit that she might commit suicide once discharged from the hospital.

School/University Setting. Interviews within the educational system dictate special considerations. Historically, problems typically encountered in academic/university counseling centers have been related to school/academic performance, leaving home/separation issues, and roommate difficulties. As society and educational systems have grown more complex, so too have the problems presented in traditional counseling programs. Examples of recent issues include eating disorders, date rape, and drug and alcohol problems as well as sexual orientation and experimentation issues. In addition to those counseling centers serving the needs of the residential student, the commuter student population, especially in big cities, has grown. Hence, the spectrum of psychopathology in these counseling centers often reflects disorders that are observed in the metropolis at large. Historically, school counseling centers are not established for individuals with chronic and acutely severe symptoms such as psychotic or suicidal behaviors. These cases are typically triaged to facilities designed to service such needs. Nor is the focus of counseling centers on long-term care; the number of sessions may be restricted. As a result, the interviewer should not engage clients in a comprehensive battery of tests; in fact, time may not allow for an in-depth history. Because problems often presented at these centers tend to be less severe, the interviewer may not need a comprehensive interview.

The interviewer is often confronted with a delicate ethical issue of confidentiality. It is common for rules in student handbooks to conflict with ethical codes of confidentiality. Hence, in many institutions, those psychological problems that can interfere significantly with student work and behavior are violations of student conduct codes and are to be reported to the appropriate university administrative committee. In fact, in some university settings, counselors are to report inpatient hospitalizations to a representative of the academic program of the hospitalized student. Not only does the administrative referral conflict with ethical principles of mental health professionals but are a breach of statutory law. There are many potential risks for the student client in reporting his/her utilization of mental health services to academic administration, including suspension, probation, and letters in permanent files. These administrative actions may potentially follow students when they apply for jobs and for admittance to professional and graduate schools. Once students are aware of the potential impact psychological services have on their privacy and academic standing, their resistance may increase, and it may be difficult to garner all information necessary for an adequate conceptualization and treatment plan. Further, caution should be exercised in ensuring complete disclosure of limits of confidentiality to the client at the outset while exercising extra precaution in privacy (i.e., limit the detail in session notes).

Outpatient Psychological and Medical Facilities. The interviewer is exposed to a fuller range of psychopathology on outpatient units than in crisis facilities. Clients with both mild and severe psychopathology are served in an outpatient facility. While those with psychosis, suicidal ideation, and organic brain dysfunction may be seen in outpatient facilities, they are not in crisis significant enough to warrant hospitalization. Consequently, the interview in these settings will be different from that implemented in crisis settings. First, goals of the interview are different such that the form of therapy has been selected (e.g., outpatient treatment). In addition, there is generally no mystery for the client as to the purpose of the interview, unlike medical units and perhaps school settings. Consequently, there is less resistance during the interview process; this is particularly true in the case of self-initiated referral. Therefore, the interviewer will have more time and less trouble in conducting a comprehensive interview. The interviewer's goal should be to gather relevant information about the symptoms and its context in order to develop a conceptualization of the problem. Once in place this conceptualization will be the blueprint for further intervention, if warranted.

The interview in this setting is typically guided by the problems and the fortitude of the client. For example, if the client is demonstrating significant anxiety while discussing her recent rape, it would be inadvisable to pursue questioning about details of the assault. Generally, in outpatient settings, the interviewer is afforded the luxury of time to establish a working relationship and allow the patient more latitude in setting the tempo of therapy.

Other issues that arise in outpatient settings include a greater exchange of information between therapist and client than one would see in other settings. Outpatient clients are inquisitive about their role in the treatment process and therapist's expectations. In addition, questions about fees, length of time for treatment, their diagnosis (e.g., do others have it?), and possible types of treatment are frequently posed by outpatient clients. These questions need to be addressed candidly and swiftly as the interviewer's forthright answers enhances trust. For example, if a therapist tells a client with a longstanding eating disorder that she expects treatment to last no longer than 6 weeks and 12 weeks have already elapsed, the client is likely to prematurely terminate treatment. There is no crystal ball to determine the length of treatment especially because success depends in part on individual differences. It is prudent to respond to length of treatment questions by delineating the difficulties in projecting a specific date for treatment termination. It is also useful to explain that unlike general physicians who can prescribe medications to eradicate an organic problem, psychological intervention does not work in this manner. This latter explanation is particularly relevant given the number of clients seeking outpatient services who assume psychological treatment is delivered similarly to medical treatment. After completing the interview it is also useful to give a ballpark estimate for length of treatment; this should be based on treatment outcome literature. If an interviewer cannot approach a best estimate for length of treatment it is useful to offer a temporary goal: "Let's give it 8 weeks and reevaluate where we've been and where we're going."

After the initial interview, the interviewer needs to give some feedback and recommendations to clients, even if clients do not request such information. It is important to summarize chief complaints and the manner in which they interfere with client functioning. Interviewers may give clients terms to enhance their understanding of their symptoms but not necessarily a clinical diagnosis. For example, if a client is experiencing shortness of breath, fear of dying, fear of leaving home without a safe person, etc., it would be much more useful to the client to learn he/she is experiencing overwhelming anxiety as opposed to agoraphobia. However, if the client requests a specific diagnosis, it would be prudent to disclose this directly. By addressing concerns about diagnosis directly, the interviewer is helping the client develop a realistic perspective for treatment, engendering hope, and decreasing the client's isolation by explaining others share their disorder.

Jails, Prisons, and Courthouse Settings. These settings are typically adversarial. Depending on the reason for referral, the interviewer may be confronted with interviewees who range from being very resistant to overly solicitous. Privacy may be hampered when conducting these interviews as fellow inmates, guards, attorneys, guardians-ad-litem, etc., may be within listening proximity to the client. The interviewee's motivation to be truthful, forthright, and forthcoming with information is varied given the perceived referral question. Because these evaluations are often court mandated, confidentiality of records does not apply. Interviewers need to be frank with respect to their role in the interviewers' lives and the limits of confidentiality.

It is important for the interviewer to look for consistencies in behavior and self-report when conducting these interviews. Furthermore, interviewing and observing other individuals in the interviewee's life is important to determine the veracity and amount of information obtained about the interviewee. For example, referrals concerning parental custody involve the court evaluator interviewing both parties vying for custody as well as other people involved in the child's lives (e.g., guardian-ad-litem, the child protective agency worker, the child's therapist, stepparents, grandparents). These interviews are important to verify information and behaviors noted in the parents' interviews. It is obvious that parents suing for custody desire to present their best behavior to the court evaluator. Further, each side may attempt to malign the other to enhance its chances of "winning" custody.

In other court cases, the interviewer may be restricted by time. There is not the flexibility as there is in other settings. This is particularly true as the interviewer attempts to coordinate his/her schedule with others at the jail/prison (e.g., attorneys). Further, if there is an emergency hearing, the interviewer may have very limited time to interview the interviewee and make recommendations to the court. An abbreviated history and mental status examination are often the only tools available to the interviewer in this situation.

CONFIDENTIALITY AND DUTY TO WARN AND PROTECT

Confidentiality is one of the most critical components to the practice of psychology. Without the therapist's ability to maintain the privacy of clients' communications and records, effective evaluation and treatment are not possible. Confidentiality is so important that it is protected by the American Psychological Association, other professional associations, and by state law. It is imperative that clinicians from all areas (psychology, social work, marriage and family therapists, etc.) become familiar with the laws in the state that govern their particular branch of practice.

As previously mentioned, confidentiality can be a tricky process and must be handled with care. It is always best to err on the conservative side (if in doubt, do not release information without written consent or court order).

Again, the setting in which the interview takes place, as well as the referral source, may impose different amounts of pressure on the interviewer to stretch the limits of confidentiality. Caution should be exercised in releasing information to anyone but the client and, except for unusual circumstances (e.g., court-ordered evaluations), the one who is interviewed is the client.

Legal limits of confidentiality need to be delineated at the beginning of therapist–patient contact. In most jurisdictions a breach of confidentiality is legal when it protects the physical welfare of others (i.e., suicide, homicide, child abuse), although disclosure of such information may differ by state. With respect to homicidal ideation, a variety of maneuvers, such as the following, are employed: therapist has a duty to warn an intended homicide victim, therapist must have the patient committed to a facility, and appropriate authorities (i.e., police) must be notified of the client's plan.

Students sometime question the practice of informing parents, at the outset of therapy, the limits of confidentiality in reporting communications of child abuse to appropriate governmental authorities. A lower rate of abuse disclosure has not been observed in families informed of confidentiality limits than those families not informed. It was discovered, however, that parents, who are initially instructed of the obligation to report suspicion of abuse to the authorities, are more likely to "accept" the abuse report and continue in treatment than those not informed. They are not likely to feel betrayed when fully informed of the limits of the law and of the legal obligations, at the beginning of treatment. Interviewers should also be aware of limits of confidentiality with minors and with those who have legal authority to access children's medical/psychological records. There are many clinicians who will not work with children unless the guardians agree to protect the privacy of child records. However, if the parent ultimately desires the records, he/she can legally access the records without permission of the child client. In some states, children may obtain psychological services without the permission of the guardian/parent. The number of sessions, the specific treatment conditions (e.g., emergent or not), and the age at which a minor can enter treatment independently, vary with state law.

Given the number of people who could potentially access records (i.e., whomever the client releases the information to, third-party payers, those issuing court orders, etc.) it is prudent to take care when writing in the record. It is wise to pretend you have a judge, a cadre of attorneys, insurance company personnel, physicians, an ex-spouse, teachers and guidance counselors, and others relevant in the client's life (past, present, and future), looking over your shoulder while you write in the record. For example, during training, a therapist was treating a child for Munchausen's by Proxy. The school needed information about this child to help plan her educational program. Concurrently, the patient's mother was requesting a treatment summary for her own records. In order to protect the child, we attempted to dissuade her from having such a summary. Prior to sending the summary to the school, the therapist summarized the information over the telephone for the guidance counselor and told her a report would be sent but not to release it to the mother because it could potentially interfere with treatment. The counselor said not to send her the report because law dictated that an external therapist's report would become part of the school record which was then subject to release to the parent. Although the mother had not requested school records, it was imminent because she had consented to release the psychological report to the school. Although one must be careful when writing in charts, it is important to provide enough detail to facilitate treatment planning, especially should the client transfer to another agency or practitioner or need services in the future. Chart notes should be written to facilitate client's reimbursement from the insurance company, and to address any disagreement or malpractice claim that arises in conflict over services rendered. Some states have passed legislation dictating the contents of sessions notes (date, time, place, issues addressed, disposition, plans for future treatment, etc.). Finally, client documentation needs to be kept under lock and key.

Diversity Issues

As mentioned previously, the client brings to the interview a previously determined context, including race, cultural background, gender, age, physical disabilities, and religion. Although historically the literature is sparse in examining the impact such factors have on evaluation and treatment, in recent years professionals have begun to emphasize unique characteristics the consumer brings to the mental health service. This is particularly important given the increasing number of minorities who are being referred for treatment. The race variable is a complex one, because it includes different cultural heritages, experiences, and value systems. For example, the term *Black* was previously reserved for those individuals with dark skin tone, irrespective of ancestral roots. The term was applied universally without considering the individual's culture. There are black-skinned individuals from Europe, Africa, the Caribbean, and Cuba. There are some significant distinctions within subgroups (e.g., between southern African American families and northern African American families; Boyd-Franklin, 1989). These distinctions are important because the context from which the individual originates varies from the culture and is not solely determined by skin tone. But people of color do have common experiences such as discrimination and racism. Boyd-Franklin (1989) discussed the myth of the Black Family, indicating that such an entity does not exist given the "great diversity of values, characteristics, and lifestyles that arise from such elements as geographic origins, level of acculturation, sex, education, religious background, and age . . ." (p. 6).

Clinicians need to be sensitive to diversity issues not only for the purposes of understanding the clients' symptoms as manifested in their subcultural context, but also to enhance the interviewer–interviewee relationship. For example, with respect to the former, it is not unusual to observe conflict between first-generation American adolescents and their Cuban parents concerning issues of separation and growing up (e.g., dating). The Cuban family is likely to merge several generations, under one roof or within a large complex of attached or adjacent homes. This integration of families may appear as pathological enmeshment to the novice non-Hispanic therapist; however, such generational merging is traditional and historically considered a necessity. Problems emerge for families from two different cultures when there are conflicting values and the lack of flexibility to address such conflict. Therapists need to investigate the meaning of the client's background, ethnicity, race, and other diverse characteristics that can impact symptom presentation. The clinician's level of comfort with a diverse range of characteristics will dictate how he/she handles these issues.

Diversity issues can affect the client–interviewer relationship. If the client has experienced much discrimination and racism by Caucasians, and the interviewer is Caucasian, it is likely that trust of the interviewer will be impaired. In addition, novice therapists are often uncomfortable in interacting with individuals with different characteristics. Problems with client diversity may be the result of failure in empathy, lack of life experience and exposure, ignorance, and anxiety. For example, several young trainees from wealthy families and lacking in many life experiences had difficulty early in their training in understanding their clients' inability to attend sessions. These clients were poor; hence, they could not afford a babysitter, gas money, etc. One of the clinicians was incredulous to learn that her patient, who attended every weekly session for 9 months, had been homeless and living in a van for the duration of therapy.

Age is another client characteristic to consider when approaching the interview. Although beyond the scope of this book, the interview proceeds much differently with children than with adults. The interview also varies by age of adult. Older adults typically experience more physical problems than younger adults; as a result, the interviewer must disentangle the impact organicity has on symptom presentation. Interviewers need to refer these clients to appropriate medical personnel to rule out potential physical problems that mimic psychological ones. At the very minimum, all clients prior to intake should have a medical examination. In addition, interview may proceed at different rates given the age and level of impairment (if any) of the elder interviewee.

Data have not consistently detected age differences in response to treatment nor to drop-out rates. And although the literature demonstrates that more women than men seek psychological services, overall, once enrolled in treatment, men and women are equally responsive to intervention. There also has been considerable debate as to the impact of therapist gender on treatment outcome. Although some argue that treatment success depends on the match between therapist and client on gender, empirical data have not supported this premise. There are some unique situations that would dictate the preselection of a therapist by gender such as a severely traumatized client who had been raped or exposed to domestic violence.

Issues Specific to Novices

Novice therapists tend to give advice, to make judgmental statements, and to have problems with empathy. Many new therapists were parented with a sense of responsibility to help. Consequently, the urge to fix the problem is often overwhelming for the new therapist who is then prone to give advice. The problems in giving advice are multifaceted. First, advice evolves from the interviewers' own experiences and perspective and not the interviewees. Such advice may conflict directly with the client's moral and value system.

Second, typically when clients seek services they have already attempted many potential solutions to their problems, especially the obvious ones. It is likely then that the advice a therapist imparts to a patient includes a course of action the client already unsuccessfully attempted. Such advice can increase the client's sense of hopelessness and frustration; furthermore, the credibility of the therapist may be hampered by previously attempted solutions.

Third, beginning therapists often have difficulty in relinquishing their own moral and value system which interferes with the ability to understand and validate the client's orientation to life. During the role-play portion of an interviewing course, a student was assigned the role of a young single college student who was pregnant but ambivalent about carrying out the pregnancy. The student playing therapist, in this situation, had great difficulty with objectivity and as hard as he tried, he repeatedly channeled the interviewee toward advising her not to choose an abortion. The therapist's goal is to allow the client to explore the problem within his/her own context.

New therapists also struggle with either asking too many superfluous questions or not exploring important sensitive areas. With respect to the former, trainees can be distracted by "detective work" of symptom presentation and diagnosis and assume the role of interrogator rather than facilitator. The interviewer is intent on finding out as much as possible about the individual without regard to the client's own understanding and context of the symptoms. Yet other trainees experience difficulty in their avoidance of socially sensitive topics. Ironically, these therapists believe it is impolite to explore particular areas of clients' lives. For example, one novice therapist was interviewing a boy with post traumatic stress who had been sexually and physically abused by his father. Further, prior to the parents' divorce,

6 months prior to treatment, the mother reported a history of domestic violence between herself and the client's father. Approximately 2 months after the father had been arrested and imprisoned for the child abuse, the mother came to session with a black eye, painstakingly covered with make-up. The mother did not offer an explanation for the injury nor did the clinician query her as to its origin. The clinician admitted to feeling embarrassed for the mother. Unfortunately the information concerning the origin of the injury had potentially far-reaching implications, including the safety of the children. Perhaps the mother was repeating her pattern of affiliating with violent men, exposing her children to possible harm. The therapist addressed the black eye at the next session and discovered that the client and her children moved to her mother's and adult brother's residence. The drug-abusing brother had struck the client. So in fact this information was crucial to the protection of the children (and mother) and their treatment.

SUMMARY

The purpose of this chapter was to delineate goals of the clinical interview and to introduce the requisite tools for accomplishing these interviewing objectives. Finally, a variety of critical issues that can impact the interview and its process was presented. Case examples were provided throughout the chapter to provide a richer and more meaningful context for the beginning interviewer.

REFERENCES

American Heritage Dictionary (1983). *The American heritage dictionary of the English language.* Boston: Houghton-Mifflin.

Boyd-Franklin, N. (1989). *Black families in therapy.* New York: Guilford.

SUGGESTED READING

American Psychiatric Association (1994). *Diagnostic and statistical manual of mental disorders (4th ed).* Washington, DC: Author.

American Psychological Association (1992). *Ethical principles of psychologists and code of conduct.* Washington, DC: Author.

American Psychological Association (1994). Guidelines for custody evaluations in divorce proceedings. *American Psychologist, 49*(7), 677–680.

Evans, D. R., Heran, M. T., Uhleman, M. R., & Ivey, A. E. (1993). *Essential interviewing (4th ed).* Pacific Grove, CA: Brooks/Cole.

Gaw, A. C. (Ed.). (1993). *Culture, ethnicity, and mental illness.* Washington, DC: American Psychiatric Press.

Hersen, M., & Turner, S. M. (Eds.). (1994). *Diagnostic interviewing (2nd ed)*. New York: Plenum.

Rodriguez, O. (1987). *Hispanics and human services: Help seeking in the inner city* (Monograph No. 12). New York: Fordham University Press.

Swenson, L. (1997). *Psychology and law for the helping professions.* Pacific Grove, CA: Brooks/Cole.

2

Beginning the Interview and Confidentiality

Maureen Kenny
Florida International University

The first interview is generally the initial contact between client and therapist and sets the stage for the relationship. This chapter advises the practitioner about how to initiate the interview in a variety of clinical settings with regard to structure, conduct, and how to develop the therapeutic relationship. It approaches the initial interview in a straightforward and comprehensive manner. What is presented is not intended to be a "cookbook" of interviewing, but rather a guide to certain techniques. The ethical and legal issues of confidentiality, which are critical to any therapeutic relationship, are also examined. Further, this chapter explores the importance of a sense of trust between client and therapist.

BEGINNING THE INTERVIEW

The initial interview provokes anxiety in both the client and the beginning therapist. The two main goals of the first interview are to make the client feel comfortable and to obtain all the necessary information for treatment planning and initiation. To accomplish both these goals, the therapist should be relaxed and skilled. If clients do not feel comfortable (i.e., understood, empathized with, and respected), they will not disclose requisite information that the therapist needs for treatment.

Where does the client's anxiety about therapy come from? Many clients are ambivalent about seeking help. Clients may know they need help but may also recognize that this involves opening painful wounds. Some people believe that seeking mental health services is a sign of weakness or craziness. In addition, some clients do not know what to expect. The media's portrayal of mental health professionals is often intimidating and can instill fear.

The therapeutic relationship, if handled and conducted professionally and ethically, is unlike any other relationship the client will ever experience. Friends, in an effort to help, tell friends what to do and give unsolicited advice. They often judge or criticize one another. And many clients have suffered at the hands of parents who believed they were helping (i.e., "This hurts me more than you."). But in the therapeutic relationship, there is no judgment. The client is accepted unconditionally. It may take the client some time to understand this unconditional acceptance.

GREETING THE CLIENT

Keep in mind that clients must feel comfortable with the therapist. It is not as important what therapists say, as how they act. They must convey a sense of concern, empathy, and caring about the client. Therapists should respect the client, which begins with addressing clients by their last name (e.g., Mr. or Mrs. Smith). Wait for the client to invite being called by the first name. Therapists should shake hands with the client, just as they would if they were meeting anyone for the first time (see Fig. 2.1).

When greeting a client, therapists should make it clear what they prefer to be called. Some practitioners like to use their title (e.g., Dr. Smith). Others, perhaps those working with children, desire to be called by their first name in an attempt to lessen the professional distance. In addition, therapists should indicate what position they hold at the agency. For example, if the therapist is an intern and under supervision, this should be made clear to the client (e.g., "Hello Ms. James. I am Ms. Parker and will be conducting your interview today. I am a psychology graduate student who is completing my training here at the community mental health center. This means that I am under the supervision of a licensed practitioner."). The therapist should also relate any information about training or expertise that might be of interest to the client (e.g., "I understand that you recently lost your husband. I have extensive experience working with grief victims. I trust that I can help you too.").

UNDIVIDED ATTENTION

The therapist attempts to create a safe, comfortable, and nonjudgmental space for the client. During interview time, the focus should be completely on the client. To reduce distractions, do not allow any interruptions or breaks

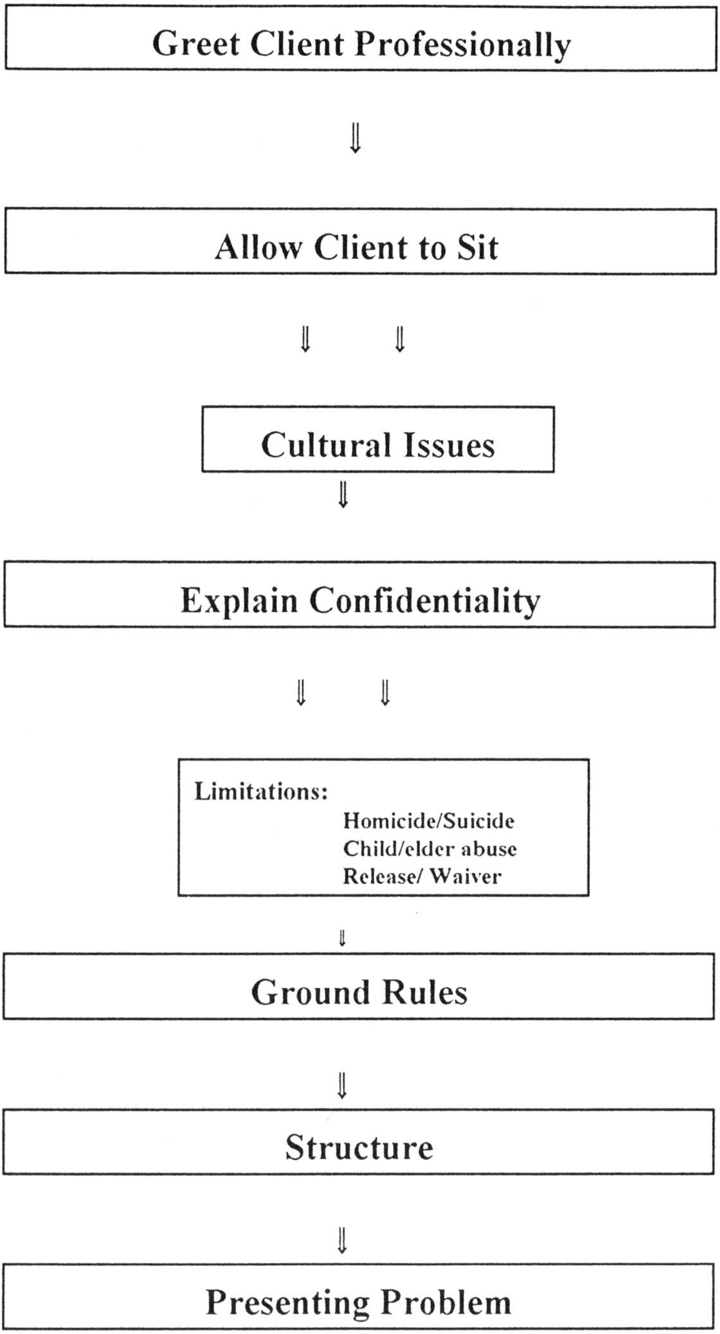

Greet Client Professionally

⇓

Allow Client to Sit

⇓   ⇓

Cultural Issues

⇓

Explain Confidentiality

⇓   ⇓

Limitations:
Homicide/Suicide
Child/elder abuse
Release/ Waiver

⇓

Ground Rules

⇓

Structure

⇓

Presenting Problem

FIG. 2.1. The initial interview.

in the session. Place a "Do Not Disturb" sign on the door, put the phone on hold, and turn a beeper to its silent, vibrating mode. A therapist who takes a phone call during a session communicates to the client that there is something more important to do. The client may feel shut off while waiting for the therapist's attention and may have difficulty returning to the material being discussed before the interruption.

Therapists should allow clients to take whatever seat they desire. Therefore, a variety of seats should be available, each differing in its distance from the therapist. A therapy room set up with several chairs and a small couch would be ideal. The therapist's chair should be easily identifiable, maybe by its size or lushness, so that the client will not accidentally take that chair.

Therapists should be culturally sensitive to the needs of their clients. For example, a class demonstration showed a great variability in the students' choice of physical proximity to the therapist, which seemed to relate to their cultural background. In addition, some therapists desired to be physically closer to the client. In one case, a therapist edged her chair closer and closer, and the client kept pulling back. This "dance" continued until the client was almost out the door! Although the therapist's comfort is critical, it is more important that the client feel relaxed.

STARTING THE SESSION

Once seated, how does the therapist begin the interview? Some like to engage in "chatter" with the client before moving into the "official interview." Asking if the client had difficulty finding the office or making some comments about the weather can relieve some of the initial anxiety and "break the ice." However, such niceties should not stall the beginning of the interview. Remember, the purpose of meeting with clients is to help them make sense of their difficulties.

The first session is generally conducted differently than those that follow. The therapist asks questions and gathers information. The therapist is much more active in deciding what to talk about than in subsequent sessions. This should be explained to the client at the outset. Therapists should make it clear to clients that in later sessions, the agenda will be up to them.

OPENING STATEMENTS

There are several opening statements for the interview that seem to work: "Tell me how I can help you," "What's been on your mind lately?," or "What has been happening that led to your coming here?" These broad-based questions should encourage clients to open up about why they are seeking psychological help. They provide an opportunity for them to describe their problem. Beginning the interview with more specific questions may increase their anxiety level.

However, it may be necessary to ask the client specific questions to get started. Some clients need to be guided through the interview. A vague question, such as "Tell me about yourself," is too ambiguous for some clients. A more helpful question would be, "Tell me about your family while growing up," or "What is your relationship like with your siblings?" This provides the client with a starting point.

GROUND RULES

During the first session it is essential to set *ground rules*. Although this term has been used by many theorists to incorporate many different concepts, its most basic meaning is those rules by which the therapy will operate. This refers to the scheduling and canceling of appointments, the fee structure, length of sessions, and what is expected of the client during the hour. Customarily, there are few rules that govern the client's verbal behavior once inside the therapy room; the client is free to discuss anything. However, one common rule implemented for the safety of clients dictates that they cannot hurt (physically) themselves or the therapist, and they can expect the same in return. Whatever the rules, the therapist should make them clear to the client at the outset. Examples include: "If you are unable to attend a session, please call the office 24 hours in advance, otherwise you will be charged," or "Our sessions will be every Wednesday at 5:30 pm and will last 45 minutes. Your copayment is expected at the end of the session. If you have to cancel, please call as soon as you can. Also, if you miss three consecutive appointments, we will have to discuss termination."

THE PRESENTING PROBLEM

In some cases, the therapist receives some information about the client prior to the initial interview. This is usually demographic information and what is termed a *presenting problem*. The presenting problem is usually what has led the client to seek help. It may or may not be the most important issue, although other issues may become more apparent in the interview. Although the presenting problem provides a starting point for the therapist, it is best to obtain the information firsthand. Do not rely on information obtained by the previous interviewer. Clients occasionally express dismay at having to repeat the information, but most clients will cooperate if the therapist effectively communicates the reason. For example, "I understand that you have already told Dr. G. how you feel, but I want to make sure I know exactly what is going on with you. So please, tell me about what brought you here."

The presenting problem should be identified early in the session (see chap. 4 concerning the nature and history of the presenting problem). At a minimum, the therapist should find out how long the client has been experiencing this problem, in what ways it disrupts the person's life, if this is the first time this problem has occurred, and how the client has dealt (or not dealt) with it in the past. One way to obtain the presenting problem is simply to ask the client. The following example illustrates how to elicit the presenting problem:

Therapist: What led you to come for therapy?

Client: I felt I needed some help.

Therapist: What specifically did you feel you needed help with?

Client: I have been feeling really anxious lately, ever since my bag was stolen.

Knowing what brought the client into treatment early in the session determines how the therapist proceeds in the interview. If a client speaks about feeling very depressed and as though life is not worth living, the therapist needs to assess the seriousness of the suicidal ideation. But, if the client reported ambivalence over adopting a baby, then the therapist might begin to explore the client's mixed feelings.

A student in an introductory counseling skills class submitted a videotape of himself conducting an initial interview with a client. For approximately 45 minutes he acted as if he were a drill sergeant, shooting out questions at the client. He never stopped to reflect on the client's feelings or ask him to expand on his responses. He had an interview form in front of him with questions that he was clearly determined to follow. At the end of the 45-minute interview, he finally asked the client: "So what brings you here today?" The client appeared frustrated and confused. The client was clearly upset at the delay in his being able to relate his concerns.

The preceding example demonstrates several points. First, therapists must stop and listen—really listen—to the client. Listening includes putting down paperwork. This therapist was more concerned with his agenda (filling out forms and gathering information), than with listening to the client. The therapist's own compulsion to complete his paperwork inhibited him from connecting with the client on an emotional level.

Consider another example illustrating the importance of listening. An advanced student conducting an intake asked all the "right questions" and filled in the intake form diligently. However, at one point, the client, a middle-aged woman presenting with marital difficulties, began to cry. Such display of emotion was not about to stop this therapist. He kept right on asking his questions! The interview proceeded something like this:

Therapist: How long were you married before the separation?

Client: [*sobbing*]

Therapist: How long were you married for?

Client: [*trying to pull herself together, looking around for a tissue*]

Therapist: [*almost impatient*] I need to know how long you were married before your separation.

Of course, in the process of collecting his information, the therapist lost the client. This is analogous to the medical joke in which the operation was a success, but the patient was lost. You must remember that given the demands of the situation, clients are likely to respond to most questions. Clients will follow the therapist's lead, even if they are being led down the wrong path.

SILENCE AS AN INTERVENTION

Another important skill for a therapist is being able to keep silent. Despite sounding simple, it is not an easy technique to master. Beginning therapists seem to feel they must fill every moment with words so that clients are getting their money's worth. Silence is an intervention. It is perfectly fine to allow clients time to collect their thoughts. Often the material a client comes forward with after a silence can be very meaningful. By allowing silence, the therapist communicates that the therapy space is a safe one in which the client may or may not speak.

Consider the following example of a beginning therapist's desire to talk. At this point in the interview, the client had been providing some of her marital history:

Therapist: Your second marriage?

Client: Yeah, it lasted 14 years, we actually lived together for 8 of those 14 before getting married. We broke up a lot and got back together, then broke up again. Actually I moved back to my country . . . that is where I met him. My son was with me at the time. . . . I did not want to leave my son behind like my parents did to me. I did not know my parents for the first 12 years of my life. . . .

Therapist: What country was that?

In this example, there was no reason for the therapist to ask questions; the client was willing and talkative. The therapist's own anxiety and inability to remain quiet was disruptive.

In another example, a student therapist had a client who was very verbal and did not have any difficulty communicating:

Client: I have a feeling of just not accomplishing what I am supposed to. . . . I am feeling shameful. . . . I just feel terrible. . . . That's all I know. . . .

Therapist: What would you like to be doing that you are not doing?

This therapist, unable to tolerate the silence, quickly jumped in by focusing on what the client could be doing. This interrupted the client's train of thought, and seemed to minimize the client's pain by changing the focus.

A useful activity for students to experiment with is to listen to their session tapes with a stopwatch. They are instructed to listen for silences and time them. They usually find that the long silences in actuality last only a few seconds!

NOTE TAKING

The amount of information to be obtained and remembered during the first interview may seem overwhelming. This raises the issue of note taking. Many therapists in training are either video or audio recorded so that a supervisor can review the session later. In these instances, note taking seems unnecessary because the tape can be reviewed later and notes can be taken from the tape. Watching or listening to these therapy tapes is also an educational process for therapists because they can look at themselves and their clinical skills more objectively. In cases where therapists do decide to take notes, the client should be informed at the start of the session (e.g., "I am going to jot some notes down for myself, so that I am able to get all the information I need. I want to make sure that my report is accurate."). Note taking may eliminate the fear of "missing" something. It can also be helpful in highlighting areas where more information is necessary. Notes can be reviewed quickly at the end of the session (mentally) and further inquiries can be made (e.g., "You mentioned earlier that you have been working as a travel agent for 5 years, did you have any other employment prior to that?").

Nevertheless, there are several potential drawbacks to note taking. First, it may be distracting for the client. A client may become preoccupied with what the therapist is writing and begin to think about that rather than the reasons for coming to therapy. Moreover, clients may begin to notice when therapists do and do not write something down, and then increase their verbalizations around those areas where notes are taken, thinking that these are more important. Finally, the client may wait for the therapist to finish writing or try to peer at what has been written.

GETTING INFORMATION FROM THE CLIENT

Questioning is essential in the beginning interview to find out what clients mean when they use a term. It is not enough for a client to talk about feeling depressed. The therapist must ask what "depressed" means to the client. One person's notion of depression may be a person who cries a lot and decreases food consumption. However, for another, depression may mean that life is not worth living anymore and suicide is a viable option. A therapist looking for a client's definition might ask questions such as the following: "You say you have been anxious. Can you tell me more about that?" or, "You were upset with your father for his behavior. What does upset mean for you?"

This type of questioning becomes essential when a client begins to use psychological jargon. As psychology gains a spotlight in pop culture, people begin to use terms erroneously. For example, a male client stated that he was codependent. When asked what this meant for him, he replied, "Well I attend a codependent support group." Pressed further to relate this concept, he was unable to do so. He responded that his girlfriend had told him he was codependent and attributed their relationship difficulties to this "problem." At this point it was impossible to tell if he was codependent, but it was clear that he did not know what the term meant.

Beginning therapists must also be sensitive to their own use of jargon. Jargon can be confusing, alienating, and upsetting to the client. It is best to use terms and language that the client can relate to and understand. For example, a good way to summarize feelings of low self-esteem might be: "Since being fired from your job and having your girlfriend break up with you, you are feeling down on yourself and not as good as others." The same message filled with jargon sounds like this: "So as I see it, your early lack of good enough mothering, coupled with several narcissistic injuries, has left you with little ego strength and a resultant lack of self-esteem." In the latter example, the client may be left confused and feeling stupid.

FOCUS ON THE CLIENT

As clients relate their history to you, it is vital to keep the focus on them. Frequently, people wish to share whatever it is that their husband, boss, or friends are doing to "drive them crazy." Remember, therapists cannot change those people; they can only help the client. Thus, all questions should be directed to the client. Asking extensive questions about significant others can take the spotlight off the client. If a client begins to talk about someone else in an effort to avoid self-evaluation, then a way to get them back on track would be to ask, "How did that make you feel?" or "I understand that is important, but I'm interested in knowing how it affects you."

STRUCTURING

Structuring is often cited as an essential component of a beginning interview. It entails setting the stage for the interview and letting the client know what will happen. This reduces ambiguity and eases the client's anxiety. One important component is to inform the client of the length of the session. Many clients come to the therapist's office with the experience of a doctor's appointment lasting only several minutes. A first meeting with a client may last 90 minutes.

The structure will change depending on the setting of the intake. For example, in an agency setting, the client may first see the therapist, then the office manager who will assess the fee, and finally the receptionist who schedules the next appointment. It is important to inform the client about this in advance. Again, keep in mind that a client who is new to mental health services will be unsure what takes place. Many clients have strange ideas about psychotherapy. A simple way to brief a client about the process would be, for example: "For about 90 minutes today I will be asking you some questions to get to know you and understand what brought you here today. When we are finished, you will meet with Jane, our biller, who can verify your insurance and go over fees."

Therapists are also obligated to inform the client at the first interview if they will be handling ongoing therapy. When the intake therapist is not going to be the ongoing therapist, this is often difficult for clients to understand. They may become angry at having to retell their story to someone else. Another possibility is that clients may form an immediate attachment to the intake therapist and believe no one else can help or understand them. Reflect the client's feelings of frustration and be empathic. The following scenario highlights what might happen:

Therapist: I will be doing the intake interview with you today, but when you return next time, you will be seeing Dr. Jo. She will be your therapist.

Client: Oh! So then I have to go through all this stuff again! Why can't I just see her now?

Therapist: I see that you are quite upset at not being able to see Dr. Jo today. Unfortunately, the way the clinic operates is that I meet with everyone first to fill out the paperwork.

Clients should also be advised that a therapist is being chosen based on what is best for them. For example, if the chief complaint is anxiety, the case will be assigned to a therapist who specializes in that area. Or, if parents are coming to discuss their child, let them know that there are designated child therapists who will work with their child. The following are some examples of how to explain this situation:

Therapist: I know that you have spent a great deal of time and energy telling me about your difficulties and you may have to fill in Dr. Dune on some of the details when you see him. He is the resident specialist in eating disorders and I think he will best be able to help you.

Therapist: Mr. and Mrs. S, well, when you first called I thought that Jason [*the son*] was your main concern. But as I think we can all see after this meeting, you two seem to be disagreeing a lot on what is best for him. I think our marital therapist would be the one who would be best able to help you. My field is mainly children and I am not sure that that is the most appropriate treatment at this time. How do you feel about that?

Therapists working privately may be handling most of their own incidental work, and so the client may deal only with them during their first visit. This type of situation could be structured by saying, "Today we will discuss what has been going on with you lately, some of your history, and then we will schedule another appointment time that is convenient for you so we can begin examining your concerns. Today's appointment should take approximately 60 minutes."

INCONGRUENCIES FROM THE CLIENT

Therapists should be aware of discrepancies between the client's verbal and nonverbal behavior during the interview. Such incongruencies can indicate that it is uncomfortable for the client to discuss a certain issue or that perhaps the client is not being completely honest. Whatever the reason, it should be addressed. For example, a therapist in training had a client who appeared to be angry toward her. The client provided curt responses and had limited spontaneous speech. The therapist reported to supervisors that she did not like or feel connected with the client. The therapist continued with sessions, ignoring the obvious tension between them. It would have been more appropriate to say, "I sense that you do not want to discuss much today" and then process the client's reaction to the statement. By addressing the client's obvious feelings, the therapist opens the door for clients to talk about them if they choose. The therapist is also modeling direct and honest communication with the client.

HOW LONG WILL IT TAKE, DOCTOR?

Instilling a sense of hope in the client during the first hour can be useful. Therapists should be honest about whether they can help the client. For example, if the therapist will not be able to help the client or the client is in need of services that the therapist cannot provide, then an appropriate referral should be made. Let the client know what to expect: "I think we can work on increasing your communication skills with others"; "I believe as you begin to discuss all the tragedies that you have experienced lately, you will begin to feel better and less depressed"; or "I think your problems are something that we can work on here."

Clients are often eager to know exactly how long it will take before they feel better. Many parents want to know how long it will take to "fix" their child. Some clients start with the intention of coming in a few times and then deciding if they want to continue. Let clients know that it is difficult to work under these constraints. Do not provide a client with a specific time frame because this is impossible to predict. Therapists should be upfront about time expectations: "It will take a few weeks for me to get to know you and understand what has been going on with you. I am not sure that you will feel better in 4 weeks. You have been experiencing these problems for a while and it will take some time to alleviate your pain."

Time is also an issue for insurance coverage and cost of therapy. If clients are allowed 12 sessions by their insurance company, then therapists should let them know if progress can be achieved in that amount of time. Ethically, the client should be informed that it may take longer. Another approach in such cases would be to designate a more manageable goal. For example, consider a client who has been having difficulty in all interpersonal relationships, leading her to feel angry, frustrated, and lonely. A more appropriate goal might be assertiveness training, which could lead to some improvement in relationships and alleviate some of her anger. One way to approach this with the client is to say the following:

> It seems as though you have experienced a lot of pain and difficulty throughout your life in relationships with others. This has left you angry, perhaps because you have been unable to assert yourself and your needs with others and then are left feeling used. I think, given the short amount of time we have to work together, one way to improve your feelings would be through the use of assertiveness training. This would help you to more clearly state your feelings and needs to others without getting angry. What do you think about that?

Competence in all of these interviewing skills takes time and practice. The beginning therapist should strive to make the client feel safe, comfortable, and accepted. Reducing initial anxiety, allowing for time to think, and listening attentively are essential to forming a therapist–client alliance.

Self-Review Checklist Following Interview

- Was I empathic?
- Did I allow the client to speak openly?
- Was I judgmental toward the client?
- Were the silences appropriate?
- How much information am I missing?

CONFIDENTIALITY

A therapeutic relationship is not possible without confidentiality. It is essential that what a client chooses to tell a therapist remains between the two of them. Confidentiality ensures clients that nothing will be disclosed to anyone without their permission. Such privacy enables the client to fully disclose intimate information without fear. (Several exceptions to this rule are discussed later.)

A discussion of confidentiality with clients should include defining it and then making sure they have grasped the concept. Ask if they understand what the term means. Ask if they have any questions. The issue of confidentiality may be covered verbally in the interview as well as in the informed consent forms a client signs prior to beginning the session. Be aware that the terms used to describe confidentiality to clients are critically important. For the most part, this discussion concerns adult clients. One way to describe confidentiality to a client would be to simply state: "I am ethically and legally obligated to keep the information that you tell me in confidence. This means that I cannot reveal to anyone, without your consent, any of what transpires between us. You, however, are free to tell anyone you want about the therapy." You should avoid using a word like "secrets," because it can have a negative connotation for some clients.

Confidentiality also prevents the therapist from disclosing if the client is receiving services. For example, if the wife of a client calls to say that he is a "lousy husband," the therapist cannot confirm that he is a client. The following scenario illustrates this point:

Mrs. Whitt: Hello Dr. Clem. I know my husband has been seeing you and I just wanted to let you know the real story. . . .

Dr. Clem: I am sorry Mrs. Whitt, legally and ethically I cannot even tell you IF your husband is seeing me.

Mrs. Whitt: That's okay. I know he is. I just wanted to let you know that last night he was out all night drinking.

Dr. Clem: I am sorry Mrs. Whitt, I am not at liberty to talk to you [*hang up*].

In this example, the therapist has been polite but firm, and has not broken confidentiality. It would be good practice, however, to address the wife's phone call with the husband in the next session.

At times it may be tempting to share details of sessions with others—including family, friends, and colleagues. This temptation must be avoided. If it is necessary to seek assistance from a colleague with a clinical dilemma, then be sure to disguise all identifying information about the client:

> A very cute, 4-year-old girl was being seen by a psychologist. She would announce her arrival for each session by showing the receptionist her latest toy. She had managed to charm all the office staff with her perky personality and great looks. One day after her session, the psychologist walked her out to the front door. On coming back into the office, the therapist was asked by the receptionist, "She is so cute! What could she possibly coming here for?" The therapist was forced to respond, "Yes, she is real special, but you know I can't tell you what is going on with her. That information is confidential. I do appreciate your concern about her, however."

The psychologist was able to maintain confidentiality despite pressure from the receptionist.

When to Discuss Confidentiality

There should be no dilemma about when to discuss confidentiality with a client. Most ethical principles advise discussing it as early as possible in the relationship. Does this mean during the first session or over the phone prior to the first session? Although there is no one clear answer, the start of the relationship seems to make sense. It is probably best to wait until meeting the client for the first time in the office to fully explain the concept, visually see their response, and then gauge their understanding. But there may be times when it is necessary to discuss confidentiality over the phone during the first contact. For example, a mother was scheduling a time to bring her daughter in for some psychological testing. The testing procedure was reviewed and the mother was informed that she would be getting a test report. She immediately asked if the report would be sent to the child's school. At that point, it was necessary to inform her of confidentiality and that no report would be sent unless she signed a release form.

Breach of Confidentiality

Laws regarding confidentiality differ from state to state, so check local statutes. However, there appear to be at least four universal situations in which confidentiality can be broken: clients sign a release of information or some other form clearly designating to whom you may speak or release information, cases of child or elder neglect or abuse, when the client has filed a malpractice suit against you, or if clients appear to be a threat to themselves or others (e.g., homicide or suicide). It is best to take a straightforward approach when telling clients about the limitations of confidentiality:

> The only time that I would have to break confidentiality, would be if I thought you were to attempt to harm yourself or were planning to harm someone else. This means, if you tell me that you are abusing a child or elderly person, I would have to report that to our local child protective services. Also, if you told me that you were intent on killing yourself or someone else, I would also have to break confidentiality, to get you help or to warn the other person.

Again, always ask the client if there are any questions about any of these situations.

If a situation arises when it is necessary to break confidentiality, let clients know that you are concerned about them and do not want to hurt them. Relate that telling someone else is in their best interest. Convey the message that confidentiality must be broken to obtain assistance or greater services for the client.

Waivers/Releases of Information. This is the clearest and least stressful situation in which confidentiality is broken. Here, the client voluntarily gives permission for the therapist to release information. Examples of this are when the parents of a child client sign a release of information to request that the therapist speak to a teacher. Another situation would be a client who asks the therapist to consult with a physician regarding his condition. In these cases, a form would clearly designate the party with whom the therapist may speak.

Child Abuse. Most states have laws requiring certain professionals, including therapists, to report known or suspected cases of abuse or neglect. The therapist is required to identify the victim of the abuse and the perpetrator, if known. Mandatory reporting helps each state keep track of abuse and neglect statistics and to assist families, if necessary.

Remember, the aim of breaking confidentiality is to help the client. Child abuse must be reported not to punish the family, but rather for the sake of the child's safety. Explain this to the client. For example, if the client is a child, then say something like: "Johnny, I am concerned about the way that your father has been disciplining you. The marks from the electrical cord have hurt you a lot. I am going to need to tell some people who can help about what has happened so that they can help you and your Dad." If the parent is the client and abuser, then a proper response would be: "Mr./Mrs. Pape, I know that you feel helpless sometimes when dealing with Johnny, but it is against the law to hit him with an electrical cord. I am going to have to report this to the authorities. I understand that his behavior is out of control at times, but I know we can work on more effective ways of disciplining him. You have hurt him a lot by hitting him and I know that you don't really want to hurt him like that." Most parents will cooperate.

Malpractice Suits. If a client files a malpractice suit, the therapist is allowed to reveal confidential information during the court proceedings. According to the rules, if clients file suit against therapists for what occurred during the therapy, then therapists have the right to defend themselves and to reveal the details of the therapy. Clients have waived the right to confidentiality by bringing suit against the therapist.

Suicide/Homicide. If clients express any intention to cause serious harm to themselves or others, then the therapist may break confidentiality. This includes a client who expresses clear suicidal plan and intent. In these cases, the therapist should either notify the family of the client or admit the client to a facility that can provide 24-hour supervision (i.e., a hospital). This issue also comes up when a client has intentions to kill someone. Most state statutes note that there must be a clear and imminent danger. In these cases, the therapist has a duty to warn the identified victim. This means making all possible efforts to contact and warn the intended victim. If the person cannot be contacted directly, then police should be notified. It then becomes the police's responsibility to notify the intended victim. In either case, the therapist must carefully evaluate the client's intention and decide how serious the threat is to the client or to others. Again, therapists should explain to the client why the pledge of confidentiality must be broken.

Ethical Dilemmas

Occasionally, a client who is familiar with the rules of confidentiality may be reluctant to reveal information. For example, consider a client who had been in therapy previously and had often been suicidal. It became evident during the first session that the client was depressed and might be contemplating suicide. When the client was directly asked if she was thinking about killing herself, she stated: "I can't tell you that . . . even if I was, I wouldn't tell you." In this type of situation, the most a therapist can do is to try to communicate concern and to explain why it would be necessary to break confidentiality.

As stated earlier, in order to avoid any misunderstandings, confidentiality should be discussed as soon as the professional relationship begins. The following example highlights the possible consequences of not doing so. A student therapist under supervision was seeing a man in individual therapy. As an adjunct to the individual therapy, he was to have a family session once a month. His family consisted of three children and a wife. On the first occasion when the man came with his family, the student therapist encouraged family members to share whatever was on their minds, as it would "stay in the room" (her way of describing confidentiality). The oldest boy, age 8, reported that his father had hit him repeatedly with a belt. The therapist knew she was obligated to report this abuse to the authorities, but had not reviewed the limits of confidentiality with the children prior to their disclosure. When the therapist informed the family that she would have to report the abuse, the family was very angry and the children felt betrayed.

Beginning therapists should also realize that they are not compelled to break confidentiality in cases of crime. In other words, if they know that a client murdered a man several years ago, they do not have to disclose this information. The main issue is about danger. Is this client going to kill someone else now? If there is no reason to believe this to be true, then maintain confidentiality.

HIV + Clients

An emerging issue in the literature concerns clients who are HIV positive. A person diagnosed with HIV can infect others and thus may present an imminent danger. This is the logic behind breaking confidentiality in these cases. But break confidentiality to whom? and when? Although clinicians disagree on these issues, there is an emerging consensus on some aspects. If there is a clearly identifiable partner of the infected individual who is unaware of the client's HIV status, then it is believed that the therapist must first encourage the client to inform this partner. But, if the client does not, then the therapist has a responsibility to inform the partner.

Obviously, the impact of breaching such confidentiality is far reaching. It may result in the loss of a partner, discrimination at work, and emotional difficulties. At a minimum, the therapist needs to explore these possibilities with the client.

Issues of confidentiality are not easily outlined or followed. Despite legal statutes and ethical principles, it may be difficult for a therapist to break confidentiality. Thus, the clinical judgment and experience of the therapist seem most important. Therapists are encouraged to research state statutes and to consult any guidelines given by their professional organization.

SUMMARY

This chapter has provided some directives for handling the beginning interview with clients in different settings. The importance of structuring the interview to help guide the client and reduce ambiguity was stressed. The notion of the first interview as stressful for both the client and the therapist was addressed. Guidelines for approaching the client—keeping in mind cultural and ethnic differences—to obtain information for planning treatment were provided. And the use of silence as an intervention was also underscored.

Finally, the ethical and legal principles of confidentiality were outlined. The importance of maintaining confidentiality with all clients was emphasized. The instances in which it is okay to break confidentiality were reviewed, and some guidelines for discussing these instances with the client were provided.

SUGGESTED READINGS

Corey, G., Corey, M., & Callanan, P. (1993). *Issues and ethics in the helping process: Clients' rights and confidentiality*. Pacific Grove, CA: Brooks/Cole.

Fox, R. (1993). *Elements of the helping process: A guide for clinicians*. New York: Haworth.

Moursund, J. (1993). *The process of counseling and therapy*. Englewood Cliffs, NJ: Prentice-Hall.

Zaro, J., Barach, R., Nedelman, D., & Dreiblatt, I. (1977). *A guide for beginning psychotherapists*. New York: Cambridge University Press.

3

Rapport, Empathy,
and Reflection

Faye E. Johnston
Vincent B. Van Hasselt
Nova Southeastern University

Michel Hersen
Pacific University

The very essence of this text, from the inception, is to present to students of psychology a foundation from which they can glean the "nuts and bolts" of psychotherapeutic practice. For this chapter, in particular, it is necessary to transcend any particular theoretical perspective because when one refers the clinician's inherent gifts of empathy, rapport, and reflection to his or her clients, theoretical perspective is not applicable.

Rapport, *empathy*, and *reflection* are universal terms when applied to therapist skills. Other chapters in this text offer specific tools for the acquisition of intervention skills and the variety of helping mechanisms specific to each client, while addressing the choice of interventions relevant to the presenting client problem. The purpose of this chapter is to lead the student to consider the most inherently fundamental tenants requisite for successful intervention as a clinician—rapport, empathy, and reflection. Without implicit consideration of these most basic therapist skills, all other learning and practice in therapist education becomes mechanical.

The human ingredients that are displayed or employed in the expression of clinical rapport, empathy, and reflection are the connections from which the client gains the ability to feel safe enough to explore and consider change. Each of these skills is addressed separately, focusing on workable, practical definitions to a thorough review of the "how to" and "how not to" use of each. There are numerous, learned interpretations of these skills, based on the invaluable plethora of noted theorist opinion. Attempts to accurately measure these therapist skills have often proved how these abilities are empirically elusive. "Being there" for your client requires a combination of internal and external cognitions and behaviors to occur simultaneously, while these emanate to and from you and your client(s).

The goals of this chapter are to enhance your awareness of and to acknowledge the challenge of acquiring these all-important skills. Our intent is to provide a "working" explanation of these global skills and to demonstrate, through case illustrations, how easy or difficult it is for all clinicians to maintain these skills in the applied to client intervention.

One question often posed is, "Can an individual learn how to be empathic, demonstrate rapport, and provide reflection to a client?" The answer is often as complex as each individual, therapist, or client. However, it is the basic premise of this chapter that these skills can be acquired and appropriately utilized by any clinician who is dedicated to helping others. Prerequisites to such attainment are close introspection for the motives of pursuing this field and very definite estimates by the therapist of his or herself.

As you read and absorb this chapter, permit yourself to question your use of reflection, rapport, and empathy in your own daily living. How do you respond to the frustrated salesperson, the tired convenience store manager, your immediate friends or family? Begin checking your responses with those in your world, and this special assignment will be the beginning of the necessary steps, or behavior rehearsal, for your work as a therapist.

RAPPORT

What is rapport? Why is therapist/client rapport so intrinsic to the success of therapy? How do you achieve rapport with your clients? Many questions, complex answers. Why complex? Because building rapport between you and your client will always be your challenge. It will be up to you to assess your client's needs and goals, establish trust and safety, and acknowledge that frequently your client will be uncertain as to the actual reasons he or she has come into therapy in the first place. Suffice it to say that you must always be prepared to maintain this rapport, as the original conditions under which you first establish rapport with your client can and will change from session to session. Expect this phenomenon, and nourish the opportunity for these transitions, as this implies the freedom for client growth and change.

Let us first define what rapport means. This term is not so elusive when expressed in more specific therapist techniques.

1. *Establish an environment in which you and your client are at ease.* Environment implies both physical (e.g., office setting, therapist posture, and gestures) and psychological components. Always remember that, initially, your client does not know what to expect. He or she has never met you before and may be apprehensive, defensive, or anxious about the decision

to participate in therapy. Many clients feel that there is some disabling stigma attached to therapy. Your role will be to convey to your client an awareness of all these possibilities and an openness to whatever your client may present. Your professional ease and patience will provide the client with the security requisite for the establishment of rapport. Discussing basic client information will assist you in the initial determination of your client's presenting symptomology, while helping the client to feel comfortable in your presence.

2. *Assess your client's problems and respond with empathy.* (Empathic responding is defined and addressed in the next section of this chapter.) It may often be difficult for your client to be specific in the expression of the issues central to their concern. Frequently your client may express these issues vaguely, abstractly, or globally.

Client:	There doesn't seem to be any light at the end of the tunnel.
Therapist:	So things seem pretty dark for you right now?

Client resistance (for any reason) may pose a challenge for the therapist. Clients may be intensely resistive; thus, if the clinician keeps in mind that the client must be permitted time and patience for the establishment of trust, then favorable results can be anticipated. Remember, your client's resistance may stem from an enduring set of defense mechanisms that he or she may recognize are not benefiting the client; however, letting go of these mechanisms and searching for alternatives can be very frightening for a client.

3. *Assess your client's level of insight and establish your alliance with your client.* Clients may present with full, limited, or no insight into their problems. If you are unable to correctly estimate your client's awareness into his or her problems, rapport will be diminished. Obviously, the client who has complete insight into his or her presenting problems will promote the foundation of rapport more easily. Frequently, however, clients may have limited insight into their true concerns, and may be very defensive about the exposure of these issues. Always include your client in the exploration. Remember, this is the client's agenda, not yours. Recognize that some insights may take time, and that your client will be willing to explore more freely, if he or she senses that they are not being pushed.

Client:	[*A middle-aged married female*] I really am not the one with the problem. I don't know why I'm here really, because my husband is the one who needs therapy. He's the one with the problem.
Therapist:	Perhaps, you could tell me a little more about what you think your husband's problems are and how those problems are affecting you?

In this case, the therapist did not push the client, but encouraged her to feel that anything she wanted to say was important. This type of therapist response provides the client with a sense of ownership of the session, and thus, affirms rapport.

4. *Demonstrate the instillation of hope, new perspectives, knowledge of your awareness of the client's problems, and deter doubt.* If a client believes the therapeutic process may provide new perspectives, hope for change or acceptance, and the possibility for growth, then he or she will experience the freedom and safety to explore.

Client:	I have heard that treating depression is really difficult, and I know that I have been depressed for so long that there isn't much hope for me.
Therapist:	There are many new, and varied treatments for depression, and we will work together to find just the right choices for you.

5. *Assist your client in understanding his or her role as a client.* Commonly, a new client will have only a vague picture of what may be expected of him or her during the therapy process. This is especially true for clients who have never participated in therapy. However, even with a client who has had previous therapy, their expectations or concerns about the process are new, because you are a new therapist. For the client who has had no previous therapy experience, it will be important for you to outline the process, and to solicit and answer your client's possible questions. For the client who has participated in previous therapy, it will be equally important for you to evaluate those experiences, encouraging your client to share their thoughts with you freely and openly. Understanding your client's expectations regarding his or her work and relationship with you will be at the heart of your rapport together.

Client:	You should know that I have been in therapy before, a few years back. It was a waste of time.
Therapist:	It would be very helpful for me to hear more about that, if you feel like you would be able to talk about that experience.

As indicated earlier, the skills inherent in the establishment of an effective client–therapist relationship are many and varied. Understanding your role as the therapist and how that role must be adjusted to the needs and expectations of each individual client requires that you will have the knowledge, skills, flexibility, and willingness to prepare you to meet your clients challenges. This understanding, combined with your own self-awareness, will enable you to enter your client's world and establish the trust and respect that are the foundations of rapport.

EMPATHY

Much has been written about the subject of therapeutic expression of empathy, and yet, this incredibly important therapist tool defies universal definition. Why? Perhaps because empathy may be, like art, "in the eye of the beholder." Historically, empathy was cited as a concept in the late 19th-century philosophical literature. Descriptions of the projection of real psychic feeling from one person to another, and an emphasis on what was described as perceptive awareness, were some of the earlier attempts to define this concept. The debate regarding the accurate nature of empathy remains considerable. Empathic response is born from a keen understanding of one's self and serves as another means for the therapist reflect the client's needs, thus assisting in the establishment and maintenance of rapport.

As indicated previously, each of these basic therapeutic skills achieves its optimum client benefit by co-existing. Experienced clinicians have described empathy as a necessary and almost sufficient condition for client progress and as a psychological "nutrient," without which human life could not be sustained. In order for you to utilize empathy, it will be important to accurately reflect, or mirror your client's feelings, experiences, and behaviors. The accuracy of your perceptions of what the client is expressing is based on your awareness of the client's affect, your understanding of what has happened to the client, and, finally, what your client's role may have been in the experience.

Always keep in mind that no two clients are the same. How does this basic tenet affect you, as the therapist? Only that you will need to remain open, flexible, and resourceful to the needs of each individual, with an honest respect for their uniqueness. This will also be one of the many reasons why your work as a therapist will remain challenging and very rewarding. Let us examine some basic guidelines that will assist you in developing your empathic style and formalizing your empathic skills. Simply put, empathy is understanding, not sympathy. Empathic response allows your client to know that you are accepting, understanding, and confirming his or her "world," without making judgments about that world. Accurate, empathic responding requires that you perceive the client's feelings and experiences/behaviors attached to those feelings.

For example, when a therapist responds, "You feel sad because moving means leaving all your friends," "You feel" relates to the client's feelings, while "because" acknowledges your understanding of the client's behaviors/experiences. So often, clients will be unable to identify the exact feelings that are attached to each experience. Or, they may be flooded with feelings, unable to sort these feelings out and match them to the experience. This confusion of feelings and experiences is often the precipitant to bringing the client into therapy. Think of this challenge as if the client's issues represent a multi-piece puzzle.

The client brings into the therapeutic process many pieces of a puzzle, and is often unsure what actual outcome or picture will emerge. It remains for the therapist to help the client sort out these pieces (feelings and experiences; piece by piece) in order to develop a clear picture, or frequently, pictures of relief, change, acceptance, or renewal.

At this point, you may be asking yourself, "How am I going to be able to manage all this at one time, and still be able to respond to my client accurately?" This question is asked by every clinician at one time or another, and substantiates our belief that, with practice, the novice clinician can formulate these skills. Because no two clients are the same, each new clinical experience will permit you to expand on these basic fundamentals. Before we explore the "how to's" of empathic responding, you need to be aware that your communication skills and style are intrinsically involved. Here is where your awareness of, understanding of, and willingness to pursue the client's issues must be utilized. The key to this process is remaining focused on your client at all times.

Client: I have seen several other therapists before you, and I am just about to give up on this whole mess . . . I am so tired of starting over again, but I keep hoping that I will be able to get some control back over my life.

Therapist: You seem to have some real concerns about how therapy might help you. You seem to have real hopes that you can find some solutions this time.

Client: Yes, I do have some doubts, but I have always believed that I can change, I just don't know how.

In the above example, the therapist responded nondefensively, and helped the client begin to focus on possibility for change.

Client: [*A male client, seeking therapy for the first time, is very anxious about the therapeutic process, but does not share this with his therapist, choosing instead to answer sarcastically*] So what's it to you?

Therapist: I'm wondering if you are feeling a little scared and intimidated by therapy?

Client: How did you know? I'm really scared to tell anyone about how I've been feeling.

Because the therapist was able to "look past" the client's sarcasm, and identify the client's resistance as his initial fear, the empathic response gave the client permission to release some of his fear, and begin to share his feelings.

Very frequently, you will encounter a client who is expressing a combination of emotional states and content, and it will be up to you to guide the client. As a cardinal rule when this occurs, and you may be uncertain whether to address the client's affect or the content, addressing the affect first will often help the client to become focused on a central theme or issue.

> *Client:* I have tried over and over again to get along better with my boss. Things seem to be going well for a little while, and then, out of nowhere she is yelling at me. If I do things the way she says, and they don't work out, I get yelled at. If I do things the way I think they should be done, she doesn't like that either. I don't know what to do.
>
> *Therapist:* That must be extremely frustrating for you.
>
> *Client:* Yes, that's it, I stay frustrated all the time, and then it becomes harder to do my work.

In this example, the therapist was able to "look past" the client's content, and help the client to identify the feeling associated with the content.

Consider a few more examples of this type of client challenge:

> *Client:* [*The client is a 62-year-old widow who is tearful.*] My daughter, my only child, has just left for college.
>
> *Therapist:* You must be very proud of her, and yet feel very alone right now.

In this example, the therapist was able to reflect back to the client an accurate understanding of her conflicted emotions.

> *Client:* [*Discussing her recent marital separation*] My ex wasn't a good husband, but he seemed to care for the kids. That was the way things went. Now that we are separated, I don't know if he will help with the kids.
>
> *Therapist:* You are hoping for some financial support from your husband, but you are really concerned what will happen if he doesn't help to provide for them.
>
> *Client:* I guess I haven't realized how scared I really have been since this happened.

Often an empathic paraphrase of the client's statement can assist the client to get to deeper feelings.

The "how to" of empathic responding involves understanding the uses of empathy, and then the practical application of these responses based on some basic "do's" and "don'ts." Inherent in the development of therapist empathy are goals that represent the fundamentals of effective listening. Basic, fundamental questions you may want to ask yourself about each of your clients involve how your client perceives herself or himself, and how the client perceives others. Ask yourself how your client relates to others, and what strengths does he or she present? Early identification of clients' coping and defense mechanisms will also facilitate the establishment of rapport. Of considerable relevance to these mechanisms will be your client's values and beliefs about life. Your awareness of these beliefs will provide a foundation for your work with your client.

In examining the uses of empathy as they apply to the therapeutic relationship, it is reasonable to state that empathic responding: (a) assists in building the client–therapist relationship, while providing support to your client, (b) encourages client response and exploration, (c) assists the therapist role by providing methods to clarify client response, and (d) provides the foundation for the use of other interventions (e.g., confrontation, challenging).

These are several key phrases that you as the therapist can acquire to improve your empathic responding. Frequently, your clients will reach an issue, and become blocked, or demonstrate resistance.

Your client may respond, "I just don't know" or (more firmly) "I don't know." At this point, your response of "It must be hard not to know" can often open the floodgates of expression for your client.

Other empathic phrasings may begin:

"It must be (difficult, hard, etc.)"

"It sounds like . . ."

"It seems like . . ."

"You feel (sad, anxious, annoyed, relieved, etc.) because . . ."

Remember, empathy takes into account your client's actual feelings, experiences, and behaviors. This can be challenging for the therapist, because often what the client may be immediately saying is not representative of the central issues. Also, keep in mind that too much empathy can deter the process, and that for some clients, the discussion of their feelings is a threat.

Client: [*An adolescent female*] My mom yells at me all the time about the way I dress. She yells at my older sister too about the same things, then tells her that she should dress like I do.

> She never yells at my younger brother for some of the same things she yells at me for doing.

Therapist: So your mom's inconsistency is really confusing to you.

Client: Right! I never know what to expect!

Here the therapist captured the client's feelings regarding her experience.

Client: [*A single woman in her mid-40s*] Last week I attended a family birthday party with my mother. Besides the family, there were other family friends, and we were all in a discussion. I was expressing my opinion to the group, which is hard for me to do, because I'm shy, and my mother openly disagreed with me.

Therapist A response: It's probably hard to admit, but I bet you were angry.

Client: Well, I'm not sure about that.

Therapist B response: So your mother did it again.

Client: Yes! And it made me feel so embarrassed.

The *Therapist A* response was just too assertive for this client who had already indicated her difficulty in expressing herself. The *Therapist B* response indicated a sensitivity to this client's feelings, and, thus, permitted the client to express the feeling herself.

As you practice empathic responding, remember that you must set aside your judgments and biases. The use of empathy keeps your client focused on the important issues. You must be fair, flexible, and totally aware of your client's verbal and nonverbal messages. Noting your client's responses to empathy will be a beacon for you to guide your client's progress. Understand that empathy is one of many tools you will master and rely on in your work. This text will provide you with other strategies, offering you and your clients a myriad of choices for therapeutic success.

REFLECTION

For practical purposes, and for your ease in understanding the meaning and importance of the therapist tool *reflection*, this section will address this technique as two potential entities. The first refers to the therapist's reflection of client feelings; the second concerns the therapist's reflection of the client's content. Actually, these two parts equal the sum of reflection as an intervention skill. However, there may be occasions when you will choose to use both simultaneously, or separately.

Before we proceed, it is useful to analyze what true client reflection really is, and what value this skill may have for your client. Frequently, during the initial client session, we can explain to them that part of our role as therapists is to reflect back to them, like a mirror image, what they are feeling and saying. In no way does this mean that the therapist will mime or mimic the client response; nor will the therapist "parrot" back the words of the client. The true "therapist mirror" becomes an invaluable method for the client to learn about him or herself.

At this point, you may be wondering, "How do I do this?" First, understand that this skill takes practice. A novice therapist will often be concerned with achieving rapport, listening carefully, and working hard on responding appropriately. Keep in mind that your original motivations for becoming a therapist, combined with your education and supervision, will provide the foundation for the practice of all of your intervention skills. Many of the world's most respected clinicians adhere to the philosophy that, as therapists, we are always learning and practicing. Further, our professional goals are not based on mastery of techniques, but on the growth and development of every client we serve.

Reflection of clients' feelings may appear to be a simple task. Certainly, there may be very obvious client expressions that are easily reflected by the therapist. More often, however, clients will present a mixture of emotions, and it will be your job to attend to not only what your client is saying, but also to how your client is talking. Carefully observing your client's behavioral mannerisms, posture, voice intonation, and expressions, while hearing the client's words, will provide a more accurate picture of what really is going on.

Client: [*smiling graciously*] My husband doesn't know the meaning of the word *partnership*. He believes that everything we have worked together for is under his control.

Therapist: I'm a little confused. You are smiling, and yet, you sound so resentful.

In this case, the therapist observed the client's smile, heard the resentment in the client's voice, and was able to ask for clarification to assist the client in identifying her feelings.

Clients will tell you many things about their feelings via nonverbal behaviors. Crossing and uncrossing their legs, hand gesturing, teeth clenching, opening and closing their eyes, avoiding eye contact, shifting in their seat, and tensing or relaxing their bodies all are indicators of feelings and cognitions that the client may have difficulty expressing.

Therapist:	You have told me about what your boss expects you to do, and about the details involved with your work. Perhaps you could tell me a little more about how you feel about your relationship with your boss?
Client:	[*A young male, who has been relating details about his work, shifts in his seat, uncrosses his legs, and crosses his arms over his body*] I'm not sure what you mean?
Therapist:	It seems like you have experienced some tense times with your boss, and I was wondering if you could tell me more about that?
Client:	How did you know? (uncrossing his arms) You're right, you know. I have felt so much pressure, because I don't seem to be able to get things the way he wants them, no matter how hard I try.

In this case, the therapist was able to observe the client's nonverbal behaviors, and realized that these represented the deeper feelings and reactions this client was having in his work relationship. Accurate reflective moments, like the aforementioned, will serve as the building blocks requisite for client–therapist rapport and, ultimately, a safe, comfortable climate in which your client can openly discuss his or her issues.

Reflection of feelings differs from empathy, in that you are actively assisting your client in identifying, accepting, and "owning" his or her feelings. Remember, empathic response lets your client know you are understanding his or her total picture; you are letting the client know that you are there with them. (Review the section on empathy, if the difference is unclear to you.) Reflection then becomes a skill to assist your client in identifying different feeling states and also in expressing those states.

Client:	[*A young, newly married female*] I know my mother means well, but she calls me all the time, especially at dinner time, to see how things are. She is constantly giving me advice, telling me how to cook and clean, and she even asks me about how Steve and I are doing romantically.
Therapist:	That must be very frustrating for you.
Client:	I am frustrated, and I feel torn, because I love my mother, but I wish she would just stay out of my marriage. It's hard enough being newly married, without her interference!

In this case, the therapist reflected the client's frustration, which permitted her to express additional issues currently affecting her, such as the concerns of being newly married.

Again, as it bears repeating, "less is more" when responding to your clients. Accurate reflection of feelings can be delivered in a simple phrase, and the fewer the words, the better: "You must be feeling . . ." "That must be . . ." "Could you be feeling . . . ?" "Sounds like you are feeling . . . ." Each of these will assist your client in identifying feeling states and attaching the feeling to the experience. Clients often need your guidance to help them explore the actual feeling associated with an experience. Reflective statements create the atmosphere in which the client may, for the first time, be able to give him or herself the "permission" to feel.

Reflection of client content requires that you accurately paraphrase or summarize your client's statements. Remember, for this skill, you are reflecting the "essence" of what your client is saying, not the exact words or phrases. This skill is pivotal for a client to be able to identify problem areas or issues, and to begin to formulate goals for addressing them. Think of this skill as one that will assist your client in "getting to the heart of the matter."

> *Client:*   [*A 45-year-old married male*] I'm not sure why I'm here. My
>   firm is letting people go, my son is involved in a messy
>   divorce, and my wife resents all the extra time I'm spending
>   at work. I don't seem to be enjoying my life like I used to.
>
> *Therapist:* There seem to be a number of problems bothering you, all
>   at the same time.
>
> *Client:*   Yes, I can't really focus on any of them anymore. It's like
>   they all run together, and I end up feeling hopeless.

In this case, the therapist chose to reflect the client's message by summarizing the content of his statements, thus enabling this client to express his true feeling. If the therapist had focused on only a part of the client's statement such as his relationship with his wife or his concerns about losing his job, the client would not have been able to express his over-all feeling state.

Here are some other examples of reflecting client content:

> *Therapist:* Are you experiencing any other concerns?
>
> *Client:*   [*A 39-year-old married female*] Well, as a matter of fact, there
>   is the problem with our 16-year-old daughter. We seem to
>   be having trouble with her. She doesn't want be home by her
>   curfew, and she is coming home later and later.
>
> *Therapist:* The fact that your daughter isn't home by her curfew is a
>   major problem.

In this case, as with all paraphrasing, the therapist's response is expressed to match the client's statement. It will be important for you to match your paraphrase in a similar grammatical structure to that of your client.

Client: *[A 66-year-old married male]* As I told you, my wife's illness has really put a strain on our finances, and I didn't expect these kind of problems, so soon after retiring. I really miss going to work every day.

Therapist: It seems like you are having difficulty coping with your wife's illness, and at the same time, also dealing with your retirement.

In this case, the therapist was reflecting the essence of the client's statements, thereby assisting him to focus on his issues to affect change.

Frequently, your role as a reflective therapist will be to assist your clients to organize their concerns. Often, clients will randomly "spill out" their difficulties to you and reflective summarization will help your clients grasp the meaning of and to prioritize these concerns, which is the first step in managing them.

Client: *[A 52-year-old married female]* My father lives alone, and recently he has been very ill. My husband is beginning to resent all the time I'm spending going back and forth to take care of him. My sister lives out of town, and my brother lives close by, but neither one of them seems to want to help, so I've stopped asking them. I've talked to my husband about moving my father in with us, but, he doesn't seem to keen about that idea. I've looked at nursing homes in the area, but I don't want to make that decision by myself.

Therapist: It seems like you are considering a number of solutions to this problem, and you are unclear which to choose. Why don't we begin by discussing each possibility separately?

In this case, the therapist acknowledged the client's confusion, and also validated the client's attempts at problem solving.

Remember, reflection of content means maintaining your focus on the client's message. Your response must be geared to the content of that message. You may have ideas that you feel would assist your client. However, sharing your ideas shifts the focus from your client, and may disable your relationship. Ownership of both the issues and the solutions must be the client's, not yours. If your client always feels that you are "mirroring" their issues, thoughts, values, beliefs, and feelings, they will feel the personal power to address their concerns and attempt change.

SUMMARY

The goal of this chapter was to insure your understanding of and appreciation for the myriad of skills that encompass the use of therapist rapport, empathy, and reflection. There are countless texts, journals, and books dedicated to the explanations of each of these constructs. However, for the sake of brevity, we have highlighted the key features of each. Just as each client is different, each therapist also differs in behavioral style and interpretation of clinical techniques. Yet, there must be some "common ground" among us. This common ground is more readily observable when we focus on the use of rapport-building techniques, empathy skills, and reflection devices than any other therapist tool. Why? Because regardless of our theoretical perspective, no matter where or how we were trained, our work involves the establishment and maintenance of a relationship with a client, and without these fundamental skills, that relationship can not exist. Does this statement imply that these skills are the only tools possible for client change? Most assuredly not, because as you work with your clients, you will discover that your work will challenge you to continually draw from a wide variety of clinical and theoretical resources.

This chapter defined and described rapport, empathy, and reflection as useful tools, building blocks, to the client–therapist relationship. The essentials of rapport-building techniques include the use of empathy and reflection. The effectiveness of empathic response depends on quality of rapport with the client. Accurate reflections of client feelings and content rely on the foundations that empathy has established and rapport has developed. On completion of this chapter, you should be able to understand the differences between these skills and, similarly, appreciate their close relationship. You may choose to use these skills interdependently or to utilize them seperately. An effective therapist can be exceptionally reflective, yet only moderately empathic, and establish good client rapport. Other therapists utilize empathy strongly in their client approaches, and do so successfully.

The essence of this chapter is that client–therapist rapport is essential to your work. You will discover that the use of the rapport-building techniques, empathic responses, and accurate reflective skills will serve your clients well in your endeavors.

SUGGESTED READINGS

Duan, C., & Hill, C. E. (1996). The current state of empathy research. *Journal of Counseling Psychology, 43,* 261–274.

Egan, G. (1990). *The skilled helper.* Belmont, CA: Brooks/Cole.

Evans, D., Hearn, M., Uhlemann, M., & Ivey, A. (1993). *Essential interviewing.* Belmont, CA: Brooks/Cole.

Kottler, J. (1986). *On being a therapist.* San Francisco: Jossey Bass.

Kottler, J. (1992). *Compassionate therapy—Working with difficult clients.* San Francisco: Jossey-Bass.

Othemer, E., & Othemer, S. (1994). *The clinical interview—Using* DSM–IV: *Vol. 1. Fundamentals.* Washington, DC: American Psychiatric Press.

Rogers, C. R. (1980). *A way of being.* Boston, MA: Houghton Mifflin.

Storr, A. (1980). *The art of psychotherapy.* New York: Routledge, Chapman, & Hall.

Teyber, E. (1992). *Interpersonal process in psychotherapy.* Belmont, CA: Brooks/Cole.

4

History of the
Presenting Complaint

G. Stennis Watson
Alan M. Gross
University of Mississippi

The current symptoms of a presenting complaint are rarely adequately conceptualized or treated apart from the context in which they occur. Behavior, affect, and cognition are controlled by a variety of conditions, such as the effect of learning history, biology, personal and social relationships, cultural norms, innate strengths and weaknesses, socioeconomic background, education, and vocation. The therapist should be interested in current levels of functioning and conditions that affect current functioning at all times. Additionally, effectiveness of therapeutic intervention often increases when the therapist possesses knowledge of historical conditions associated with the presenting complaint. This chapter explores several historical events that affect many clients and suggests sources for obtaining historical data.

Assessing historical correlates of a presenting complaint aids the therapist in conceptualizing it and developing an intervention strategy. In some cases, historical data may direct the therapist's attention to important symptoms that would be otherwise overlooked. In other cases, such as persons provisionally diagnosed with mental retardation, a pervasive developmental disorder, or attention deficit hyperactivity disorder (ADHD), history of onset is crucial to diagnosis. For example, if a child presents with all the current behavioral symptoms necessary to diagnose ADHD, the therapist still must ask when the symptoms first appeared. If ADHD-like symptoms appeared prior to age 7, then a diagnosis of ADHD may be considered. If the symptoms appeared after age 6, then an ADHD diagnosis is ruled out.

The quantity and nature of historical data required to conceptualize and treat complaints are determined by the disorders associated with the presenting complaint. In some cases, such as a child presenting with ADHD-like symptoms, a substantial history may be required. The therapist needs to know the present symptoms, when they appeared, how they changed over time and across environments, and must be able to rule out a medical (e.g., a metabolic disorder or head trauma) or psychological condition (e.g., mild mental retardation, oppositional behavior, or substance abuse). Furthermore, history may suggest a course of intervention. If ADHD-like symptoms were of late onset and are manifested in only a few well-specified environments, then a purely behavioral intervention may be most effective. If symptoms were of early onset and pervasive across environments, then a combination of medical and behavioral interventions for ADHD may be most appropriate. If ADHD-like symptoms occur in a child with a personal or family history of metabolic disorders, then the child should be referred for a complete medical examination in addition to any psychological intervention that is attempted. In other cases, very little history may be needed beyond onset and duration of symptoms and treatment history. For example, a therapist may need minimal historical data to treat an adult presenting with a snake phobia.

History taking involves two simple questions: What problems are associated with the complaint? and What problems are differentiated from the complaint? The therapist needs enough data to be able to identify the complaint as a particular disorder and to be able to rule out other disorders. The following are general questions that may facilitate the process of conceptualization and intervention:

What is the source of the complaint, if it can be determined? (etiology)

What is the history of the symptoms per se?

What events typically precede or follow symptomatic affect, behaviors, or cognitions? (antecedents and consequences)

To what extent are the symptoms controlled by environment, or by physiological and developmental events? (nature and nurture)

What desirable outcomes have been associated with the complaint, either for the client or for someone in the client's social sphere? (secondary gain)

What coping skills has the client displayed relative to the presenting problem? (strengths)

Remember, however, that both insufficient and excessive data collection can have detrimental consequences. Insufficient data collection may lead to inaccurate case conceptualization, and excessive data collection is a waste of time. The effective volume of data to be collected is determined by the nature of the presenting complaint. The therapist must understand the symptoms and nature of suspected disorders, ask questions formulated in light of such understanding, and attempt to stay within the domains of suspected disorders. For example, if a college student presents with vague complaints about an inability to concentrate on lectures and assigned readings, then the therapist may suspect one of several underlying conditions: anxiety, depression or dysthymia, environmental stress, an insufficient reward system for academic success, or a medical condition. The therapist should know signs of each of these disorders and gather sufficient data to rule out improbable disorders. If depression is suspected, then the therapist should establish a history of disturbance of sleep, appetite, sexual interest, or affect. When an insufficient reward system is suspected, these questions may be unnecessary, or even detrimental, to therapeutic rapport. In general, the amount of data collected is determined by the amount of data needed to develop an accurate conceptualization and intervention for the disorder.

HISTORY OF PRESENTING SYMPTOMS

The most obvious place to begin gathering historical information is with primary symptoms of the presenting complaint. When did the symptoms begin? Were they chronic or remitting? How did they respond to changes in the environment? What antecedents and consequences have been associated with the symptoms? The focus is on symptoms per se and variation in symptoms over time. For example, a parent brings a third-grade child to a therapist and complains that this child does not pay attention in school. The therapist should investigate whether symptoms began in the third grade or were present earlier, whether symptoms are associated with a particular teacher or time of day, whether symptoms appear only when peers are engaging in similar behaviors, or whether symptoms appear when the child is seated in a particular location. These questions can aid the therapist in determining whether the child has the ability to attend, and whether the child does attend in some situations. The child whose inattention is pervasive may be considered for ADHD, but the child whose inattention appears only when seated with certain peers or when seated in the rear of the classroom should not be considered for ADHD.

Often, clients' descriptions of complaints are vague. It is the therapist's job to help clarify their symptoms. Depressed clients may state that they feel blue, but fail to tie sadness to specific events. A vague description of subjective distress can give the therapist a general picture of the client's depression, but does not permit the kind of fine-grained analysis needed for intervention. Therapists should ask the client when dysphoria began and whether it has remained consistent over time. The therapist should also ask the client about a history of unintended weight loss, changes in sexual interest, loss of pleasure in hobbies, feelings of agitation or frustration, changes in sleep patterns, or fatigue over a given time period. By sharpening and specifying historical symptoms of the presenting complaint, the therapist can develop a sense of both the duration and severity of the complaint.

In some cases, the history of symptoms is a good predictor of the course of the disorder. For example, if schizophrenia is suspected, then the therapist should investigate the age of onset of symptoms, the chronicity of symptoms, and the type of symptoms (negative or positive). If the client displays a single psychotic episode with sudden onset in adulthood, then the prognosis is much better than when a client has unremitting symptoms beginning in adolescence and including extreme social impairment and impaired affect. Clients with a single episode may need only time-limited therapy and support until they can return to a normal life. Clients with early onset and chronic symptoms will probably require long-term therapeutic and social support.

Psychiatric History

A client's psychiatric history can provide insight into the types and intensity of distress that has been experienced, convergent evidence concerning case conceptualization and diagnosis, prior therapeutic interventions that have been effective or ineffective, and prognosis for improving the client's functioning. Therapists should know whether clients have been treated previously by a mental health professional, and if so, whether they received treatment on an inpatient or outpatient basis. Therapists should also inquire into the type (e.g., individual or group psychotherapy) and orientation of therapy (e.g., cognitive, behavioral, or interpersonal). If the client has previously received medications, then the therapist may want to know which medications, for how long, and why those particular medications were prescribed. (A single medication can be used for a variety of disorders: e.g., the use of benzodiazepines to treat insomnia, anxiety, and convulsions.) An important question is whether treatment was effective, in the opinion of both therapist and client. Case descriptions and diagnoses made by previous therapists can direct the current therapist's attention to chronic or reemergent symptoms in the current presenting problem.

Prior psychiatric histories should be evaluated with a critical eye, for several reasons. First, symptom profiles evolve in response to environmental and physiological changes, and the client who presents with a particular constellation of symptoms at one time may present with a different constellation of symptoms at another time. For example, a person with schizophrenia may be in a state of florid psychosis in a prior psychiatric report and in a relatively adaptive state at the present. Abatement of symptoms, however, does not prove beyond a doubt that the schizophrenia has been cured; rather, the disease may be controlled by medication, or the client may be in a state of temporary remission associated with decreased stress in the environment. Second, persons may have multiple disorders, either sequentially or concurrently, and observations reported in a prior history may accurately reflect a problem other than the current presenting problem. Third, mental health professionals are subject to selection biases when they report their observations of clients. Stated simply, symptoms that were salient to them may not have been the most important symptoms, or they may have made diagnoses based on poor criteria. Therefore, a positive prior psychiatric history is an important, but not infallible, guide to case conceptualization and treatment planning.

It is equally important to know if a client has no prior psychiatric history. A negative psychiatric history may show that the client has not experienced significant distress in the past (or caused significant distress to others), or it may mean that a client's level of adaptive functioning has remained sufficiently high so that there has been no need to seek psychiatric intervention, even though some distress may have been present. It would be most helpful if a negative prior psychiatric history always demonstrated minimal prior dysfunction. However, a negative psychiatric history may mean that the client (or persons in the client's social sphere) has a high threshold for distress, a strong sense of denial of psychiatric symptoms, or the intelligence to avoid detection. Furthermore, the therapist should be aware that a client's psychiatric history may appear negative when there is, in actuality, a history of intervention unreported to the therapist.

When a client with a negative history of prior psychiatric intervention reports significant distress to self or other persons, nontraditional records of psychiatric distress may be available. A person with substance abuse problems may have multiple arrests for driving under the influence of alcohol or public drunkenness. A person with antisocial tendencies may have a record of arrests for assault. A person with tendencies toward self-injurious behavior may have a history of admissions to a general hospital for acute treatment of suicidal gestures. In each of these cases, records of psychiatric disorders exist, not as psychiatric histories, but as police reports and medical records. Therefore, the therapist should be alert to the possibility of alternative sources of psychiatric history.

Substance Abuse History

A client's use of alcohol, prescription medications, and illicit drugs is closely related to psychiatric history. Prescription drug use is assessed by determining whether the client complies with medical advice. Alcohol and illicit drug use are assessed by asking if clients drink or use drugs, which substances they use, how often they use them, and how much they ingest (in numerically quantifiable terms, e.g., more than two drinks? fewer than six drinks? twice a week? every night?). A negative consequences assessment may be helpful: Have you ever blacked out? Have you done anything while intoxicated that you would not have done while sober and that you regretted later? Has substance use caused you legal, occupational, or marital trouble? Have you suffered from any medical disorders related to substance use (e.g., pancreatitis)?

Substance abuse is important because it may produce psychological distress. For example, alcoholism is associated with memory loss in Korsakoff's syndrome, and amphetamines can produce acute psychotic states. Furthermore, drug use may reflect attempts to self-medicate emotional distress, such as depression or anger. Therefore, the therapist should be aware that substance abuse can both produce psychological dysfunction and mask dysfunction associated with other disorders.

Medical and Developmental History

Psychopathology is often associated with physiological disorders. For example, memory loss may be associated with strokes, tumors, traumatic brain injuries, Alzheimer's disease, temporal lobe epilepsy, aging, or general neuropathy. Common medicines can cause distressing side effects such as sexual dysfunction (impotence), fatigue, or ringing in the ears. Therefore, the therapist is wise to develop at least a minimal medical profile of the client. A full medical history may include a chronology of serious illnesses and surgery, physical trauma (especially head and spinal injuries), surgeries, metabolic disorders, respiratory and cardiac functions, and medications. Knowledge of a client's medical history can facilitate prediction of the general course of a client's disorder (see chap. 6). For example, a client with Alzheimer's will invariably display a loss of memory function, social withdrawal, eventual mutism, and ultimately, death. The therapist who is informed about a client's Alzheimer's diagnosis can facilitate transitions that the family will have to make as they care for the client. However, a client with a surgical brain lesion may show no deterioration of function, and the therapist's role will be to aid the client and family in adapting to the present level of functioning for an extended period of time. Knowledge of a client's medical history may predict necessary psychotherapeutic interventions. For example, clients often display symptoms of depression following cardiac bypass. A cognitive therapist may want to challenge client beliefs specifically related to cardiac surgery in the treatment of postoperative depression. Finally, knowledge of a client's medical history can help a therapist know when to refer a client for medical treatment. For example, if a client with a history of diabetes begins to show fatigue, then the therapist needs to refer the client for medical intervention as well as to consider the possibility of depression.

The therapist needs to know whether a client achieved normal developmental milestones, especially when treating clients with disorders beginning in childhood. Did the client sit, crawl, stand, or walk in normal sequence? Did the client talk or enter puberty at about the same time as peers? Were motor and intellectual functions age appropriate? Frequently, developmental delays are subtle and go unnoticed until a child begins school.

It is important to find out why a client failed to demonstrate age-appropriate behavior. One such example is delayed toilet training, which may reflect a variety of conditions. A child with mental retardation may have an innate neurological deficit that results in delayed toilet training manifested across all environments. A child seeking attention from parents may demonstrate inappropriate toileting in a limited number of environments, such as at home but not at school. The behavior is the same for both clients (i.e., failure to use the toilet in age-appropriate fashion at home). However, the cause and treatment are quite different for these clients. In the case of the child with mental retardation, the treatment may include both modification of the environment to support the child more effectively and a behavior modification program to help the child use the toilet. In the case of the child who can toilet appropriately but chooses not to, a straightforward program of behavior modification may be employed.

FAMILY HISTORY

The history of a presenting complaint may be related to a client's interactions with significant social systems, the family being the most prominent. Basic questions concerning a client's family include the size of the family, the client's place in the birth order, the client's role in the family, and the nature of the relationships among family members; socioeconomic status; employment and educational histories; and a sense of family values and religious traditions.

General knowledge of family background sets a context within which the client's presenting complaint may be evaluated. For example, if a client reports conversing with God or an angel, then knowledge of the client's religious background is quite important. The client whose religious background does not include ecstatic experiences may be suspected of auditory-visual hallucinations. However, if the client's religious background includes ecstatic experiences, then the client may simply be describing experiences consonant with learning history, may be using metaphorical language derived from the religious tradition, or may be describing hallucinations preceding a psychotic break.

Family history helps specify the learning histories of clients and may help identify a client's tendency to behave in certain patterns. For example, the oldest children in large families may be taught to be independent and to take care of younger siblings as part of their learning history; the youngest children in the same families are less likely to be taught to take care of younger children than the oldest children. Under severe stress, learned patterns may emerge as predominant coping mechanisms such that the oldest children become focused on taking care of others or on attending to a multitude of details, whereas the youngest children expect others to take care of them. Thus, the pattern of relationships manifested in a client's family may provide clues to the origin of maladaptive relationships that the client manifests and may suggest therapeutic interventions.

General knowledge of family relationships helps establish that pattern of relationships that may be expected from a client. For example, if a client complains of present marital dissatisfaction and a series of failed marriages, then the therapist may choose to investigate relationships among the client's nuclear family. If the client's nuclear family had poor communication skills and a history of relationship disturbance, then the therapist may need to help the client gain skills in communication. On the other hand, if the client's family appears to possess adequate communication skills, then the therapist may need to explore issues other than communication training in order to aid the client in developing adaptive relationships.

Finally, family history may suggest to the therapist whether or not a client's family is capable of supporting a client who is severely ill. The illness may be associated with a high degree of family dysfunction that preceded the client's problems, or the disorder may disrupt the family system. In either case, a severely debilitated family may not be able to offer the support that a client with moderate to severe problems needs for adequate life functioning. For example, a family with a child with autism may be taxed beyond the emotional, financial, and social resources it possesses, and an appropriate therapeutic response may be to help the family develop new resources for coping with the child's illness.

Especially when serious psychopathology is suspected, the therapist may want to take a detailed psychiatric history of the client's family in addition to general family information. A detailed psychiatric history of the family is in most respects like that taken of the client. For each family member, the therapist investigates the presence or absence of symptoms; onset, nature, and duration; and the nature and effectiveness of any treatments. Of course, the therapist should use discretion in the quantity of data sought, because all family members are not of equal importance in their influence on the client. For example, knowing that a parent or sibling of a client is schizophrenic is much more important than knowing that a distant cousin is schizophrenic in terms of that person's influence on both learning history and genetic inheritance.

A detailed family history can alert the therapist to certain disorders that appear to be passed along (by genetic inheritance or learning) in families. The clearest example is Huntington's disease, which has 100% penetrance in families with the disorder. Other examples include autism, familial Alzheimer's disease, and substance abuse. Knowledge of family history does not provide a guaranty that a client will or will not display a particular disorder, but it does add to the predictive and explanatory power available to the therapist.

INTIMACY WITH FRIENDS AND SIGNIFICANT OTHERS

A history of friendships and romantic relationships may be instructive in conceptualizing a client's problem and developing an intervention. Issues of interest include whether the client has shown the ability to initiate intimate relationships or to sustain them once initiated. The therapist may inquire about how many close friends the client has had, either over a lifetime or in a specified time frame, how friendships were initiated, how the client related to these friends (e.g., level of disclosure, common activities, sources of tension, amount of time spent together), and causes of friendship termination. The therapist may pose the same questions about romantic relationships and also inquire about the level of sexual intimacy and level of commitment (e.g., exclusive dating relationship or monogamous marriage) that either party made to the relationship.

For example, if a college freshman comes to a university counseling center early in the semester complaining of loneliness, then the therapist may ask about family and intimate relationships in high school. If the client had a steady dating relationship and a circle of close friends, then the therapist may interpret the client's loneliness as an adjustment disorder that can be resolved with time and mild social support from the therapist. On the other hand, if the client has not had close friends or a healthy dating history, then the therapist may consider the complaint in light of poor social skills, dysthymia, or a personality disorder. A client who reports having made few friends over a lifetime cannot be expected to have appropriate skills to initiate friendships without substantial new learning. And, in some instances, a history of few friends may suggest that the client has some behavioral patterns associated with serious pathology. Likewise, a lack of intimate romantic relationships may indicate either the need to learn new patterns of relating to significant others, or it may indicate serious pathology. On the other hand, if a client has related to romantic companions in healthy ways, then the therapist can be relatively certain that the present complaint is not related to a learning problem, but may reflect environmentally induced stress or some newly emergent dysfunction.

SOCIAL SUPPORT SYSTEMS

Knowledge of a client's social support systems is informative for several reasons: for actual support supplied to clients in times of needs, as environments where a client's level of social skill may be assessed, and as training grounds for learning and practicing critical social skills. Furthermore, rejection by social groups with which a client wants to affiliate causes stress and may generate expectations of rejection if the client is rejected repeatedly. A client who has a history of healthy affiliation with social support systems is likely to have more innerpersonal and interpersonal resources for coping with stressful events than a person who has an impoverished history of social affiliation. Furthermore, a history of strong social support systems demonstrates that the client has basic skills necessary to develop relationships that facilitate adaptive living. Lack of social support systems may reflect a variety of issues, including a client's inability to relate to others, desire to be separate from others, or poor opportunity to develop social support groups.

A thorough evaluation of social support includes number and type of reference groups with which the client is affiliated, the type of support the client receives (both subjectively and objectively assessed), and the costs of belonging to these groups. Common support systems are family, friends, clubs, coworkers, and religious groups. The key issue is whether a client's social support network is adequate to facilitate an adaptive lifestyle. Therefore, the quantity of affiliations is less important than the quality of affiliations, and the cost–benefit ratio for belonging to a group is important. From a practical perspective, group membership gives the client an opportunity to engage in meaningful activities, meet other persons, and develop value systems, all of which are associated with life satisfaction.

For example, when a client presents with complaints of loneliness, the therapist may want to investigate the duration of the problem by exploring the client's social support history. If the client reports an impoverished social history, the therapist may suspect that the client has a long-standing history of social detachment, and therefore, loneliness. An approach to treating the client's loneliness may be to help the client identify appropriate social groups, develop skills that facilitate the client's incorporation into the social groups, and target social skills the client may continue to cultivate.

ABUSE HISTORY

Current evidence suggests that childhood abuse (physical and sexual) is a relatively common phenomenon and a history of abuse may appear in the adult client as borderline personality disorder, eating disorders, dissociative disorders, and somatization disorders. Because abuse has a relatively high rate of occurrence and because it has potentially serious psychological consequences, a therapist must consider the possibility that clients have been abused as children. However, the therapist investigating the possibility of abuse must exercise caution, as evidence suggests that client's memories can be shaped by the questions a therapist asks. The therapist must avoid twin pitfalls: failing to uncover abuse that occurred and leading the client to believe that abuse occurred when it did not.

The therapist investigating a possible history of abuse is advised to be direct and objective, to use neutral terminology, and to be empathic and sensitive to the client's needs without losing a therapeutic perspective. Therapists should be aware of any tendency they have to side with a victimized client. For example, if a therapist suspects a history of childhood sexual abuse, then the therapist may ask the client if an adult or another child ever touched the client on the breasts, genitals, or buttocks with a purpose other than to bathe the child, treat the child for an injury, or perform a medical examination. If the client responds affirmatively, then the therapist must ascertain who touched the child, for what purpose, how the child was touched, at what time in the child's life, and how many episodes occurred. Based on the client's answers, the therapist may accept that abuse did occur and formulate an intervention strategy, doubt that abuse occurred (and, if the client is alleging abuse, begin to explore reasons for the allegations), or determine that further investigation is required. Therapists should not assume that a client's vague feelings or fuzzy memories are evidential proof that abuse took place. Rather, they are symptoms of distress to be explored and included in a conceptualization of the client's complaints.

An equally difficult issue arises when a therapist suspects that a client is an abuse perpetrator. In that case, the therapist must ask questions similar to those posed to a victim of abuse: Have you touched anyone on the breasts, genitals, or buttocks who did not have the capacity to consent? Who, when, where, and how often? As with potential victims, the investigations of perpetrators should be direct and objective, and should avoid the use of leading language.

Unlike many of the other historical issues that a therapist examines, a positive history for abuse (either as a victim or as a perpetrator) introduces serious ethical and legal responsibilities. If victims cannot protect themselves (e.g., a child or a person with impaired judgment), then the therapist has an obligation to protect, possibly notifying legal and human service agencies or parents. If victims are competent adults, are able to protect themselves, and may benefit from responding to the abuse and the abuser, then the therapist may allow them to choose how, when, and where the abuse is to be confronted.

EDUCATIONAL AND VOCATIONAL HISTORY

Frequently, an estimate of premorbid functioning can facilitate evaluation of intellectual or personality changes associated with a disorder. Educational and vocational histories can provide accurate and reliable baseline data to assess changes. Basic questions relate to highest level of academic achievement, grade performance relative to peers, occupational choices, and success within a chosen occupation. Obviously, these data aid the therapist who is treating a stroke patient in a rehabilitation center. Potential recovery of function is often associated with level of premorbid intelligence and achievement, and the upper bound of recovery is related to abilities the client evinced prior to the stroke. Likewise, a therapist working with a person with mental retardation can use vocational and educational data to help the client select from among various life choices. For example, two clients with mental retardation may have similar estimates of intelligence. However, one has a job-related history that is more successful than the other. Job performance information may help the therapist who is asked to make recommendations concerning a client's potential for independent living, probability of successful training for a skilled occupation, or types of jobs in which a client may be successful.

Knowledge of a client's premorbid level of functioning may assist the therapist in evaluating personality changes associated with disease processes. One of the most famous case reports in neurological history involved Phineas Gage, who sustained damage to the medial ventral frontal lobes in a work-related accident. Prior to the accident, he had been described as a personable fellow who showed great responsibility in his work. Following the accident, Gage demonstrated erratic, quarrelsome behavior, and did not maintain a steady job. Knowledge of Gage's premorbid vocational functioning allowed psychologists, even substantially after the accident, to estimate the level of damage to Gage's personality associated with his brain damage.

SUICIDAL AND HOMICIDAL HISTORY

Clients who report violent ideation or intentions should be assessed for suicidal and homicidal risk. This includes present feelings, thoughts, and behaviors. However, past behaviors of violence to self or others may be even more predictive of future violence than present cognitions and feelings. For example, if a client presents with severe depression and reports a desire to die, then the therapist should inquire into past behavior. The client who has made numerous suicidal gestures, especially in the recent past, should be treated as a high risk for suicide, even if firm plans for suicide have not been made. (Equally important is the history of close family members who have committed suicide, because this has predictive value for the client's behavior.) On the other hand, a client who has no past history of suicidal gestures may be treated as a moderate or high-risk client based on present ideation and intention. Likewise, the client who presents with violent feelings toward others, but with no history of acting on those feelings, must be treated differently than the client who has a past history of violence toward others. In the case of the client with a negative history for violence toward others, the therapist may monitor feelings and actions, using psychotherapeutic interventions and contracts with the therapist concerning violent acting out. A history of past violent behavior suggests that the client has the capacity to act in violent ways, and proactive steps must be taken to prevent danger to other persons, as well as to treat the underlying causes of the violence.

SOURCES AND MEANS OF COLLECTING HISTORICAL DATA

One of the primary sources of historical data has been the semistructured client interview. After establishing rapport with the client, therapists use that presenting complaint as a guide to explore current and historical issues that affect case conceptualization and treatment intervention. Clearly, the client is an important source of information. The client has access to a breadth and depth of data that few, if any, others have concerning the client. Furthermore, only the client can provide direct access to subjective feelings or thoughts in conscious awareness. However, there are some significant liabilities associated with a semistructured client interview: the therapist's selection bias and limited knowledge, the client's limited capacity or willingness to report accurately or fully, and restricted point of view. Various approaches can be used to supplement data collected in the semistructured interview.

Liabilities stemming from a therapist's limited knowledge or selection bias may be counteracted by a structured interview. If therapists use a predesigned format, then there is less danger that they will fail to collect some essential data that were overlooked because the therapist had limited knowledge about the client's disorder or symptom history, or because the therapist attended to nondiagnostic symptoms and failed to attend to diagnostic symptoms. In some cases, a comprehensive interview schedule may be followed. For example, if the therapist is conducting an assessment to determine a child's foster placement, and if the therapist has limited access to the child's records, then the therapist's task may be to collect as much data as possible in a limited time. In other cases, a domain-specific interview schedule may be followed. For example, if a client presents with symptoms of posttraumatic stress disorder (PTSD), and the therapist will be able to engage in continuing assessment of the client, then a dedicated PTSD interview schedule may be the most effective means of gathering data. The comprehensive interview schedule does allow the therapist to gather most of the information necessary to a wide range of disorders, but it may require a substantial amount of time or provide only cursory examination of the most important content areas. The dedicated interview schedule avoids these pitfalls of the comprehensive schedule, but it does require that the therapist be accurate in the provisional diagnosis.

Limited capacity and willingness to report past life events are common in the context of a diagnostic interview. Clients may have diminished capacity due to age-related problems, language deficits, or memory failures. For example, a very young child or an elderly person with Alzheimer's disease may be able to give limited data concerning their histories. On the other hand, clients with normal cognitive capacity may be unwilling to reveal their history out of shame, a desire to present themselves in a positive light, or fear of social or legal consequences. For example, a client may be unwilling to discuss sexual impotence, excessive alcohol use, or pedophilia. In cases where clients cannot or will not report their histories, collateral histories taken from other persons who know the client may be invaluable. Collateral sources may include family members and friends, teachers, employers, physicians, other mental health professionals, and police officers. School, medical, vocational, psychiatric, legal, and informal (e.g., letters or a diary) records and other such written documents often augment human collateral witnesses, and have the advantage of being less subject to memory failures than personal interviews. Of course, the therapist must be aware that collateral sources have limited points of view and are frequently biased in their presentations.

Finally, clients have limited points of view. For example, clients who present with complaints of anxiety may be able to describe the role of other persons (e.g., parents, teachers, employers) and stressful events (examinations, occupational changes, financial restrictions) in generating their anxiety. However, they may not be able to describe their own role in creating or maintaining their anxiety. The collateral witnesses and written documents described here may provide an enhanced picture of the client's mental health. Therefore, the astute therapist will seek convergent evidence from a variety of sources.

SUMMARY

Current symptoms and functioning are necessary for conceptualization of and intervention in a client's presenting problem. However, by themselves, current symptoms may be insufficient to complete this task. Treatment conceptualization and planning may benefit enormously from knowledge of the history of presenting symptoms, psychiatric disorders, substance abuse, medical disorders, developmental patterns, family, friendships and romantic relationships, social support, sexual or physical abuse, educational and vocational achievement, and violence to self or others. A variety of methods is available for assessing the history of the presenting problem. A traditional means is the direct client interview using a semistructured format. Alternatively, the therapist may engage the client in a comprehensive, structured clinical interview designed to assess history broadly, or the therapist may use a domain-specific interview that covers a particular disorder in great detail. For information that the client does not provide, the therapist may turn to collateral witnesses or written documents. Finally, the therapist must use judgment in gathering historical data. There are no absolute measures of how much to gather. The therapist must keep in mind the nature of the assessment, restrictions on time and financial resources that can be devoted to assessment, and the nature of the disorder suspected.

SUGGESTED READINGS

Cormier, W. B., & Cormier, L. S. (1991). *Interviewing strategies for helpers: Fundamental skills and cognitive behavioral interventions* (3rd ed.). Pacific Grove, CA: Brooks/Cole.

Halleck, S. L. (1991). *Evaluation of the psychiatric patient: A primer.* New York: Plenum.

Hersen, M., & Bellack, A. S. (1981). *Behavioral assessment: A practical handbook* (2nd ed.). New York: Pergamon.

Hersen, M., & Turner, S. M. (Eds.). (1994). *Diagnostic interviewing* (2nd ed.). New York: Plenum.

Morrison, J. (1995). *The first interview: Revised for the* DSM–IV. New York: Guilford.

Sullivan, H. S. (1954). *The psychiatric interview.* New York: Norton.

5

Social History

Bunny Falk
Nova Southeastern University

Have you have ever watched a "learn to paint" television show, and just as you are about to switch to a different station, the artist says, "So today we are going to learn how to paint Da Vinci's Mona Lisa"? Your curiosity intensifies and you watch with great interest as the instructor applies the paint to the canvas. As you watch, you begin to wonder, when are the rudimentary outlines of varying color going to come together and start looking like the Mona Lisa? And then, slowly but surely, the artist adds a line here, a dab of color there, and that unmistakable face appears. Just as the artist skillfully adds fine details to the broad brush strokes to form the face, so too will skillful therapists obtain a clear and concise social history of their client.

A social history provides the context in which clients (and their presenting problem) developed. Biological predispositions aside, no one is born dysthymic, obsessive-compulsive, or phobic. Something or someone contributed to the emergence of the client's difficulties. A client's **history** is more than a set of facts; it is **HIS STORY**. The therapist's job is to facilitate the telling of that story; because without it, the therapist may be treating a disorder instead of a person with a disorder. Anyone can place eyes, nose, and mouth on a canvas and call it a face. But it takes the details, the nuances, and subtleties to produce a portrait.

This chapter provides practical information about, and "field-tested" suggestions for, conducting the social history portion of an interview. There is a brief discussion of the purpose of a social history, which is followed by descriptions of several useful formats. Because some therapists prefer to approach the social history as a series of subcategories (e.g., family history, marital history, medical history, etc.), there is a discussion about how to obtain the basic information (usually obvious to the client) within each category, as well as relevant information the client may assume is unimportant or unrelated to the problem. Throughout, sample questions, statements, and transitions are offered to demonstrate the point being made. When reading these examples, and perhaps trying them out on clients (or role-play partners), keep in mind that these suggestions are meant to be helpful, not a script to be followed word for word. After seeing a videotape of Albert Ellis interviewing "Gloria" in a counseling skills class, several students attempted to adopt Ellis' confrontive style as their own. The result was disastrous. Therapists, as interviewers and clinicians, will achieve greater effectiveness by developing their own style.

PURPOSE OF THE SOCIAL HISTORY

Whether referred to as social history, relevant background information, background history, or psychosocial history, the purpose of this part of the interview is to obtain sufficient information to conceptualize the origins of the client's difficulties. After listening to clients describe their distress and/or symptoms—including onset, course, and duration—the clinician will understand the *problem*. Regardless of theoretical perspective, effective treatment strategies depend on the clinician also understanding the person with the problem.

As mentioned earlier, clients' stories provide the context within which they develop both adaptive and maladaptive strategies for living. Early childhood experiences, personality styles of family and friends, interpersonal relationships (or lack of them), educational and work experiences, health status, socioeconomic status, experiences with intimacy (both sexual and emotional), and encounters with legal or governmental systems are some of the elements that impact on a person's life. No two people experience life in quite the same way. This is true for clients as well as therapists. It will not be enough to elicit documentary-style reporting of details about the client's life. The therapist also wants to hear the client's perceptions of, as well as the meaning and feelings associated with, the things they report. The point here is to avoid conducting the interview as if it were an interrogation. Asking one specific (close-ended) question after another in rapid succession does not provide a safe, accepting, and nonthreatening environment that invites clients to tell their stories.

Students almost always report having the same "getting stuck" experience when they "ran out of things to ask." To avoid this predicament, therapists should remind themselves that they are not computers that have been pre-programmed with 150 social history questions. Therapists who continuously refer to a list of questions stored in memory are probably not asking questions that would naturally (and spontaneously) occur.

Listen carefully to what clients are saying. Follow their lead and satisfy the need to know by asking "What was that like?" or "How did that (person or event) change things for you?" For example, a client might answer a question about socioeconomic level during childhood in the following way: "My family was one of rather limited means, in fact, I do not remember ever having a doll." At this point, the therapist might wonder what she means by "limited" or how she feels about having no toys as a child. There is the temptation to assume that not having a doll was terrible (because it would be awful for you); therefore, the therapist decides not to inquire about her feelings but instead asks: "What do you mean by limited?" This is not a bad question to ask, but this therapist would probably find out much more by asking something like: "What was that like for you?" The client might reply: "Of course I wanted what the other girls had, but we were very poor. But you know, my father felt so bad about not having the money to buy me dolls, that he made me a doll house with all the furniture and the little people. Made it all for me. I was always very close to him. He understood me so well." The therapist's broad invitation to tell how she felt allowed the client not only to clarify what "limited" meant (poor, little money), but also to talk about her perception of the relationship she had with her father.

Successful interviewing takes practice. New clinicians report discomfort when asking clients for more than the cold, hard facts. As such, they stifle their natural curiosity about why things have happened the way they have. Students often believe the purpose of the interview is to focus solely on the client's difficulties. After all, the client came into therapy looking for relief from symptoms or resolution to a crisis; therefore, the clinician should find out as much about the problem as possible. Be reassured: That is exactly what you are doing. If the old adage, "We live what we learn, and we learn what we live" holds true, then the social history will point both therapist and client toward relief and resolutions.

DESCRIPTION OF THE SOCIAL HISTORY

The social history portion of the intake interview (and ultimately the written intake report) is usually the lengthiest because it is the most comprehensive. Interview format generally follows the logical flow of a person's life. Occasionally, more than one session will have to be devoted to the intake assessment. Clinicians should obtain information in the all of the following areas, if possible:

1. Family of origin
2. Extended family
3. Present family constellation
4. Educational level attained—including description of interpersonal aspect of the school experience
5. Occupational training/job history
6. Marital (significant other) history
7. Interpersonal relationship history
8. Recreational preferences
9. Sexual history—including inquiry about abuse
10. Medical history—including significant family medical history and/or current medications
11. Psychiatric/psychotherapy history—including hospitalizations and/or medications
12. Legal history
13. Alcohol and substance use—including recreational and social use
14. Nicotine and caffeine consumption

Some clinicians prefer to organize their inquiry by thinking in terms of broader categories. For example, family history may include Areas 1, 2, and 3. Relationships may encompass Areas 6, 7, and 8. Some clinicians may not explore areas, such as education, occupation, and legal history beyond superficial facts. Others see every area as having an equal potential for revealing important information. Obviously, the more time the clinician can devote to conducting the interview, the more in-depth the inquiry.

Typically, clinicians use the first two sessions (50 to 90 minutes) to conduct the intake interview. However, even if less time is allowed, remember that the client will continue to reveal useful information throughout therapy, as long as opportunities are provided for them to do so. When time is short, begin by saying something like: "We have limited time to talk today, so I'd like to ask you to tell me things about yourself that you think I should know," or "Why don't we start with your telling me the things you think are important for me to know today?"

MAKING THE TRANSITION FROM PROBLEM TO PERSON

When time is not limited, let the story of the client's life unfold. Because clients have come to the session either in crisis, or in search of symptom relief, they may want to talk only about the presenting problem. At some point, the clinician must change the focus of the session (i.e., off the problem and onto the person). Execution of these transitions is made easier by telling the client something like the following: "I think at this point I'd like to change our focus a little—if I knew more about you, that would be very helpful," or "I want to take some time now to get to know you better. Tell me . . . ." Keep in mind, implementing a change in focus structures the session and permits the best use of the interview time.

FAMILY HISTORY

It is not uncommon for clients to become upset while recounting their presenting problem. For some clients, especially those talking about the problem for the first time, the anxiety, sadness, or anger exhibited may escalate to extreme levels. As the clinician probes for more details surrounding the presenting problem, other clients become more guarded. In either case, this is a signal from the client that the therapist is getting close to very sensitive and/or painful material. Clients may not be ready to face their situation. Therefore, to place some distance between clients and their present distress, point them in the direction of family history. Ask where they were born and raised, and then ask about their family of origin. Interfamilial patterns of communication, characterizations of family members, and presence of past or present conflicts all shed light on clients' current distress. Additionally, it is important to know if symptoms or problem behaviors, similar to that of the client, are (or were) present in other family members. Cultural norms for some clients will mean that their extended family plays a key role in all aspects of their life. Sometimes, with as many as three generations living in one house, the client's problems are compounded by blurred roles, boundaries, or failure to fully individuate. Taking the time to explore the influential forces waiting at home for clients when they return from therapy assists the therapist in neutralizing those who would sabotage any progress in an effort to keep things as they were.

An effective way to keep track of information is a family genogram. Developed by family therapist Murray Bowen (1978), the genogram resembles a family tree but uses symbols to represent each person about which the client reports information. The genogram is a pictorial representation of the client's family of origin and extended family, and provides specifics about each individual (e.g., birthdate, marital status, illnesses, etc.). Also, recurring problems, conflicts, or patterns of behavior are easier to see. Some clients are hesitant to talk about family members for fear of appearing disloyal or being judged. Asking what their Uncle Eddie died of (i.e., cirrhosis of the liver) is far less threatening than asking a client to identify all the alcoholics in the family. Providing dates, cause of death, relocations, and such on the genogram reduces uneasiness and enables the information-gathering process to get started. The following are examples of questions or statements that encourage clients to expand the description of their family:

Who was (or is) in your family?

Tell me what was it like to grow up in your family? How would you characterize your relationship with the members of your family?

Many families have a tradition that they share, it might be how they celebrate birthdays or how they settle an argument. Tell me about a tradition in your family.

How did (or does) your family celebrate the holidays (any holiday)?

Who did you go to when you needed someone to talk to?

How did you know when you were "being good (or bad)"?

All families have times of crisis: How did (does) your family deal with those times. Tell me what they do.

Remember, clients will answer most questions; specific questions yield specific information. For many clients, this may be their first therapy experience. Unsure of what to expect, the client will follow the therapist's lead. Broad inquiries imply that interest goes beyond the basic facts.

EDUCATIONAL HISTORY

After the family, school experiences are the next important in shaping individuals. Clients' shared memories and perceptions of time in school provide a way to assess how well they fared not only in the educational process, but also in the socialization process. If the process went well, clients will probably have much more to say than if it was rough. Even the sternest ("she was the meanest old lady") third-grade teacher can provoke fond memories.

A complete lack of memories is even more noteworthy. Traumatic or negative events during early childhood may make it difficult for the client to recall not only the specific event, but also the everyday occurrences common to all young children. A good way to explore any thoughts the client has regarding not being able to remember would be to ask: "What sense do you make of not being able to remember anything about this time in your life?" or "What do you think about having no memories?"

A person who was successful in forming friendships in school, usually continues to have success in relationships later in life. A lack of relationships throughout the school years may indicate a failure to master basic social skills. Confidence, self-esteem, or lack thereof may have its origins during this period of the client's life. Take note of how clients describe themselves. Is there a single event to point to as a success or proud accomplishment? Or, does the client summarize school days as a dismal failure? The question "What was school like for you?" may get a one-word answer like "Horrible!," but "How so?" invites an explanation.

Naturally, a review of educational information should also include how well the client performed academically. Report cards are not always an accurate representation of intellectual functioning. Clients who have been very successful in their field, but report that they flunked out of high school have certainly capitalized on their strengths. In contrast, there may be clients who report great grades, scholarships, good college, and a great job that they have been asked to leave because of drug use.

OCCUPATIONAL TRAINING/JOB HISTORY

Inexperienced clinicians would rather ask something like, "What do you do [for a living]?", rather than begin inquiring with a direct, "Are you currently working?" Students sometimes express concern about "embarrassing" an unemployed client. Their lack of insight into how judgmental that sounds is surprising. The direct question does not imply any pejorative notion on the clinician's part, only a temporal one. A "No" answer may mean retirement, leave of absence, sabbatical, or—if the client is a seasonal employee (like a teacher)—summer vacation. Of course, it may very well mean unemployed. If so, it is important to know if the client is looking for a job. Here again, the interviewer cannot assume that not looking for a job has clinical significance. It may mean, for example, retirement, an opportunity to return to school, or winning the lottery.

A good indicator of successful occupational functioning is to obtain a job history. Explain that some people remain in the same job with the same company their entire lives, whereas others have a difficult time finding one thing that holds their interest and frequently change jobs. Then, ask a question like: "Tell me which sounds more like you?"

One thing to explore is whether clients work in the field in which they were trained. This may provide wonderful insights into family dynamics that might not otherwise come to light. Consider an attorney who originally was trained to be a dentist. When asked why he took such a circuitous route to law school, he explained that his father had always wanted a doctor in the family. He was accepted at dentistry school and not medical school, and he decided to attend because he thought he was still giving his father the doctor he wanted. But, the kicker is, he hated being a dentist! And so, after his father died, he went to law school.

MARITAL HISTORY

Marital history means much more than how many times a person has been married. This is also an opportunity to learn about any other relationships the client perceives as significant. Marital status is one of the items usually found on the demographic form given to the client by the receptionist in an office or clinic. Most often the client is asked to circle one: S, M, D, or W.

Why not use the client's status as the place to start? You might say to the client: "Circling a letter really doesn't let you say much about being divorced, you probably have a lot to say," or, "Writing *married* in a blank doesn't let you say much about it; why don't you take me through your marriage?" If clients seem unsure about how to begin, help start the story by suggesting that they describe how they met; what was the early attraction? If clients do not keep the narrative going, there are several queries that can provide valuable information about client satisfaction:

Tell me one thing you would not want your partner to change.

Tell me one thing you want your partner to change.

What would you refuse to change about yourself, even if your partner asked you to?

How do you think you would characterize your relationship in 5 years?

Unfortunately, many intake forms do not have an indicator for committed relationships of unmarried or gay or lesbian couples. Often, clients are not sure how to indicate their "relationship" status. So ask them: "Are you currently in a relationship?" This probably will uncover more accurate information than asking if the client is married. Always follow a specific question like this with a more open-ended inquiry, such as: "How would you characterize the relationship?" or "In all relationships there are good times and not so good times. Tell me about some of those times."

Older adults pose special interviewing considerations. It is not unusual for older women to have outlived more than one husband. As they get older, the need for companionship may place the older person in the multiple-marriage partners category. It might be inaccurate to assume that the older client cannot maintain committed relationships simply based on number of marriages. On the other hand, noteworthy information may be missed if the reasons for a lengthy widowhood following a reportedly "idyllic" marriage are not explored. It would be helpful to ask, for example: "You described your marriage as [wonderful]; tell me what the last 10 years without a partner have been like." If the client describes these years as terrific, then find out more about the marriage.

INTERPERSONAL RELATIONSHIPS

In addition to marital or other committed relationship, does your client have friends? Have the client talk about friends, coworkers, neighbors, and how these relationships are working.

RECREATIONAL PREFERENCES

This simply means: How do clients have fun? A therapist whose work involves substance or alcohol abusers will report that one notable deficit is lack of recreational skills. Chemically dependent individuals often have no "clean" frame of reference when it comes to recreation. Also, if clients have obsessive-compulsive tendencies or traits, fun is not something that comes easily to them. Their answers will indicate an inability to tolerate spontaneous or "childlike" behavior. They view fun/recreation as wasteful or silly. What's more, they will not hesitate to tell you so.

SEXUAL HISTORY

Even experienced clinicians have difficulty obtaining an adequate sexual history. The client will sense the level of discomfort in the clinician and take the hint; uneasiness, stilted, awkwardly phrased questions, and abruptness send the message that sexually related topics and problems will not be tolerated by the therapist. If this is the case, clients with a history of sexual dysfunction or abuse may be unsure about what to do. Also, older adults are often treated by clinicians as if they have no interest in sex, or are incapable of sexual feelings and desires. This is absolutely incorrect.

A therapist could begin taking sexual history by asking clients if there has been any change in their level of interest in engaging in sexual relations, or in satisfaction. If any change is indicated, ask what clients think has caused it. Clients may suggest that any differences have more to do with a partner than with them. Questions like "How have you discussed these differences with your partner?" and "How will you resolve the differences?" will reveal if the partners can talk about sexual intimacy.

Many clinical supervisors view inquiry into the presence of sexual abuse as necessary. Unfortunately, students and inexperienced clinicians either ignore the topic completely or approach the subject in an insensitive and threatening way. The best way to become acquainted with alternative ways to approach the subject with clients is to go to the literature on sexual abuse or adult survivors of sexual abuse. A question like, "Have you ever been forced to engage in sexual activity against your will, or without your permission?" usually elicits an informative response.

MEDICAL HISTORY

An adequate medical history will always include information about current physical conditions receiving treatment, hospitalizations for medical reasons, all surgical procedures, serious dental problems, name of the client's primary physician or family doctor, the date of the last checkup, and the name and dosage of all currently prescribed medications. Also ask the client about favorite over-the-counter remedies. Rather than have the client rely on memory for names and dosages of medications, when you schedule the intake appointment, ask them to bring all of their medications with them. It is not uncommon to find a client who, for example, has a bottle of Ativan prescribed by Dr. Jones, also has a bottle of Ativan prescribed by another physician in a nearby town. Or two different physicians may have prescribed drugs with an antagonistic effect. It is important to keep in mind that more antidepressants are prescribed by family doctors and general practitioners than by psychiatrists. Proper medications can be an ally, but improper or unknown drugs can be a therapist's worst nightmare.

Family medical history is crucial to the medical history. Ask clients, "Are you aware of any medical problems in your family?" If clients are unsure, then ask, "Who might you ask to get that information if you don't know firsthand?" Many medical conditions have an effect on emotional functioning. As such, untreated physical symptoms may not only pose a medical problem, but also an emotional one. Therefore, ask clients: how they have been feeling, and to describe their energy level as compared to 6 months or a year ago.

PSYCHIATRIC/PSYCHOTHERAPY HISTORY

It is important for the therapist to know if the client has been previously diagnosed with a psychiatric disorder. If so, do not assume the diagnosis is absolute. This does mean that the client has entered the mental health care system and the problem may be recurrent. Clients may not remember anything more than seeing a psychiatrist at some time in the past, or that they spent time in a hospital for emotional reasons. Any names, dates, or name of facility may make it possible to obtain past records. If they can recall details of prior hospitalizations, then try to determine the reason for the hospitalization, type of treatment provided (medication only, Electro-Convulsive Treatment [ECT], individual and/or group psychotherapy). It is also important to find out how the client views the experience: "How was it helpful?" or "What was different as a result of your hospitalization?"

Prior outpatient treatment or psychotherapy also indicates that the client has entered the mental health care system at an earlier time. The situation leading up to such treatment would not be as serious as one requiring inpatient treatment. Here too, details can assist the therapist in understanding the client's impetus to seek help previously, as well as pinpoint what the client perceived to be helpful the last time.

LEGAL HISTORY

A good way to approach legal history is to ask: "What encounters have you had with the legal or justice system?" Clients will answer this type of question more accurately than if asked if they have had legal problems. Legal problems can mean anything from lawsuits, speeding tickets, to time in jail for a DUI. Let clients reveal the nature of their legal experiences. Multiple traffic offenses, criminal activity, or violent crime portray far less impulse control and judgment than an occasional speeding ticket or parking fines. On the other hand, a client who evinces extremely litiginous behavior may have characterological pathology.

ALCOHOL AND SUBSTANCE USE/ABUSE

Asking clients something like "I like an occasional beer or glass of wine (with or without dinner). How about you?" is a nonthreatening way to inquire about alcohol use. Today it has almost become chic to confess about having had a sustance abuse problem, so clients seem less reticent about discussing this area. However, if relationship, job-related, or legal problems seem to coincide with the substance or alcohol dependence, then they often become reserved again. Clients who are in denial will not respond favorably to any inquiries, even when faced with evidence to the contrary. In these situations, therapists should confront inconsistencies in behavior, home/job situations, and so on. Here again, consult the literature for guidance as to taking drinking history, and so forth.

NICOTINE AND/OR CAFFEINE CONSUMPTION

Although today's health care consumer is far better informed than ever before, many clients may not be aware of the "other addictive drugs": namely, nicotine and caffeine. Thanks to the aggressive stand the U.S. Food and Drug Administration is taking with the tobacco companies, the addictive nature of nicotine is being given tremendous media coverage. This is not as true for caffeine. Consumption of either substance is meaningful, so ask clients about it: for example, "How has your doctor's edict, quit the coffee and the smokes, changed things for you?" or "What will be the most difficult thing about doing as your doctor asks—to quit smoking and drinking coffee?"

BRINGING THE HISTORY TAKING TO CLOSURE

When the second hour of the intake interview is drawing to a close and after asking for information in more than a dozen areas, how does the therapist bring this part of the interview to a close? Remember, although this interview may be ending, the opportunities to learn more about the client are beginning. Every session provides a new chance to hear more of the client's story. Because the therapist–client relationship is in the early stages of trust and rapport building, a very effective way to promote a successful colaboration is to ask clients about any feelings they have concerning what has been covered. Ask something like, "Can you think of anything else that I should know today? We will have many more opportunities to go back to many of the things we talked about today."

SUMMARY

The social history allows the therapist to paint a portrait rather than draw a sketch. Make an effort to leave no stone unturned when gathering information. Inquiries in the aforementioned 14 areas will provide a thorough understanding of the context within which the client's difficulties developed.

Interviewing is a skill that develops over time. The best way to learn it is to do it. When role play or interviewing opportunities present themselves (especially with live supervision), seize the chance. Do not shy away for fear of looking foolish or making a mistake. Tape practice interviews and all sessions while in training and then listen to them. This is a great way to hear misspeaks and to decide how to improve.

The following is a list of ingredients for a good social history interview:

1. Listen to what your client tells you. This will give you direction for further query.
2. If you must talk, say or ask something noteworthy.
3. Interview. Do not interrogate.
4. Be curious—it comes naturally and spontaneously. Don't stifle it.
5. You can't remember everything; you will remember what is important.
6. Be aware of cultural differences.
7. Invite your client to
   "Tell me . . ."
   "Give me an example . . ."
   "What sense do you make of it?"
   "How was that for you?"
   "What helps, what makes it worse?"

"How would you characterize . . ."
    or
"How would you describe . . ."
"Tell me what you think I should know about . . ."

SUGGESTED READINGS

Bowen, M. (1978). *Family therapy in clinical practice.* New York: Jason Aronson.

Bugental, J. F. T. (1987). *The art of the psychotherapist.* New York: Norton.

Egendorf, A. (1995). Hearing people through their pain. *Journal of Traumatic Stress, 8,* 5–28.

Fontain, J. H., & Hammond, N. L. (1994). Twenty counseling maxims. *Journal of Counseling and Development, 73,* 223–226.

Hersen, M., & Turner, S. M. (Eds.). (1994). *Diagnostic interviewing* (2nd ed.). New York: Plenum.

Lukas, S. (1993). *Where to start and what to ask: An assessment handbook.* New York: Norton.

Meier, S. T., & Davis, S. R. (1997). *The elements of counseling.* Pacific Grove, CA: Brooks/Cole.

Morrison, J. (1995). *The first interview.* New York: Guilford.

McGoldrick, M., & Gerson, R. (1985). *Genograms in family assessment.* New York: Norton.

6

Medical History

Oscar G. Bukstein
University of Pittsburgh School of Medicine

The medical history is part of any complete evaluation for emotional and/or behavioral problems. The substantial progress of neuroscience research during the past several decades has provided substantial evidence for the conclusion that some psychiatric disorders are the result of abnormal brain mechanisms. This potentially places psychiatric disorders on the same level as medical disorders: that is, having a physical or biological (i.e., organic) etiology. The medical basis of psychiatric disorders, as well as other potential relations between medical illness, treatments for medical illness, and behavioral/emotional disorders, further underscores the importance of the medical history in an assessment interview. A substantial literature supports the principle that preexisting or concurrent medical problems affect psychological functioning, and vice versa. Medical history information becomes critical in developing a comprehensive understanding of a client's life circumstances and psychosocial functioning.

THE PURPOSE OF THE MEDICAL HISTORY

The primary purpose of the medical history portion of the assessment interview is to obtain data from the health domain of the client's life. Information from this domain may tell much about clients and their current status. For a differential diagnosis of the presenting problem(s), information about current health status may point to a medical illness as a factor in the etiology of the emotional or behavioral symptoms reported or exacerbation of preexisting or concurrent behavioral or emotional symptoms. Many specific medical illnesses are manifested by a variety of psychological symptoms, which are identical to those symptoms seen in specific psychiatric syndromes. The potential mechanisms for psychological manifestations of medical illness include direct physiological effects of the illness on the brain, alteration or distortion of sensory input or disruption of the sleep–wake cycle, specific or toxic effects of medication or other treatments, and impairment in the individual's ability to cope with the illness. Most psychiatric diagnoses require eliminating organic or medical causes prior to assigning a psychiatric diagnosis. During a diagnostic evaluation, the clinician must consider any and all medical causes or contributions to the presenting emotional and/or behavioral symptoms.

Psychiatric symptoms or disorders may also be the result of reaction or maladjustment to a medical illness, either acute or chronic. Medical illness and the individual's adjustment to severe or chronic illness can manifest themselves in a variety of psychological responses, both adaptive and maladaptive.

In addition to contributing information to adequately explain the presenting problem(s), the medical portion of the assessment interview can add important information to the clinician's general database on the client. This database includes the client's general health status, past medical history, current health providers(s), and current treatments.

CLASSIFICATION OF MEDICAL PROBLEMS IN *DSM–IV*

In the *Diagnostic and Statistical Manual of Mental Disorders* (*DSM–IV*), there are several ways of classifying medical problems and their relations with psychiatric disorders. Using the multiaxial system, the clinician can indicate medical problems or the effects of such problems on psychosocial functioning on several axes. In Axis I, Clinical Disorders, there are several clinical entities that are, in fact, medical conditions. Delirium, Dementia, and Amnestic Disorders are defined by their relations to specific medical conditions, substance use, or trauma. Within the category of Mental Disorders due to a General Medical Condition, Catatonic Disorder, Personality Change, and Mental Disorder Not Otherwise Specified are listed as ". . . due to . . . (specific medical condition)." Substance-Related Disorders, especially intoxication, withdrawal, and complications from the use of a specific substance are physiologically induced conditions. Sexual Disorders and Sleep Disorders have prominent medical components. Somatoform and Factitious Disorders can be defined in terms of their presentations of medical symptoms. The section Other Conditions that May be a Focus of Clinical Attention

TABLE 6.1
Subtypes of Psychological Factors
Affecting a Medical Condition (*DSM–IV*)

Mental Disorder Affecting . . . (specify the general medical condition)
Psychological Symptoms Affecting . . . (specify the general medical condition)
Personality Traits or Coping Style Affecting . . . (specify the general medical condition)
Maladaptive Health Behaviors Affecting . . . (specify the general medical condition)
Stress-Related Physiological Response Affecting . . . (specify the general medical condition)
Other or Unspecified Psychological Factors Affecting . . . (specify the general medical condition)

---

lists several psychological factors that may influence medical problems (see Table 6.1). Although not a psychiatric diagnosis per se, these factors may affect the course of medical problem(s), interfere with treatment, and may be a risk factor for additional morbidity or mortality. This category is reserved for psychological factors where there is a clinically significant effect on the course of the medical problems and/or place the individual at greater risk for a poorer outcome, and where there is evidence of an association between the psychological factor and the medical condition.

Specific medical conditions relevant to the understanding and treatment of the psychiatric problems (Axis I and III) are listed on Axis III. Axis III should include all major medical disorders, acute or chronic, because these may potentially influence the psychiatric problems whether or not there is a direct relation.

On Axis IV, psychosocial and environmental problems, problems that affect the diagnosis, treatment, and prognosis of mental disorders are grouped together in nine categories that include problems with access to health care services. Finally, Axis V includes the client's response to medical problems along with psychological problems to determine the individual's overall level of psychosocial functioning.

DEVELOPMENTAL DIFFERENCES IN THE MEDICAL HISTORY

Despite several important similarities in the medical history across age groups and other specific populations, there often are salient differences between these groups. These differences primarily reflect the expected differences in the prevalence of medical problems between these populations but also issues of development relevant to specific age groups. For children and adolescents, the medical history should include a review of growth and development, including difficulties with pregnancy, labor, delivery, and postnatal problems, and attainment of developmental motor and language milestones (e.g., age of walking, talking, and toilet training). Use of well-child care, an appropriate immunization record, and the occurrence of childhood illnesses are typical areas for inquiry. Even variations in normal development can take on a medical aspect, as these deviations can be the result of a variety of medical conditions. For example, delays in attainment of developmental milestones, such as walking, talking, or control of toileting, can be signs or evidence of medical problems (e.g., cerebral palsy).

Medical illness commonly produces a transient regression in the behavior of children. Severe or chronic illnesses, although rare in children, can have a profound effect on the development and psychological adjustment of children. Medical problems can interfere with attainment of normal developmental milestones and development of academic and social proficiency.

For adolescents, medical-related inquiry focuses on attainment of physical maturation and progression through the physical stages of puberty. A history of sexual behavior, substance use, and other risk-taking behaviors should be elicited. Although uncommon, significant acute or chronic medical illness can interfere with the developmental tasks of adolescents. For example, dependence on parents to attend to intensive treatment regimens and parental overprotection may prevent an adolescent from achieving a measure of independence. In adolescents or children with diabetes mellitus, both child and parental reactions often result in depression and frequent adolescent noncompliance to the treatment regimen.

As an individual matures and ages, several medical illnesses become more prevalent. Cardiovascular disease, gastrointestinal problems, and other chronic illnesses affect an increasing proportion of individuals. These illnesses can affect a person's role functioning, including satisfactory maintenance of social, marital, parental, and vocational roles.

Finally, for the older patient, declining general health status, medical illnesses (especially degenerative problems such as stroke or Alzheimer's disease), and treatment can have profound affect on the individual's mental health. Illness often forces individuals into a more dependent role, especially in older age, so such a dependent position can have profound effects on mood and adaptive functioning.

PRIMARY COMPONENTS OF THE MEDICAL HISTORY

Whether the clinician chooses a brief screen of the medical domain or a more intensive survey of medical history and status, the primary components of the interview remain the same (see Table 6.2). These primary components are a history of current and/or past medical problems and treatment; current health care, including current provider(s) and treatments (must include current medications, both prescribed and over the counter); a history of significant past medical problems and treatment; any current health precautions,

TABLE 6.2
Primary Components of the Medical History

Current Medical Problems/Treatments
Past Medical Problems/Treatments
Health Care Providers
Health Precautions
Review of Systems

including drug and/or food allergies; and a review of systems allowing the client to endorse any physical symptoms that may be affecting functioning or producing distress.

The detail to which each of these primary components is explored depends on the training and level of medical education of the interviewing clinician and the purpose of the interview. For bachelor's- or master's-level mental health clinicians, screening the primary health or medical components may be sufficient. Psychiatrists or professionals with higher levels of medical training should have the training and knowledge base to proceed with a detailed inquiry when necessary.

History of Current and Past Medical Problems

Medical problems can both cause emotional or behavioral symptoms or syndromes, or result from the client's reaction to emotional or behavioral symptoms or syndromes. Whereas the specific relationship, if any, between medical and psychological problems may be evident on completion of a thorough assessment, information about current and past medical problems can allow for further medical assessment or other inquiry into a potential relationship.

Current Medical Problems. Clinicians should ask about any problems for which the client is presently being treated. Current medical problems can affect the mental health of the individual on several levels. Perhaps the most obvious effect is the psychological adjustment of the client to an acute medical problem. Medical illness threatens the integrity of a person in terms of loss of functioning, disability, and possible physical mutilation, pain, and potential mortality. Loss or limitation of functioning may include impairments in family relationships, inability to earn a livelihood, and a decrease in former activities. The relationship of individuals to their environment can change from active to passive, where the person is dependent on others. The client must deal with the reaction of others, including doctors and other medical professionals, family, and employers. In addition to these general and often highly variable effects on the family, social and occupational functioning, and the general quality of everyday life, the client with a medical illness or problem must deal with the side or adverse effects of specific medical treatments. Areas for inquiry include general adjustment to illness, attitude about illness, compliance with treatment regimen(s), access to appropriate medical care, and support from others.

In addition to the more general effects of medical problems on the psychological well-being of the client, there are specific effects of medical problems or treatments that emerge as emotional or behavioral symptoms. Endocrine disorders, infections, cardiovascular disease, respiratory, renal and liver failure, and neurological disorder can produce a wide variety of depressive, manic, anxiety, or nonspecific neurovegetative symptoms. Medical treatments, especially in the form of drug therapy, can also cause or exacerbate psychiatric symptoms. Tables 6.3 through 6.7 list both basic and specific types of medical disorders and drugs that cause or exacerbate psychiatric symptoms.

During the course of an assessment interview, a clinician should attempt to elicit information about current medical problems and the course or current status of the treatment of these disorders. If clients are unable to provide important information or details about their problems and treatment, the clinician may need to contact the treating health professionals following permission to release information. Unfortunately, many clients are not in treatment for the vague medical complaints they provide. The clinician may need to refer clients for a more comprehensive medical evaluation.

Past Medical Problems. Existing medical problems may be part of both the current medical status and past medical problems, especially when medical problems are chronic. The same psychosocial factors that affect adaptation to acute medical problems (mentioned earlier) can operate in an even more profound and often insidious fashion in clients with chronic medical problems. Although many clients may be able to connect medical problems with the sequelae of depression, anxiety, or other psychiatric symptoms, others may be unable or unwilling to do so. Those clients with chronic problems more often have to deal with issues of chronic or permanent disability, which can affect self-image, self-esteem, interpersonal relationships, as well as access to social and recreational activities.

Many medical problems, especially chronic conditions, can increase the likelihood of developing disorders like depression. For common chronic conditions like coronary artery disease and cancer, the subsequent incidence of depression runs as high as 20% and 40%, respectively. Rates of depression following chronic neurological disorders like Parkinson's disease, stroke, and multiple sclerosis is as great as 50%.

Although the relation between medical problems and psychological symptoms is not always etiological, mental health problems can adversely affect the course of concurrent or subsequent medical conditions. There are in-

TABLE 6.3
Medical Conditions Associated With Depression

Neurological disorders
  Cerebrovascular accident (stroke)
  Alzheimer's disease
  Brain tumor
  Huntington's disease
  Epilepsy (seizure disorder)
  Multiple sclerosis
  Parkinson's disease
Cancer
  Pancreatic cancer
  Lung cancer
  Brain tumor
Infections
  Mononucleosis
  Encephalitis
  Hepatitis
  Tertiary syphilis
  Human immunodeficiency virus (HIV)
Endocrine
  Hypo/hyperthyroidism
  Cushing's syndrome
  Addison's disease
  Parathyroid disease
Gastrointestinal
  Liver cirrhosis
  Pancreatitis
Cardiovascular
  Hypoxia
  Congestive heart failure
Respiratory
  Sleep apnea
Nutritional
  Thiamine deficiency
  Protein deficiency
  B_{12} deficiency
  B_6 deficiency
  Folate deficiency
Collagen vascular
  Lupus (SLE)
  Rheumatoid arthritis

creased rates of functional disability in those clients with chronic medical problems who also have psychological problems. Those clients with specific traits such as hostile, pressured (Type A) personality may be at increased risk for developing coronary artery disease, whereas those who are anxious/depressed may be at risk for a variety of gastrointestinal disorders (e.g., irritable bowel syndrome, peptic ulcer disease, esophageal motility disorders,

TABLE 6.4
Medications/Drugs Associated With Depression

Antihypertensive agents
    Reserpine
    Methyldopa
    Beta-blockers (e.g., propranolol)
Oral contraceptives
Corticosteroids
Cimetidine
Ranctidine
Benzodiazepines
Alcohol
Opiates
Stimulant or cocaine (withdrawal)
Cancer chemotherapeutic agents
Digitalis
Isoniazid

TABLE 6.5
Medical Conditions Associated With Mania

Neurological disease
    Multiple sclerosis
    Temporal lobe seizure
    Post-trauma
    Brain tumor
    Poststroke
    Huntington's disease
    Wilson's disease
Infections
    Encephalitis
    Tertiary syphilis
Endocrine
    Hyperthyroidism
    Cushing's disease
    Addison's disease
    Carcinoid syndrome
Medications/drugs
    Levodopa
    Symphetomimetics/stimulant
    Amphetamines
    Corticosteroids
    Adrenocorticotropic hormone
    Antidepressants
    Phencyclidine (PCP)
    Bromocriptine
    Cocaine
    Hallucinogens
    Isoniazid
    Zidovudine

TABLE 6.6
Medical Conditions/Medications Associated With Anxiety

Neurological disorders
  Alzheimer's disease
  Brain tumor
  Stroke
  Multiple sclerosis
  Huntington's disease
Infections
  Encephalitis
  Meningitis
  Neurosyphilis
  Septicemia
Endocrine
  Hypo/hyperthyroidism
  Hypoparathyroidism
  Hypoglycemia
  Pheochromocytoma
  Carcinoid
Metabolic
  Low calcium
  Low potassium
  Acute intermittent porphyria
  Liver failure
Cardiovascular
  Angina
  Congestive heart failure
  Pulmonary embolus
Respiratory
  Pneumothorax
  Acute asthma
  Emphysema
Medications
  Stimulants
  Sedative (withdrawal)
  Lead, mercury

and Crohn's disease). Certain stress responses associated with increased physiologic reality may result in an exacerbation or expression of symptoms, such as in atopic dermatitis or eczema. Not surprisingly, clients with interventions designed to improve ability to cope and handle emotional distress have an improved survival rate following treatment for their medical problems (e.g., breast cancer).

Treatment of past problems may also affect current psychiatric status. Chronic use of certain medications may produce psychiatric symptoms. Many chronic effects are a recent discovery or may be unknown because of the newness of the drug.

TABLE 6.7
Medical Conditions Associated With Psychosis or Perceptual Abnormalities

Medical conditions
Temporal lobe epilepsy
Migraine headaches
Temporal arteritis
Occipital tumors
Narcolepsy
Encephalitis
Hypothyroidism
Addison's disease
Human immunodeficiency virus (HIV)
Medications
Hallucinogens (e.g., LSD)
Phencyclidine (PCP)
Alcohol (withdrawal)
Stimulants
Cocaine
Corticosteroids

A history of treatment for trauma (e.g., related to accidents or violent incidents) provides not only medical information but also potential information about other behavioral variables, such as tendency toward accidents (perhaps due to perceptual problems or substance use) or living in a violent environment.

Health Care Providers and Current Active Treatments

The clinician should inquire about the client's current primary care physician, the date of the last visit, and the date of the last complete physical examination. Presence of an identified provider, as well as regular care (or the absence of both) are general indicators of health-seeking behavior. The clinician should list any specialists involved in the client's care (their specialty, the reason, and extent of involvement).

A complete list of current medications—both prescription and over the counter—should be made. Other types of current or recent treatments should be listed, including whether or not clients have used contraceptive agents or devices (especially for women).

For women, the clinician should inquire about childbirth history: that is, number of pregnancies, number of spontaneous and induced abortions, and course of successful pregnancies, including the adequacy of prenatal care. Regular gynecological and breast exams are also important elements of regular health maintenance for women.

Health Precautions

A list of specific medication, food, and environmental allergies is an important part of a medical history. Although not all adverse reactions to medications are truly allergic, any adverse reactions to specific medications, combinations of medications, or foods should be recorded.

Review of Systems

Although much of the information obtained through a general medical review of systems may have been obtained during other portions of the assessment interview, the clinician should survey general organ systems for problems or symptoms. By being more specific and prompting a response in terms of more specific questions, the clinician can often elicit responses that would not be obtained through a more vague, general inquiry into any physical or medical "problems." The clinician should specifically ask if there are any respiratory, cardiac or cardiovascular (circulation), gastrointestinal, musculoskeletal, or neurological complaints. Special attention should be given to questions and reports of neurological signs and symptoms, such as headaches, seizures, changes in sensory abilities (e.g., vision), head trauma, or episodes involving loss of consciousness, disorientation, or confusion. Inquiry into more sustained cognitive deficits, such as memory difficulties, should also be made.

Review of systems can include questions about lifestyle and habits: Do clients follow any particular or specialized health practices (e.g., taking vitamins)? Do they exercise on a regular basis or are they sedentary? What types of foods do they eat and how much? Are these eating patterns reflected in being obese, over- or underweight relative to expected standards of similar aged individuals? Have clients attempted to lose or gain weight in the past?

Does the client smoke tobacco? If so, how much per day and for how long (i.e., when did the individual start smoking)? Has the client attempted to quit? Record the number of attempts and relative success of each effort. Do not assume that cigarettes are the only form of tobacco intake. Among some age groups and in certain regions (young males in the rural South or Southwest United States), use of smokeless tobacco (e.g., "snuff") is common. Also, cigar smoking is currently enjoying a resurgence.

Inquiry into alcohol and other substance use is critical, as such substance use may have profound implications for both medical and mental health status. Commonly, clinicians ask vague questions about substance use and accept equally vague answers, denials, or minimizations. Assume a positive response; ask "how much do you use?", rather than "do you use?" Ask clients to be more specific about their frequency and quantity of use. Do not accept such vague replies as "not much," "just a bit," or "not often."

Ask clients specifically what their responses mean in terms of quantity or frequency.

Many people use illicit substances or abuse available agents (e.g., over-the-counter medications). Many clients use prescribed medications or over-the-counter medications in an inappropriate manner either for perceived therapeutic or recreational reasons. It is also useful to run down a list of major groups of common illicit substances. A survey of negative consequences of use and symptoms of substance use disorders is normally a part of the general history portion of the assessment. However, inquiry into substance use as part of a medical history can often provide information from a less defensive client. A nonjudgmental attitude on the part of the clinician will help to elicit a more honest response.

The clinician should also ask about possible exposure to Human Immunodeficiency Virus (HIV) through sexual behavior(s), drug use, transfusions, or other high-risk status or behaviors.

Somatic Complaints.   Although the specific medical or physical complaints elicited during the medical history portion of the assessment are important, it is often the pattern of symptoms or complaints that points to a specific medical condition or psychiatric syndrome. Indeed, a pattern of a number of vague, nonspecifics suggests the possibility of somatization, if not Somatization Disorder. There are a number of specific psychiatric disorders classified in the *DSM–IV* under the heading of Somatoform Disorders. Essential characteristics of these disorders include presence of physical complaints or symptoms that occur in the absence of identifiable physical pathology or disorder(s). Individuals affected often have an excessive concern about various bodily functions that are not explicable on the basis of physical or laboratory evidence. It is more common for clients with Somatoform Disorders to be seen by primary care physicians and medical specialists rather than by mental health professionals. Many clients with Somatoform Disorders will often seek help from a long series of medical professionals, using much time and resources. This ongoing evaluation and treatment of their complaints exposes them to harm from unneeded procedures and medications.

Somatization Disorder.   Somatization Disorder involves the presence of multiple somatic symptoms with multiple organ symptoms. The history of physical complaints should begin before age 30, occur over a period of several years, and result in treatment seeking and/or significant impairment in functioning. *DSM–IV* criteria for Somatization Disorder require at least four pain symptoms, two gastrointestinal symptoms, one sexual symptom, and one pseudoneurological symptom. These symptoms cannot be fully explained by substance use or a known medical condition or, when there is a related medical condition, the symptoms and/or impairment are in excess of what would be expected. These symptoms are often dramatically described but vague in terms of their possible attribution to actual medical illness. Reports of symptoms may be inconsistent and vary across time. Despite the often dramatic nature of the complaints and perceived distress, there may not be a high level of actual dysfunction, because the individual is able to carry on a significant portion of the life tasks. Somatization Disorder affects mostly women, and tends to run in families. Males in these families have higher rates of antisocial personality and alcoholism. Prevalence rates in the epidemiological catchment area study point to a lifetime of .4%.

Conversion Disorder. A diagnosis of Conversion Disorder indicates presence of symptoms or deficits, other than pain, that suggest a neurological or general medical condition. The symptom(s) are not under voluntary control and cannot be explained by a known general medical or neurological condition. Typical presentations of Conversion Disorder include sensory deficits (e.g., deafness, blindness), paralysis, inability to speak, or abnormal movements. Patterns of symptoms do not conform to those patterns seen in physiological disorders. Conversion symptoms, like other somatoform disorders, are more common in women than men, in individuals from lower socioeconomic groups, and among members of certain ethnic groups.

Several practical clues may be useful in identifying a case of Conversion Disorder. Such patients very often have a high level of comorbidity with mood disorders, Somatization Disorder, and personality disorders. A previous history of conversion symptoms or previous exposure to significant others with medical problems may lead to new conversion symptom(s), or the modeling of conversion symptoms based on the real medical experience of others. Presence of characteristics such as *la belle indifférence* (i.e., seeming disinterest in the severity of the symptoms), histrionic traits, and exposure to recent emotional stress are much less useful in making a diagnosis of Conversion Disorder than once believed.

Hypochondriasis. Hypochondriasis involves preoccupation with fears of having a serious disease despite medical evaluation and reassurance. The individual with Hypochondriasis misinterprets symptoms. However, this preoccupation is not of delusional intensity, nor is it restricted to concern about the individual's appearance. The duration necessary for a diagnosis is 6 months. Misinterpretations can involve exaggeration of normal physiological functioning or mild level of benign medical problems. The client may be fearful of having a specific disease or of having some vague but serious and potentially life-threatening medical problem. Although some clients with Hypochondriasis understand the unreasonable nature of their fears, many have poor insight into the excessiveness of their fears. *Body Dysmorphic*

Disorder involves preoccupation with an imagined or highly exaggerated defect in the client's appearance rather than other somatic complaints and possibility of these perceived defects as being representative of serious illness. The result of Body Dysmorphic Disorder may be repeated involvement with plastic surgeons.

Pain Disorder. A diagnosis of Pain Disorder involves presence of pain as the predominant focus of clinical attention, an important role for psychological factors in the onset, severity, exacerbation, and maintenance of the pain, and the absence of a factitious etiology. Also, such pain cannot be accounted for by another psychiatric disorder. Within *DSM–IV*, subtypes of pain disorder include: (a) pain disorder associated with psychological factors, (b) pain disorder associated with a general medical condition, and (c) pain disorder associated with both psychological factors and a general medical condition. In each subtype, the associated factors or condition should play an important role in the onset, maintenance, and/or severity of the pain. Pain disorder is specified as either acute (duration of less than 6 months) or chronic (duration greater than 6 months). As with the other somatoform disorders, Pain Disorder has a high level of psychiatric comorbidity, especially with depressive and anxiety disorders.

A general approach is suggested in assessing clients presenting with somatic symptoms. The cornerstone of evaluation is for medical professionals to determine if there is a true medical condition that might respond to medical treatment. Although previous medical evaluation is very useful, the clinician should not be lulled into a false sense of security. Many medical evaluations may be inadequate for a number of reasons, especially considering the medical professional's bias against concurrent psychiatric symptoms or disorders or the difficult interpersonal traits of such clients. A significant proportion of clients receiving a diagnosis of Conversion Disorder are ultimately diagnosed with a medical condition. There is no reason why individuals with psychiatric conditions, such as depression or personality disorder, cannot have serious concurrent medical disorders. Communication between the mental health practitioner and medical professional is critical to understand these clients.

Sleep and Other Neurovegetative Functions. Sleep is an essential neurovegetative function. Disordered sleep in the form of delays in onset, frequent and/or prolonged continuity disturbances, early morning awakening, daytime somnolence or fatigue, or the need for substantially increased amount of sleep are often nonspecific and can point to a number of possible psychiatric and medical problems (see Table 6.8). In addition to inquiry about the aforementioned sleep problems, additional questions may concern presence of snoring (suggesting possible sleep apnea) or poor sleep habits, such as exercise

TABLE 6.8
Causes of Excessive Nighttime Sleep

Insufficient nighttime sleep
Poor or irregular sleep routines or circumstances
Circadian rhythm disorder
Frequent parasomnia
Chronic physical illness
Psychiatric disorders
Other causes of sleep problems
Narcolepsy
Drug effects

or the use of caffeine before bedtime. The clinician should also inquire about other neurovegetative symptoms, such as appetite and energy level.

Sexual Functioning. Satisfactory sexual functioning is an important element in the normal psychosocial functioning of most adults. Although no specific frequency or "quantity" of sexual activity is considered normal or abnormal, inquiry should be based on the general satisfaction of the individual and the presence of any deficient elements (e.g., lack of desire, pain, impotence) that affect sexual satisfaction. Beyond questions about sexual functioning, the clinician may choose to ask about attitudes regarding sex as well as the occurrence of any past traumatic experiences such as sexual abuse (see Table 6.9). Many medical conditions and medications can also interfere with sexual functioning (see Table 6.10).

Changes in Mental Status. Deficits in mental status as signs of medical illness are usually elicited in the more formal mental status examination portion of the assessment. However, the client or other informants may report past or recent episodes, where orientation to time, place, or even person is impaired, or when memory and other cognitive processes are impaired. When the mental status examination cannot identify these deficits, the clinician must rely on the history.

Cognitive loss and an abnormal level of consciousness are two common presentations. Delirium and dementia are common examples of deficits in level of consciousness and cognitive loss. Delirium and dementia, respectively, have also been referred to as "acute" and "chronic" organic brain syndromes. The mental status presentations of delirium and dementia are described in chapter 7. The clinician may elicit a history of these deficits from the client or other informants, the client's physician, or review of the medical record to help determine etiology.

Delirium represents an acute change in mental status or, more precisely, a change in the level of consciousness and attention, and the rapid develop-

TABLE 6.9
Sexual History

Objective data
   Age of onset of puberty
   Age of menarche (women)
   Menstrual history (women)
   Pregnancies, miscarriages, abortions
   Methods of birth control
   Frequency of current sexual activity
   Problems with sexual activity
      Physical discomfort
      Arousal
      Achieving/maintaining erection or orgasm
      Control of ejaculation
      Lubrication (women)
   Illness or Medications that may affect sexual function
   Risk factors for HIV (AIDS)
   History of venereal disease
Subjective data
   Attitudes about sex
   History of sexual abuse/incest
   History of sexual activity
   Partner conflicts regarding sexual activity
   Childbearing decisions

TABLE 6.10
Medical Conditions/Medications Associated With Impaired Sexual Function

Endocrine disorder
   Diabetes mellitus
   Hypogonadism
   Hypopituitarism
Cardiovascular disease
   Myocardial infarction
   Vascular disease
Respiratory failure
Chronic renal failure
Neurological disorders
   Spinal cord damage
   Damage to higher centers
Pelvic surgery
Disabling arthritis
Medication
   Anticholinergic drugs
   Hormones
   Psychotropic drugs (phenothiazines, antidepressants)
   Antihypertensive drugs
   Diuretics
   L-Dopa
   Indomethacin

ment of significant cognitive impairment in addition to disorientation and confusion. Although determining the presence of delirium through the mental status examination is discussed elsewhere in this volume, the clinician should suspect delirium in any client who presents with the acute onset of confusion and disorientation in the context of medical problems or specific medications or combinations of medications (see Table 6.11). In terms of a differential diagnosis, hallucinations and delusions noted in delirium can be distinguished from those in other disorders, such as schizophrenia or mood disorders by the presence of deficits in attention, memory impairment, disorientation and fluctuating, and fragmented psychotic symptoms. Subtypes of delirium include delirium due to a medical condition, substance-induced delirium, and delirium due to multiple etiologies.

Dementia consists of the development of multiple cognitive deficits, including memory, and at least one of the following: language disturbance;

TABLE 6.11
Medical Causes of Delirium

Intercranial lesions/brain disease(s)
  Tumors
  Head injury
  Seizures
Infection
  Encephalitis
  Meningitis
  HIV
  Neurosyphilis
Metabolic failure
  Renal
  Liver
  Cardiac
  Pulmonary
Endocrine
  Cushing's disease
  Addison's disease
Nutritional/vitamin deficiency
Medications/substances
  Anticholinergics
  Anxiolytics
  Anticonvulsants
  Digitalis
  Opiates
  L-dopa
  Heavy metals
  Solvents
Drug withdrawal
  Alcohol
  Sedative hypnotics

inability to carry out motor activate despite intact motor functions; failure
to recognize or identify objects despite intact sensory function; or disturbance
in ability to plan, organize, or think abstractly. The course of dementia is
characterized by a gradual onset and ongoing cognitive deterioration. In
contrast to delirium, where a specific medical etiology is presumed, a diagnosis of dementia cannot be due to a specific central nervous system condition
that causes progressive deficits in memory or other cognitive functions (e.g.,
Parkinson's disease, Huntington's disease, or a brain tumor). Although dementia obviously can be caused by a variety of medical disorders or exposures
to specific substances (see Table 6.12), the *DSM–IV* diagnosis is reserved
for two specific types of dementia: Alzheimer's Type and Vascular Dementia
(formerly multi-infarct dementia). A diagnosis of Alzheimer's dementia is
made only on the exclusion (by medical evaluation) of other possible etiologies. Vascular dementia requires evidence of cerebrovascular disease. The
prominent differential diagnosis of dementia includes depression (or so-called
pseudodementia), amnestic disorder, schizophrenia, mental retardation, and
normal aging.

Loss of memory is a specific type of cognitive loss. There are many
potential specific etiologies to amnestic syndromes, including medical conditions, medications, and substances. Again, the emphasis during the assessment is to obtain enough medical information to help distinguish the medical
versus functional etiology of the cognitive change, and to be sure an adequate
medical evaluation has been or will be completed.

Factitious Medical Disorders

The intentional production, or feigning, of physical symptoms can result in
a diagnosis of one of the factitious disorders. The primary motivation for
faking symptoms is so the individual can assume the sick role. These individuals are not seeking external incentives (e.g., economic gain, avoiding
responsibility). Factitious disorders are subtyped based on the predominant
symptom(s), that is, psychological, physical, or both (combined). The term
Munchausen syndrome (based on the factitious or exaggerated tales of a
19th-century German baron) has often been applied to this problem. Clients
often go from hospital to hospital until medical staff suspicions about the
nature of their illness drives them to the next venue. Most cases of factitious
disorder involve feigning physical symptoms either by reporting symptoms
of an illness without actually having the symptoms, or presenting false evidence of an illness or intentionally producing symptoms (e.g., by self-injection
or ingestion of potentially harmful or contaminated substances, medications,
or self-inflicted trauma).

Factitious disorders are often quite difficult to ascertain due to the covert,
intentional nature of the client's behavior. Factitious disorders may be sug-

TABLE 6.12
Medical Causes of Dementia

Degenerative
  Alzheimer's disease
  Picks
  Huntington's chorea
  Parkinson's disease
  Normal pressure hydrocephalous
  Multiple sclerosis
Intercranial lesions
  Tumors
  Subdural hematoma
Trauma
  Head injury
Infection
  Encephalitis
  Neurosyphilis
  HIV
  Prion disease (Creutzfeld-Jacob)
Vascular
  Multiple strokes (cerebrovascular accidents)
  Collagen vascular diseases (Lupus, cranial arteritis)
Metabolic
  Liver failure
  End-stage renal failure
Endocrine
  Hypothyroidism
  Hyperparathyroidism
  Pituitary insufficiency
Toxic
  Alcohol
  Heavy metal poisoning
Anoxia
  Chronic respiratory failure
  Cardiac
Vitamin deficiency
  B_{12}
  Folate
  Thiamine

gested by a long, involved clinical presentation inconsistent with the client's health status, textbook presentations of medical symptoms, or problems and/or client demands for specific diagnostic tests or treatments. Although a long list of consecutive providers, diagnostic, and treatment episodes are usually present, the client may wish to hide these if such past episodes raise suspicions. When factitious disorder is suspected, previous medical records should be obtained and prior health care professionals should be contacted for additional information.

Malingering is not considered a mental health diagnosis but a focus of attention or treatment (i.e., V-code condition) under *DSM–IV*. Malingering is the intentional production of physical (or psychological) symptoms motivated by external incentives such as avoiding unwanted responsibilities, negative consequences or punishment, or for obtaining drugs. The motivation for malingering should be apparent. Clues to the presence of malingering include discrepancies between the claimed disability and symptoms and the objective findings of the medical evaluation, lack of cooperation during the evaluation, poor or noncompliance with treatment, and presence of antisocial personality disorder. The context of the client's presentation (referral by an attorney) may also increase suspicion.

SUMMARY

The medical history is essential for a comprehensive assessment of behavioral and emotional problems. Although the detail and sophistication of the medical history will vary according to the clinician's training, there are primary components of the medical history that deserve inquiry. These components include current and past medical problems, treatments (including medications), health care providers, health precautions, and a review of systems. A thorough medical history may assist the clinician in considering a potential medical etiology of the psychological symptoms and the influence of concurrent medical problems on the general adjustment and psychosocial functioning of the client. The mental health clinician should work closely with health care professionals to assist in the diagnosis of any medical problems suggested by the client's symptoms, as well as to provide appropriate treatment of concurrent medical and psychiatric disorders.

SUGGESTED READINGS

American Psychiatric Association (1994). *Diagnostic and statistical manual of mental disorders* (4th ed.). Washington, DC: Author.

Brown, L. K., Fritz, G. K., & Herzog, D. B. (1997). Psychosomatic disorders. In J. M. Weiner (Ed.), *Textbook of child and adolescent psychiatry* (2nd ed., pp. 621–633). Washington, DC: American Psychiatric Press.

Lishman, W. A. (1987). *Organic psychiatry* (2nd ed.). Oxford, England: Basil Blackwell.

Stoudemire, A. (Ed.). (1995). *Psychological factors affecting medical conditions*. Washington, DC: American Psychiatric Press.

Stoudemire, A., & Fogel, B. S. (1993). *Psychiatric care of the medical patient*. New York: Oxford University Press.

Stoudemire, A., & Hales, R. E. (1991). Psychological and behavioral factors affecting medical conditions and *DSM–IV*: An overview. *Psychosomatics, 32*, 5–13.

7

The Mental Status Examination

Charles J. Golden
Philinda Smith Hutchings
Nova Southeastern University

The mental status examination is an essential and integral part of any initial interview with a client, as well as an essential tool in assessing the progress of a client over time. The traditional mental status examination is an informal, general evaluation of the major aspects of the current functioning of the individual, tailored both to the needs of the patient and the clinician. Its primary purpose is to quickly identify the current status of the client: major symptoms that could be associated with a medical or neurological disorder, the presence of major psychological and psychiatric problems (e.g., schizophrenia and major depression), and the overall cognitive and emotional functioning of the individual. When used in conjunction with good history taking and other interview and evaluation processes, it is an important and crucial part of the initial diagnostic workup of the client.

Mental status examinations may also be standardized, reduced to specific tests or questions, which are given to every client as part of a general workup. Such standardized versions of the mental status examination may be used for a specific purpose, such as identifying dementia, or may be more general and aimed at a wider audience. Standardized examinations are most useful when initial evaluations are done for research projects, to document specific symptomatology, or when evaluations are done by paraprofessionals or others without formal psychological or psychiatric training.

The traditional examination has the advantage that it uses the experience and knowledge of the therapist to pick which areas to emphasize, which areas to test (such as the degree to which attentional or memory processes

107

should be tested), and which areas are necessary for accurate and complete diagnosis. But, it also has the disadvantage of relying on the examiner's experience and insight, because results may vary depending on the skills of the individual examiner. However, despite this possibly significant drawback, the more flexible examination is preferred because of the greater range of clinical data and observations that can be generated and the flexibility it affords in different circumstances.

GOALS OF THE MENTAL STATUS EXAMINATION

The goal of the mental status examination is to determine the current status of the client. The specific data of interest may vary from setting to setting. The neurologist may be more interested in signs that point to an acute neurological condition requiring immediate medical attention. The clinician in a psychiatric emergency room may be most interested in suicidal or homicidal tendencies. The psychiatrist may be interested in indicators relevant to the need for hospitalization or specific medications. In general, however, the goal is to establish whether or not there are major problems in the intellectual, memory, or cognitive skills of the client, any difficulties with reality contact, any problems in the modulation or control or expression of emotions, any suicidal or homicidal thoughts, any psychotic thoughts, the ability of the client to handle psychological issues and stressors, and the presence of pathognomonic signs indicating acute neurological or medical dysfunction.

Beyond these specific goals, the core of the mental status examination is the ability of the examiner to observe the client and to accurately see and report how the client acts (verbally and nonverbally), feels, and thinks in an objective and comprehensive manner. The inexperienced examiner (or even the experienced examiner treating an unusual case) may not understand the meaning of what is happening, but the good examiner can observe and report precisely what has occurred. This ability to observe and report the totality of the client's behavior gives the face-to-face mental status examination the capacity not only to diagnose but to discover new things and to see the client as an individual.

This discussion emphasizes observation and accurate, objective reporting rather than the primary reporting of conclusions. Accurate and objective evaluation is an essential basis for interpretation. Interpretation of inaccurate data will always be bad regardless of the skill of the interpreter. "The client cried frequently during the examination" is much better than "The client was sad." "The client reported that he believed that his liver had been magically altered into a fish" is better than "The client had somatic delusions." This chapter does not have the space to cover the possible meaning of every possible observation, and in any case, the therapist will learn extensively through experience and supervision things that a book cannot teach. In all cases, however, accurate observation is essential and the foundation of all good clinical diagnostic work.

PRELIMINARY CONSIDERATIONS

The proper way to report observations is to record them. However, the recording behavior must not interfere with the examination itself. If the therapist is focused on writing things down, clients may feel they are being neglected or will slow down or omit part of their story to "accommodate" the therapist. The therapist may also become more concerned with writing and less with understanding what occurs. Thus, whenever possible, less obtrusive techniques should be employed. These include committing the session to memory, making audiorecordings, and videotaping the interview.

Using memory has the advantages of being readily accessible and easy to use (it does not require equipment), but it also has the disadvantages of being selective, easily confused, and not readily shown to another. When relying on memory, it is often useful to take one-word notes as a reminder of specific points that are important. In addition, remember to dictate or write notes immediately after the session so that the information is fresh and does not become confused with another client. (This is why psychological hours are only 50 minutes long; it allows time for recording.)

It is often useful to audiotape or videotape clients. These methods have great advantages in terms of accuracy and replicability, although they may lose some of the emotional content and "atmosphere" of the original examination. In addition, they may act as a crutch, which prevents clinicians from developing their own memory skills and forming an integrated picture of the client as the exam proceeds (an important skill in deciding the direction and content of the overall examination). Thus, it is important to try to develop memory and integrative skills, using recordings as a "check." Relying on them can become a disaster when the tape recorder fails or the tape is destroyed.

Any recording equipment should be fully set up and tested before the client enters the room. At most, the therapist should only have to push a single, readily accessible button. If the setup is more complicated, then the recording device should be set to run before the client enters the room. In all cases, of course, the client should be informed of the intention to record and written permission should be obtained.

When setting up a room for a mental status examination, avoid placing the desk in an intervening position. It may act as a wall or barrier to establishing a good rapport with the client. The setting should be comfortable for both participants, and neither should be in a "superior" position. Sitting side by side is never appropriate, but a face-to-face position (either directly or at a small angle) usually works best. The therapist must be able to see the client fully. For example, if the client is behind a table so that legs are not visible, tremors or anxious movements of the foot may be missed. Lighting must be adequate to see the client's features. Avoid putting seats in a position where sunlight through a window may be in anyone's face. Temperature controls must be set so that the room is comfortable (neither too hot or too cold). The room itself should not contain distractors that can draw the client's attention from the interview. Clients will occasionally ask for changes (hotter, colder, brighter, darker, higher chair, footstool, etc.), which should be accommodated whenever possible.

The clinician should dress neatly and professionally but be careful not to overdress or intimidate. Full attention should be on clients; therapists should not be involved in any other tasks. They must appear interested in the client's story and should not appear to be rushed or in a hurry (even when they really are in a hurry.) A relaxed and warm atmosphere encourages the client to give more personal information and to show less resistance to answering questions.

The mental status examination is often performed first with a new client, so it is important to try to put the client at ease before attempting more probing questions. Any topics of interest to clients are appropriate, including the weather, their trip to the clinic, their day at the hospital, the sports team whose logo they are wearing, and so on. This obviously must be tailored to the specific circumstance and reason for the interview, so there is no standard "opening line."

In cases where clients are extremely preoccupied with a problem or issue, it is often best to let them express themselves (so they feel they are heard and taken seriously) before going on to the mental status examination, even when the issue is irrelevant to the examination. For example, if a hospitalized client is obsessively concerned that the nurses will not bring fresh cold water or open the window blinds, this person could be calmed and relaxed by getting the water or opening the blinds. Always be courteous and hospitable to the client. Although this has nothing to do with the formal purpose of the examination, therapists should never be so goal oriented that they fail to remember that their ultimate goal is not to diagnose but to help. In addition, a client who is at ease is much more cooperative and revealing, which makes the therapist's job much easier.

THE MENTAL STATUS EXAMINATION

The information gathered in the mental status examination can be subdivided into two types of data: data gathered through observation throughout the examination and data requiring specific questions and procedures. Observations include appearance, behavior, attitude, motor behavior, reliability, and the outward manifestations of affect. Information gathered through the use of specific questions includes data on orientation, speech processes, thought processes, perceptual abnormalities, memory and concentration, intelligence, judgment and insight, and mood.

Appearance

Appearance means the physical description of clients and their clothing. The major interest is in identifying how clients present themselves to the world. Are clients neat, disheveled, appropriate, dirty, sloppy, stooped over, over-dressed, underdressed, and so on? Is their hair combed, makeup applied? Are shoes tied, buttons buttoned, and zippers zipped? Have clients washed and shaved or do they smell? Do they seem to have been taking care of themselves? Are they overweight, underweight, muscular, or scrawny? Do their faces seem alert and animated, or do they seem to be apathetic or listless? Are their eyes open and aware? Are their clothes in good shape or poorly maintained? Consider the following examples:

> The client was a 38-year-old, slightly balding man who looked trim and well kept. He appeared alert and aware of his surroundings. He was neatly dressed and groomed, and his dress was appropriately casual for the situation.

> The client was a 12-year-old female who looked to be 17 or older. She was inappropriately dressed in a swimsuit bikini top with skimpy and tight shorts. She had several tattoos of naked men on her left arm and on her abdomen. Her hair was long, but dirty and poorly combed. She frequently leaned forward so that her breasts were exposed. She wore gaudy makeup consisting of bright red lipstick and blush, which were put on poorly and smeared. Her clothes were dirty and torn in several spots. Her face appeared listless and she rarely looked up at the examiner. Her sneakers were dirty with holes in the side. There were several large bruises on her left thigh and on her back near the right kidney. There were scars inside her elbows, which suggested bruises from injections. Her nose was red and runny.

Descriptions of individuals who appear essentially normal would be relatively short. In the case of clients with abnormalities, however, the description can be quite long and should be as detailed as possible. In all cases, judgments about appropriateness of dress should take into account the gender, age, economic standing, and culture of the client, as well as the specific situation in which the examination takes place. Culture is especially important because dress that might be inappropriate in one culture might be fully appropriate in another. If this is not considered, serious mistakes can be made in all areas of the mental status exam.

Behavior

General behavior reflects clients' methods of presenting themselves. This generally includes eye contact, posture, gestures, manner of speech, level of cooperation, and general motor activity. Unusual behaviors, ranging from catatonic posturing to listening to voices to rhyming speech, should also be described in specific detail. The appropriateness of clients' behavior for their age and cultural background must be considered as well. The goal is to generate a description that ideally would allow another clinician to immediately recognize the client on the basis of behavior.

Client behavior is best described in concrete, operational terms rather than by conclusions, for several reasons. First, concrete descriptions are more basic than conclusions and offer the reader of the report clear referents for later conclusions reached by the therapist. Thus, subsequent therapists who see a client can more easily compare what they see to what a previous therapist saw regardless of whether they have reached the same conclusion. Second, conclusions are, in general, as much dependent on the evaluator as on the client, and as such do not represent basic information. Therapists do reach conclusions in their report, but this is better done at the end with all of the evidence available.

Good behavioral observations may be something like: "The client smiled continuously throughout the interview." However, a simple statement like "The client was inattentive" is better replaced by "The client was constantly looking away from the examiner at the window, at objects in the office, his own shoes, the floor, and the ceiling." Whereas statements like "the client acted hostile" may be correct, they are replaced more effectively by concrete behavioral descriptions such as:

> The client's face was continually in a scowl and he refused to answer any questions except to state that they were none of the examiner's business. He crossed his arms in front of his chest, and refused to make eye contact. His posture was tense and he held his own body rigid and straight. He would stare at the door, and sat pointed more toward the door than toward the examiner. Whenever he refused to answer a question, he stiffened and rotated his legs closer to the door as if he was planning an escape. His speech was terse and strained, and much louder than necessary.

Attitude

The client's attitude is strongly related to behavior. This should include both the client's attitude toward the therapist as well as the examination. Attitude is generally inferred from nonverbal behavior as well as from the client's statements, although these may be in conflict. Thus, clients may act hostile, but state that they are cooperating. Both of these events should be reported, and again the behavioral referents for any conclusions should be clear and reported within the previous behavioral description. For example, "These behaviors suggested a great deal of hostility towards the examiner and the examination, but the client insisted he was cooperative but that the wrong questions were being asked. He could not say what the correct questions were, nor would he address any questions about his behavior."

In some cases, attitude toward the examiner and the examination appear to deviate. In such cases, the attitudes should be described separately: "The client questioned the examiner's age, stating he was very interested in the psychological evaluation but he believed only an older person could understand his problems and needs. Although he agreed to answer the questions put to him, he frequently returned to the issue of age and appeared not to respect or to trust the examiner."

Motor Behavior

Although this category clearly overlaps with general behavior, the focus here is on the more specific aspects of motor behavior, which may have some importance in terms of neurological, orthopedic, or psychiatric diagnosis. This section includes a description of the overall level and speed of motor behavior, as well as specific description of the motor movements themselves.

Basic motor behavior can be described in terms of speed: slow (or retarded), normal, and accelerated. Slow motor behavior, often referred to as motor or psychomotor retardation, is reflected in abnormally slow speed of movement in all spheres. The client walks slowly, speaks slowly, and makes slow hand movements.

When the phrase *motor retardation* is used, it generally assumes that the client has the physical capacity to move faster. Thus, this term is not used when clients are physically unable to move faster due to neurological or orthopedic injuries. In such cases, a description of the client's motor skills is appropriate; the rate and accuracy with which the client can perform movements should be described. A distinction is usually drawn between gross motor movements of the arms and legs, fine motor movements of the fingers, and motor movements of the mouth and tongue related to speech.

Normal motor speed is simply the performance of motor activity at normal rates. In judging this and other similar dimensions, therapists should rely on their own feelings about the appropriateness of the motor behavior. All therapists have had extensive experience with normal motor behavior. If they are observant, they should notice when the behavior deviates from these internal norms. They may not know the meaning of a specific deficit or finding, but a description of the unusual behavior should be included.

Accelerated motor movement (psychomotor agitation) reflects movements that are faster and quicker than normal. In most cases, accelerated movement is accurate and skilled rather than clumsy. The movements are completed appropriately (from a motor perspective), but at much higher speed as though there is some sense of urgency.

Motor behavior may also be described as goal directed or nongoal directed, regardless of psychomotor speed. Goal-directed behavior has a clear goal, and motor behaviors are necessary to reach that goal (like walking down a hallway to reach an office). Non-goal-directed behavior is more random without clear significance or purpose (like fidgeting, pacing, hand wringing, or hair twirling). Hyperactive behavior reflects excessive movement and distractibility. Hyperactivity is distinct from the speed of behavior, so it may be at normal or accelerated speed and may or may not be goal directed.

The nature of the motor behavior is important as well. Whereas a general psychologist is not expected to complete a motor evaluation at the level of a neurological examination, there are many important findings that can be assessed simply through observation and very short tests. Therapists should observe the way in which clients walk into the office. Do clients need assistance (if so, ask why)? Do clients lean to one side or the other or need to hold on to the wall or to furniture to get around? Is there evidence of balance problems, staggering, shuffling footsteps, unusual gait pattern, or any other movements that appear unusual? Is there paralysis or partial paralysis on one side or the other?

When clients are sitting, what do they do with their arms and legs? Do they move only one side of the body? (This may occur in the absence of paralysis, or may reflect mild paralysis.) Are there tremors present in arms, legs, or the head? Tremors are uncontrolled (involuntary) movements that are seen as alternating movements (e.g., up and down) in the extremities. These may be seen in all extremities or only one. Movements may also be rhythmic in nature. Tremors can also be classified as either *resting* or *intention* tremors. Resting tremors occur when the muscles and limb are at rest; intention tremors occur when the client tries to execute a voluntary movement (such as picking up a pen). A resting tremor will cease when intentional activity is begun; an intention tremor will be absent at rest. A tremor may occur at both times.

Other important motor deficits include spasms, which reflect sudden movements of large muscle groups, or tics, which are brief, sudden contractions of smaller muscles. Other movements may include variable movements of a limb. These can be in a jerky fashion without meaning and without voluntary control, or can be more sinuous and snakelike movements that are repeated over and over. In addition, clients may show bizarre posture or twisting movements of the trunk, or muscle jerks that occur anywhere from once per second to once every 10 or 15 seconds.

Therapists may also make a quick test of fine motor control. One test involves having clients open and close their hand as quickly as possible over 10 seconds. The second involves touching the thumb to the second, third, fourth, and fifth fingers in order as many times as possible in 10 seconds. In each case, differences between the speed of the two hands exceeding 20% may suggest abnormalities, as does excessive slowness, awkwardness, or stiffness in the movements. These procedures are a quick and useful measure of the ability of clients to understand and follow directions and demonstrations.

Reliability

A very important but somewhat difficult estimate to be made during an interview concerns the client's reliability. Reliability refers to the degree to which the accuracy of the client's information can be trusted. This is not the result of any single test or piece of information, but rather reflects the overall observation of the client during the entire interview. Keep in mind the following questions throughout the interview when determining the client's reliability:

1. Does the information from the client lack cohesion or logic? Clients should be afforded the opportunity to explain unusual answers in order to make sure that any problems are not simply miscommunications or misunderstandings. (This should be done when there are discrepancies in any of these questions.)
2. Is the information from the client consistent with available records?
3. Is the client's information self-serving; that is, is the information framed in such a way as to make the client get tangible or intangible rewards?
4. Does the client seem too good to be true? Referrals to clinicians usually have problems. Some clients may minimize problems to look good, but purely normal people are rarely referred.
5. Does the client respond with inconsistent information in different parts of the examination, suggesting memory problems, lying, malingering, or confabulation?
6. Does the client appear to have problems comprehending what is being asked?
7. Does the client refuse to divulge certain information or refuse to talk about certain topics?
8. Does the client show evidence of reality distortion, such as delusions or hallucinations, or report experiences that are highly unlikely (but remember that what seems like a delusion or an unusual event sometimes is true)?

9. Does the client show problems with memory and an inability to pinpoint important dates or events? This may be evidenced in inconsistent responses as well. In some cases, deliberate repetition of questions is useful to evaluate this possibility if it appears likely.

If the answer is yes to any of these questions, then the reliability of the client is brought into doubt. The more yes answers that occur, the more doubtful the information. Where there is unreliability, history and the results of other procedures must be assessed carefully, and information sources other than the client may have to be viewed as primary. Even in cases where the client is reliable, the information itself may still be unreliable because of where the information was obtained. For example, one client repeatedly told the clinician that she was a diabetic who needed a strict diet. In fact, this "diagnosis" had been made by her aunt and was not substantiated by medical tests.

Orientation

Orientation is the ability of clients to specify *who* they are (person), *where* they are (place), and *when* it is (time). Individuals who can do this are often referred to as "oriented ×3." In addition, therapists may also ask clients *why* they are being seen. Specific questions include: "What is your name?," "Where are we now?," "What day is it today?," "What is the date?," and "Why are you here?"

Although the questions are relatively standard, the definition of an acceptable answer may differ with the individual examiner. All clients are expected to know their full names. Acceptable answers for "where" questions are obviously more variable, because examinations are not held in one place. When questions were standardized for the Wechsler Memory Scale (Form I), the answer to "where" was "New York City" and everyone was expected to know that. But when the test was used in a hospital in one of the multiple suburbs of Philadelphia, acceptable answers ranged from "Philadelphia" to names of the surrounding suburbs. Answers that communicate general awareness of the area at a level consistent with the average person are generally considered acceptable.

"When" questions also pose some problems. Date and day of the week may be off slightly in individuals who are incarcerated in jail or a hospital, or who have been ill for a significant period of time. However, people working on a day-to-day basis in an active life should get these right. Month and year should be completely accurate, and clients should have a reasonable idea (within an hour) of the time. The clinician should report the client's specific errors so that the reader of the report has an idea of the magnitude of the error. For example, "The client thought it was the 16th of June rather than the 17th." Such preciseness should be used throughout the report.

"Why" questions should be answered by such ideas as "for an examination," "for a psychological evaluation," or something similar. Some clients will answer, "Because they brought me here" (which is accurate), but additional questions should be asked. In some of these cases, the client has been deliberately lied to or kept in the dark, which must be considered in evaluating the answer. In a hospital setting, clients may not even know a therapist was consulted but they should know why they are in the hospital.

Speech

Evaluation of speech is a combination of observational processes and specific questions. Speech evaluation falls roughly into two major categories: *expressive speech* and *receptive speech*.

Expressive speech reflects how someone says something. Impairment in expressive speech is known as dysfluent speech. In such cases, what the person says "sounds" wrong, even if the clinician does not recognize the nature of the problem. This can range from mutism (inability to make sounds) to milder disorders such as mispronunciation of specific sounds or sound combinations. This can include stuttering, lisps, slow halting speech in which syllables are pronounced one by one, inability to repeat words, or a loss of the content of speech (e.g., dropping all but essential words, which is called telegraphic speech). A client with telegraphic speech might haltingly say "need food" rather than "I need food," a style similar to messages sent in telegrams where people were charged by the word.

Speech may be slow or accelerated. Such speech may be described as "pressured" if the words come tumbling out on top of one another as if compelled to get out. Shortness of statements, with statement length being less than six words on a continuous basis, is an impairment. Impairment also includes an inability to speak loudly, raspiness or hoarseness of voice, or other problems in voice quality. All of these dimensions may reflect relatively acute or recent problems or may reflect longstanding and more permanent impairments.

Circumlocution occurs when clients have word-finding problems that interfere with communicating their ideas. This may not be obvious in unstructured speech, but only when specific information, such as specific names of objects, is demanded. This can be tested using a formal test (such as The Boston Naming Test) or more informally by asking clients to identify some standard pictures (e.g., an automobile, house, can opener, toaster, and chair). In some cases, circumlocution may also be a thought disorder reflecting confusion. Indeed, many of the thought and speech disorders can be confused with one another, emphasizing the need for careful, concrete description of the client's behavior.

Circumstantial speech involves giving unlimited detail in answer to a question, and may involve some circumlocution as well. It is primarily characterized, however, by the obsessive retelling of detail as if even the remotest related information might be necessary. Much of the detail presented is irrelevant or nearly irrelevant to the question. In its extreme form, circumstantiality may become tangentiality. Tangential speech involves clients talking about one thing, which leads them to another thing, which in turn leads them to another topic so that the original goal of the sentence is lost. This can be associated with pressured speech, confusion, and cognitive problems, or it may reflect memory problems rather than a speech deficit itself.

In general, if speech sounds wrong to the ear, then an expressive speech problem should be considered. However, cultural and language issues must be considered: The language must be wrong for the client's cultural and language background, not for society in general. It is also possible to become dysfluent in one language (usually one acquired later in life) but not in another language learned in childhood. If therapists are not familiar with what is appropriate for the client's background, it is very important that they consult with someone who can give a better appraisal of what is appropriate.

Receptive language problems refer to the understanding of speech. In these cases, clients may not understand oral or written verbal communication. Pure cases of receptive language disorders show no dysfluency of expression, but the content of the speech may be garbled. In jargon aphasia, clients produce sounds that sound correct (they are fluent), but they fail to understand the therapist or to produce meaningful words. They speak in a jargon of their own making, which is unintelligible despite the fact that it sounds like their native language. In other cases, clients may be unable to understand questions or to interpret or comprehend them. It is useful to ask clients to follow a couple of simple commands, such as "Please pick up the pencil" and "Stand up and put your hands over your head." (However, deficits in understanding may be obvious just through routine interaction as well.) Asking clients to read and interpret several basic sentences also can be useful.

Thought Processes

Thought processes cover a wide range of potential problems, which reflect disorders in the way clients process information and in higher level judgmental and logical processes. These may reflect the impact of uncontrolled emotional functioning or may be the direct result of an insult to the brain. All of these disorders have in common the absence of a logical, rational coherence to clients' thought as reflected in their oral and written communications. In some cases, these disorders may be mistaken for speech problems or vice versa, or speech and thought problems may commingle. As with speech disorders, therapists can usually be sure that there is something there simply by noticing that the communication does not sound right or cannot be followed. Discriminating among the various forms of thought and speech problems can require practice and training, but as with all of these categories, such discrimination is rooted in objective, concrete descriptions of clients' behavior.

The disorders include such processes as *perseveration*, which may be as clear as the frequent repetition of one word, phrase, or idea, or may be the inability to switch from one topic or idea to another. Perseverative and memory disorders may cause the individual to frequently repeat the same question or story again and again.

Poverty of thought refers to an absence of thought content or ideas. *Looseness of association* refers to thought that leaps from one topic to another with little connection among the topics or to things or events that are connected only by occurring at the same time or by pure serendipity. Thus, the fact that the clock strikes six while one is chewing leads to the conclusion that chewing causes the clock to chime. This may be similar to *flight of ideas*, where individuals are overwhelmed by ideas (usually in a manic state) that they leap from topic to topic without finishing the first topic. In *clang associations*, clients may leap to new words and ideas based on the similarities between the sounds of words rather than their meaning (e.g., associating *rang* with *Tang* and moving from a thought about a bell to thoughts about breakfast and astronauts). *Neologisms* involve making up new words unique to the individual, which have no meaning in the client's native language. *Confabulation* refers to making up details and stories to answer questions, and may reflect a memory process as well as a thought process.

Thought blocking refers to an inability to discuss a particular topic because the information is blocked by repression or other psychological processes. This may be confused with actual memory disorder or dementia. *Retardation of thought* refers to slowness of thought. The individual can process the information, but does so only slowly and with great effort. Examiners often find themselves finishing statements of such individuals because of the amount of time these processes last.

In addition to processes behind thought, therapists are also interested in the actual content of the thought. Foremost among these are thoughts about suicide or homicide, which are evaluated in all clients. This area is not limited to thoughts about killing oneself or others, but extends to thoughts of harming oneself or others as well. When there is any evidence of such a thought, therapists are required to find out if the client has a plan to complete the behavior in terms of how, when, where, why, and who. In all states in this country, evidence of the intent to harm places substantial legal and procedural demands on the clinician.

Other important categories of thought content include *obsessions*, where the individual perseverates on a specific event or line of thought, almost to the exclusion of other ideas; *phobias*, where clients have an irrational fear of specific things or situations such as heights, spiders, social situations, or driving; *depersonalization*, where clients are aware of their behavior but feel they are observing themselves, living in a dream or a movie, or have been converted into robots; *derealization*, the belief that the environment has changed, that one's home is not one's home or a similar idea; and *delusions*, where clients hold an irrational belief not supported by reality.

Delusions may take many forms. A primary consideration is whether or not delusions are bizarre. Unfortunately, bizarreness of a delusion is difficult to define and very dependent on culture. Bizarreness depends on how unusual a belief is within the context of the person's culture or subculture. The belief that television controls viewers' minds is generally bizarre in all cases; there is debate about whether the belief that aliens control the government is bizarre (or even a delusion). Delusions may include the ideas that the client is special (a deity, a famous figure, or endowed with special powers), the belief that others are in love with the client without any supporting evidence, a belief in magical powers, a belief that people are talking about or controlling the client, a belief that the client is being persecuted, or a belief that the client's body functions have been altered in some way or are dysfunctional in some manner. These delusions are generally classified by their content. The most common types include (but are not limited to) those of reference (people are talking about you, the television is delivering a message to you alone), grandiosity (you are important), persecution (you are being injured), guilt (you have committed a horrible act), poverty (you are poor), somatization (you have a body part disorder), and religious (you are the devil or the second coming of God).

Any of these beliefs may or may not be bizarre. It is very useful as well to see how internally consistent and logical these beliefs are. Some delusions begin with very specific underpinnings (e.g., aliens are running the government) and then are logically related to observable evidence in a manner suggesting believability because of their underlying logic and organization, whereas others are disjointed, clearly illogical, and cannot be related to objective evidence. Because of the logic underlying some delusions, some delusional clients may appear quite convincing and even convince mental health personnel that they are correct because of the misbelief that delusions must be accompanied by irrational or unexplainable behavior.

Perceptual Abnormalities

The major perceptual abnormalities are illusions and the much more serious hallucinations. Illusions are not hallucinations but may sound that way. A client may say "I thought I saw my dead father walking in the mall," but really mean to say that she saw someone who looked like her father in the mall and mistook that man momentarily for her father. Shadows may present the illusion of monsters or people lurking in the dark. Each of these cases deals with mistaken identity or distortions of something seen or heard.

Hallucinations involve perception of something that is not there through one of the sensory modalities (vision, hearing, balance, taste, smell, and touch). When clients suggest a hallucination, it is imperative to get a good description of what they actually are reporting. For example, clients commonly complain of hearing voices. When asked where the voices come from, they may state that they are in their head or coming from the outside. When the voices are in their head, they may recognize that the voices are their own thoughts that they cannot control, or they may see them as external communications from someone or something. The seriousness and clinical meaning of each of these conditions differ considerably.

In addition to noting how the person perceives a hallucination, it is important to determine content. Content may reflect any of the categories discussed previously under delusions, such as grandiosity, depression, nihilism, fear, and so on. Hallucinations can be classified as consistent or inconsistent with a given diagnosis (e.g., a hallucination about seeing family dying is consistent with depression but not with mania).

The most common form of hallucination is auditory. Such hallucinations may reflect either psychological conditions, such as schizophrenia and depression, or organic disorders. These hallucinations usually take the form of hearing voices, sometimes clearly and sometimes in the distance. It is useful to determine, if possible, who is speaking, what they are saying, and how the client reacts to the hallucinations. A particularly severe form of these hallucinations is referred to as command hallucinations. In these cases, the hallucinations command the individual to perform a specific act, which can include causing severe harm to the client or to others. It is imperative to determine how seriously the client takes these commands and the likelihood of acting on them. Such clients must be considered seriously disturbed and often very dangerous. Auditory hallucinations for voices generally have psychological etiologies, whereas hallucinations for nonverbal sounds (music, bells, etc.) may have an organic etiology.

Of the remaining types of hallucinations, most are seen exclusively in organic disorders, although they are more rarely seen in purely psychological disorders (except for visual hallucinations of faces or figures that may have a psychological etiology). Etiology of these organic hallucinations may be from some temporary problem caused by medication (e.g., pain medication, illegal street drugs, alcohol, malnutrition, dehydration, acute medical disorder, acute head injury, and so on). They may also arise from more long-term conditions, such as seizures or chronic brain injury. Brain injuries may cause individuals with marginal functioning to develop symptoms of hallucinations or delusions. Older people taking many different drugs may develop unusual side effects, including hallucinations.

Visual hallucinations arise commonly from illegal drugs, drug withdrawal, and acute brain injuries, which may cause delirium or dementia, although they may be seen in cases with pure psychological etiologies. Visual hallucinations usually take the form of seeing scenes or objects that have been lost (such as a dead child) or frightening scenes. They may also occur in people who have lost their sight or have had optic surgery, or who have seizures affecting the visual processing areas of the brain. Individuals with visual hallucinations should be encouraged to describe the images as well as whether or not they believe the images to be real.

Olfactory and taste hallucinations are rarer and almost always the result of organic disorders. These hallucinations are almost always of bad tasting or smelling objects. They are generally very real to clients and very disturbing. They may arise from seizures and sometimes as side effects to a variety of medications. Tactile hallucinations (feelings of itching, touch, pain, temperature) are also almost always organic. They can also be the result of drug side effects, drug withdrawal, or seizures. They may also arise as in phantom limb pain from the sites of severed nerves.

Vestibular hallucinations may arise from reactions to illicit drugs creating a sense of falling or flying, but may also be reflected in a sense of dizziness or balance disorders. These again can arise from medication side effects and more directly from injury to the brain. In the latter case, the problem may either be hallucinatory or real depending on the location of the brain injury.

Other hallucinations may deal with extrasensory perception: reading the minds of others or sensing the presence of others. It is not always clear in these cases whether this is a hallucination or a variant of a delusional state. This can reflect a delusion of thought insertion, in which others insert thoughts in the client's head, or a hallucination in which the client actually appears to perceive others' thoughts as a variant of an auditory hallucination.

Finally, it is important to differentiate between true hallucinations and disorders that arise when the client is halfway between sleep and wakefulness. In this state, the client may see or hear things that are not real. Rarely do these include other senses. If the "hallucinations" only occur in this twilight sleep, they are *hypnagogic*. This can reflect narcolepsy or possibly other sleep disorders, but sometimes vivid dreams are also reported in a similar manner.

Memory and Attention

An important aspect of any mental status examination is the evaluation of memory. Memory is impaired in many disorders, most seriously in the organic disorders. For the purpose of this examination, memory is divided into several parts, whose interplay may lead to different diagnoses. At the same time, attentional processes that play a major role in memory can be examined.

The most basic form of memory is long-term memory, which can be classified as *primary life information* and as factual memory. In general, the evaluation of basic life facts begins with an examination of the orientation of the individual in which therapists find out if clients know who they are. Other questions can include where they live, what they do for a living, whether they are married, whether they have children, and basic facts about their history. This type of autobiographical (or personal) memory is rarely lost except in cases of extreme confusion (which might arise from delirium or dementia), severe aphasia where the client cannot understand the questions, and certain rare dissociative disorders. There may be temporary loss of such memories associated with acute organic disorders, such as a drug reaction, acute head injury or stroke, or other similar problems.

Factual long-term memory refers to memory for events outside of clients during their lifetime. In general, if this information is acquired, it is generally not lost. However, deficits appear in three areas: general confusion, failure to acquire information, and failure to retrieve information. A typical question for this area is to name "four presidents since 1950" or to simply discuss major events (Kennedy assassination, Vietnam, World War II, sports events, etc.) in the client's life, with topics chosen based on the individual's age, interests, and exposure to those events.

When there is general confusion, there is an inability to answer informational-type questions, although there may not actually be a loss of the information. Failure to acquire information may reflect a lack of interest, significant emotional or neurological problems, or alcohol or drug addiction during the time of memory loss. In these cases, loss will be constrained primarily to the time since the head injury, when the person was a heavy drinker, and so on, and memory for events at other times will be accessible. When there is a failure to retrieve information, there will be difficulty responding to specific questions about relatively recent and remote topics. However, such individuals may spontaneously give the information or other long-term information either as an inappropriate answer or in the course of general conversation when they are not searching to answer a specific question. This should not be confused with word-finding problems, where the client knows the answer but cannot find the words to express it (but may be able to do so in a circumstantial manner). Clients who do not have the information requested may confabulate, making up answers without realizing that they are doing so. Such confabulations may be confused with malingering or deliberate falsehoods.

The other categories are short-term (immediate) memory and delayed memory. Initially, one looks at short-term memory, the immediate recall of 1 to 7 items presented in any modality. There is disagreement across clinicians about the number and type of items to be used, but most use 3 to 5 items. In most exams, this is limited to words (red, tree, car, shack), which are articulated one at a time at a pace of one per second. The client is then asked to remember them. Average and above-average clients can remember all four, with the number missed reflecting some degree of attentional or memory impairment. In cases where one or more is missed, the list can be repeated. Visual memory can be tested by showing clients the first four Bender–Gestalt pictures for 10 seconds and then asking them to reproduce them. Evaluation is based more on getting the gestalt of the drawing rather than on motor skills, but motor deficits can be evaluated as well. This can be repeated for a second trial if there are memory errors on the first trial. Normal clients should get all four correct.

After completing the immediate memory trials, clients should be told that they will need to remember these items later. (The second trial, which is included when clients fail the first, allows for better consolidation for this later recall.) Therapists should then continue with their interview and then 35 minutes later they can assess delayed memory by asking "What were the words I asked you to remember?" and "Could you draw those pictures again that I asked you to draw?" These tests take only about 2 minutes together and give an idea of memory decay over time. In general, there should be 80% or better retention of the words initially remembered with no decay between 5 and 30 minutes on a task this simple.

When immediate memory is intact, it is reasonable to assume that attention is also intact. There are several tests that can be used to assess attention as well. Common tests involve serial subtraction, where the client is given a starting number such as 100 and then must subtract 7s or 3s or 13s (the latter for brighter clients). The arithmetic involved distresses many clients and up to two errors over six subtractions is common in normals. An easier version of this for lower intelligence clients is serial 3s starting with the number 20 and subtracting until the client reaches 2. Except in cases of intellectual retardation, there should be no errors. Another common task is to spell a word such as "world" backward. This should also be performed without error. In addition, one may use a digit span-type task in which clients are asked to remember a series of 6 to 7 numbers forward and to repeat a similar series of 5 to 6 digits backward.

Intelligence

Intelligence refers to the ability of the individual to deal adaptively with the world and represents a general factor that influences the client's performance on many tasks. This can be useful in determining the client's reliability and ability to understand and to benefit from therapies requiring understanding. Although simply talking to the individual can reveal levels of education, more formal methods can be used in the interview. Because IQ is so highly correlated with vocabulary skills, a quick vocabulary test such as every sixth item from the Wechsler Adult Intelligence Scale–Revised (WAIS–R; items 35, 29, 23, 17, 11, and 5) can be given, scored, and the total multiplied by 6 to get a raw score, which can be converted into a WAIS–R scaled score. This in turn can be multiplied by 6 to get a verbal scaled sum and a verbal IQ. Similarly, every sixth item from the Shipley–Hartford Institute of Living Scale or other similar tests may be used.

It is also common to use more abstract items in assessing intelligence, such as proverb items (e.g., from WAIS–R Comprehension) and WAIS–R Similarities items. Each of these yields some basic information on abstractive skills. This is also determined from the client's general interaction with the clinician. An example would be: "Can you tell me what this saying means: People who live in glass houses shouldn't throw stones." An abstract answer would be "People with faults shouldn't find faults in others." A concrete answer might be "If you start throwing stones you might end up breaking your glass house." A poor answer might be "People in glass houses don't have stones." If the client is asked "What does the phrase 'green thumb' mean?", an abstract answer would be "Someone good at growing plants." A concrete answer would be "Someone whose thumb is colored green."

Judgment and Insight

These are more difficult to evaluate and can be quite subjective. Insight must be separated from awareness. Awareness refers to knowing about a problem, whereas insight refers to knowing the causes and the impact of the problem and its role in the client's life.

Thus, clients may be aware that they have a memory problem, but not understand (insight) that this means they have to write everything down. Clients may be aware that they had family problems, but not have the insight to recognize they are carrying out the same behaviors with their own children. In establishing insight, the therapist must go beyond "What is wrong?" to "How does this affect you?", "What could you do about it?", and "Why does it affect you the way it does?" The specific questions vary considerably with the problems, but all must be aimed at getting under the surface awareness to see if the client truly understands the impact of the disorder.

Subjects can be classified into four major groups on these variables: individuals with no insight or awareness; individuals aware of the problem but have no insight; individuals with awareness of the problem and its causes, but unable to effect any changes from this information; and individuals with full insight and awareness who can effect change on their own. It follows that most populations seen for psychological help fall into one of the first three groups.

Judgment overlaps to a degree with intelligence, and can initially be evaluated through the client's ability to make decisions and handle simple situations or problem solving such as in the comprehension subtest of the

WAIS–R. Beyond the intellectual meaning of the word, judgment refers to the client's practical ability to deal with problem solving in realistic situations. Clients may be able to explain situations in terms of answering questions, but unable to implement or recognize the proper strategy in a real-life situation. An evaluation of judgment should come from the client's entire behavioral history, not just views expressed in the interview.

For example, clients with early dementia may recognize that they have memory problems (awareness), even recognize that people with memory problems should avoid new situations requiring new memories and learning (judgment), but not recognize that they must therefore not drive to a new town by themselves (lack of insight). After extensive psychotherapy, these clients may be aware of their problems (at least as presented by the psychotherapist), but may not be able to understand how this information necessitates change in their life.

Affect

Affect refers to the current predominant emotional expression at the time of the interview. This is assessed both through an evaluation of the client's current behavior by observation and by questioning ("How are you feeling now?"). Observation involves evaluation of the client's nonverbal communications, the ways in which things are said, the tone of voice used, the kinds of things said, and the feelings the client may induce in the examiner or others. A client can be perfectly polite and give the impression of hostility. Clients' own explanations of their affect should be questioned to elicit concrete referents rather than vague statements. Be aware of the various criteria for recognizing each mood state. The most common affects are described as normal (labeled euthymic), depressed, anxious, or hostile.

Affect may be described as *blunted* or *flat*. In flat affect, the client seems to show no emotion at all. The expression and manner is "flat." In blunted affect, the client shows emotions, but expression of the emotion is limited and does not appear to be correct. It is as if the range of the expression of the emotion has been cut off at either end, causing an expression that is recognizable but limited. Affect may also be *labile*, in which the therapist will see quick changes in affect, or *inappropriate*, where the affect expressed is inconsistent with the current content of the conversation (smiling when discussing an episode in which the client was in great pain and distress). Affect may simultaneously be described as *labile*, *blunted*, and *inappropriate*.

Mood

Mood refers to the client's emotion over recent time periods rather than the immediate moment. The length of this time period varies, depending on the complaint of the client and the relevance of the mood at different times to the client's current problems. Thus, a client whose problems reportedly began

2 months ago might cause one to use a period of 2 months unless other information suggested that the mood extended farther back in time. Moods can be called euthymic (normal), elated, irritable, anxious, phobic, terrorized, depressed, manic, and so on. Moods vary in the course of a normal day or week: The therapist's interest is in the predominant mood that has influenced or led to the client's current situation, although fluctuations in the mood state can be mentioned when relevant. For example, "The client has been depressed for the past 2 months except for brief periods when he was allowed to see his fiancee." Moods are affected both by the client's inner emotional and cognitive situation as well as by major external events.

REPORTING THE MENTAL STATUS

In general, the mental status is reported in an interview report as a separate section of one or more paragraphs. In other cases, mental status may be reported one or more times in progress notes to evaluate the client's overall progress or problems. The length of the section varies with the abnormality of the examination. A report for a normal exam is very brief. Abnormalities require more detail as well as concrete examples. It is important to write this section primarily as observations and real information, rather than as conclusions. This gives the reader the raw data on which later conclusions may be reached in the report after integration with history and other sources of data.

Although there is no one set or required way to write up a mental status examination, the paragraph typically begins with a description of the client, including dress, appearance, orientation, attention, and psychomotor behavior, as well as overall attitude. This can be followed by a statement on the client's reliability and the accuracy of the information obtained. Next is a description of the client's affect and mood and then a description of the client's speech and thought processes, including specific statements about suicidality and homicidality. Delusions and hallucinations can then be discussed, followed by statements on the client's level of intelligence, memory, and judgment, awareness, and insight. Abnormal areas are often discussed first after the general description of the client.

SUMMARY

Overall, this chapter has offered a brief and practical guide to the mental status examination. The examination offers a quick and efficient way to identify a client's major issues and problems, as well as to track progress over time. In addition, it helps to identify areas where additional evaluation or testing may be necessary, and should never be regarded alone as a complete or detailed examination. The mental status may miss more subtle problems and can be manipulated easily by the client either as a result of deliberate lying, repression, denial, intellectualization, or many other psychological processes that can distort or hide the real situation. The examination must be integrated with all other information about the client to check the accuracy and the validity of any conclusions.

SUGGESTED READINGS

Evans, D. R., Hearn, M. T., Uhlemann, M. R., & Ivey, A. E. (1993). *Essential interviewing* (4th ed.). Pacific Grove, CA: Brooks/Cole.

Hersen, M., & Turner, S. M. (Eds.). (1994). *Diagnostic interviewing* (2nd ed.). New York: Plenum.

Othmer, E., & Othmer, S. C. (1994). *The clinical interview using* DSM–IV (Vol. 1). Washington, DC: American Psychological Association.

Strub, R. L., & Black, F. N. (1977). *The mental status examination in neurology*. Philadelphia: Davis.

Zuckerman, E. L. (1993). *Clinicians' thesaurus* (3rd ed.). Pittsburgh: The Clinician's Toolbox.

8

Writing Up the
Intake Interview

Daniel L. Segal
University of Colorado at Colorado Springs

The ability to write up a clear, comprehensive, and professional intake evaluation report is a top skill for seasoned mental health professionals. However, this task often seems overwhelming to the beginning clinician, who also is facing the challenges of learning other basic interviewing and therapy skills. But imagine a clinician who conducts a whole course of treatment without formally documenting anything about why clients came for services, what problems they initially had, and what treatment recommendations and goals were established. How could this practitioner justify the type of treatment provided and gauge whether or not treatment was successful? Indeed, practices with limited documentation cannot survive in today's climate of managed health care organizations, professional accountability, and client rights. No matter what clinical specialty or type of setting in which therapists work, they most likely will be responsible for writing at least some form of an intake report. Historically, however, many psychology training programs have not provided formalized classroom training in professional report writing. Rather, students learned to write intake reports through informal means: studying old intake reports in their clients' charts or borrowing "model" reports from more experienced students or teachers. This chapter assists therapists in report writing, and offers practical and explicit guidelines to help them prepare well-written and thorough intake reports.

It should be stated at the outset, however, that there is no one right way to format and write an intake report, and there are few absolutes when it comes to report writing. Indeed, perusal of reports from diverse mental health professionals will show that the documents vary considerably. It is likely that different clinical supervisors will modify some aspect of report writing to satisfy their particular desires and the specific requirements of the setting. This should not be a source of great anxiety or concern for you. The general format and style of the report described here can be adapted easily to meet your particular needs. Moreover, the write-up of the intake report and the issues discussed here are not tied to any particular psychological theoretical orientation (i.e., psychoanalytic or behavioral). Rather, the information is intended to apply to all clinicians.

This chapter covers all sections of a typical intake report and discusses strategies to successfully organize and prepare each part. Throughout, common errors are highlighted as well as possible alternative or ameliorative strategies. Whenever possible, examples culled from real reports are provided to enhance understanding of the material (of course, identifying information has been altered to protect confidentiality of clients). Like all clinical skills, improvement comes with practice and feedback from clinical supervisors. A therapist's first report will not be as clear and comprehensive as later ones, but it is hoped that the guidelines in this chapter will make this first attempt successful and provide a solid base from which to build and improve. Also, it should be noted that intake report writing cannot be completely separated from intake interviewing. As such, some of the suggestions include tips about information that must be asked of clients or assessed during the intake session in order to show how that information might be presented in a report.

PURPOSES OF THE REPORT

The intake evaluation is usually the first formal contact between therapist and client. At intake, the clinician conducts a thorough assessment of the client's current and past problems, social history, and mental status. Treatment recommendations and feedback are provided to the client at the end of the session. Typically, during this 1- to 2-hour session, a great deal of important clinical information is amassed, although the unfolding of this complex information often is haphazard and confusing. The written intake report is the outcome of that initial evaluation and serves several important purposes and functions. First, the task helps (forces?) clinicians to organize the wealth of critical information gleaned from the intake session. Second, writing the report assists them in thinking about initial case conceptualization, diagnosis, and treatment planning. Third, the report provides a detailed description of the client's current psychological and social functioning. This record is valuable during ongoing treatment, because it can be consulted whenever the clinician is confused about something or has forgotten some important information. Student therapists often find it helpful to reread the intake before the first few sessions to refresh their memory and make sure that important issues are not neglected. Because the report is also a snapshot of the client's functioning at one point in time, it can serve as a baseline against which therapeutic progress can be measured at later dates. Fourth, the report serves as the official documentation or record of that initial intake session and remains in the client's confidential chart during and after treatment. Whereas this official report can be requested by clinicians who may provide services for the client at a later point, a copy may not be sent out until a written release of information letter signed and dated by the client is received. Likewise, at intake, therapists can request that the client sign a release of information so that they may receive documentation (e.g., intake reports, testing reports, and progress notes) from professionals who have previously treated the client. These old reports can be very helpful in understanding clients' history and changes in their functioning.

GENERAL CONSIDERATIONS AND CONVENTIONS

In the write-up, how should therapists refer to the person about whom they are writing? There are no definitive rules, but the following guidelines provide assistance. It is always appropriate to refer to the person as "the client" (e.g., "The client reports that he has been drinking six beers each night for the past 2 weeks."). Sometimes, you may want to refer to the formal name of the client, and this is acceptable so long as the name remains consistent from one usage to the next. For example, a student referred to the client's full name in the beginning of the report (Mr. Robert Johnson), but then resorted to using derivations of the name in other sections (e.g., Robert Johnson, Robert, Bobby, and Bob). If including the client's name in the body of the report, it is suggested to use the entire full name (Mrs. Jeremy Jones) or the formal last name (Mrs. Jones), and to avoid using first names only and nicknames (Punky, Slim, etc.). Use of the last name denotes respect for the person and a professional relationship. For female clients, "Ms." is preferable to "Miss" or "Mrs."

When should the intake report be written? In general, it is advisable to start organizing and writing the report as soon as possible after the completed interview. This way, the information is fresh and clear in the mind. In cases where students had the unfortunate experience of conducting several intakes before doing the write-ups, the result was confusion of the facts of the cases and an irritated supervisor. Clinics often have policies about when drafts of the report are to be completed. For example, practicum students may be required to submit a first draft version within 5 days after the intake session. A copy of the draft report is also typically placed into the client's chart concurrent with submission to the supervisor, and this draft serves as a temporary document until the final report is completed. This is due to the fact that crises can develop during clinical work with distressed persons, and incomplete information in the chart is better than no information at all. Many supervisors provide extensive feedback or comments on early drafts, and it would not be uncommon to revise the report several times before it is finally accepted and signed by a supervisor. View the supervisor's feedback as an opportunity to improve, and try to remain positive and receptive to advice during these challenging situations. Remember, the therapist's name will forever be linked to the report, so it is important to produce a competent product. Accuracy is also an issue, and therapists should keep in mind that other individuals, agencies, or the courts may gain access to the document. Clinic policy usually dictates that a final report is due within 10 days. The final document typically is signed and dated by both the student therapist and the supervisor.

Write-ups often include notification that the report itself is confidential. Just as content of a psychotherapy or testing session is confidential, so are written intake reports, psychological testing reports, and progress notes. The issue of confidentiality is typically discussed with the client at the beginning of the intake session, so that the client understands that confidentiality is not absolute. Confidentiality must be broken in certain situations: for example, when there are serious concerns about suicidal or homicidal behavior or suspected child or elder abuse. As noted earlier, clients can authorize release of the report to anyone they choose as long as consent to release the information is provided in writing. In cases where clients do not give their consent (i.e., the records are subpoenaed by a judge), the issue becomes more complicated and should be discussed with a supervisor.

PROFESSIONAL WRITING

When writing the intake report, remember that information is being taken only from one source: the client. Consequently, the information is not necessarily factual, but rather is only the client's view of the situation. Because intake interviewers do not know much about the veracity of the client's statements, it is advisable to regularly preface statements in the report with qualifiers. The following are some options (and examples): "The client reports (states, relates, says, describes, notes, elaborates) that he was married seven times." Other conventions are to write that "According to client . . . ," "As described by client . . . ," or "The client reportedly (was discharged from the army due to drug problems)." Avoid using "alleges" and "claims" because these sound judgmental. Make sure to preface statements that are potentially controversial or untrue. For example, it is best to write that "The client *describes* his father as a severe alcoholic" in contrast to writing that "The client's father *is* an alcoholic." Similarly, write that "The client *says* she was sexually assaulted by her previous therapists" rather than "The client *was* sexually assaulted by her previous therapist." Use judgment here and preface more statements than not. Usually the present verb tense is used throughout the report (e.g., "The client characterizes [not characterized] his relationship with his wife as close and supportive"). An exception is the mental status examination section, which typically is written in the past tense (e.g., "Speech was [not is] tangential"). In any case, make sure to remain consistent within sections or the report will look sloppy.

Objective writing is also a challenge for the beginning clinician. The trick here is to translate client statements into objective, behaviorally specific terms. In one report, a student wrote that "the client partied a lot during college." Obviously, this is what the client said, but the write-up needs more objectivity and specific data or it will start to look like one long quote from the client. When asked to rewrite and clarify the communication from the client, the student was able to revise the sentence as follows: "The client reports a long history of alcohol and recreational drug use dating back to 1987 when he was a student at the state university. He relates that he regularly drank beer to excess (approximately 3 to 10 beers) about 3 to 4 days each week, and smoked marijuana on the weekends." This is much more objective and specific than the previous comment. Consider the following example, "The client wants his wife to get off his back!" A possible rewrite of this sentence would be to say, "The client notes that his wife regularly nags him about his lack of participation in household chores, and he elaborates that he wants her to stop but is unsure how to handle the situation." Try to replace the client's slang and colloquialisms with objective, clinical terms. For example, replace "crabby" with "irritable," "cracked-up" with "became psychotic," and "nervous" with "anxious." Make sure to give as many specific details about the client's current functioning and history as possible. For example, instead of writing that "the client grew up in a small southern town," state that "the client grew up in Ocean Springs, a small town in southern Mississippi." It is also helpful to provide specific dates in the report when possible. Instead of noting that "the client was hospitalized during her adolescence after making a suicide attempt," write that "in June, 1993, the client (age 16) reportedly was hospitalized for 11 days at Memorial Hospital following a suicide attempt consisting of swallowing 50 aspirin." As you can see, more details and dates are better than fewer!

A related problem in some reports is the excessive use of quotations. Many students remember interesting and vivid quotes from the client, and they want to include them. However, a reliance on quotes is often at the expense of clarity, specificity, and objectivity. Consider the following example: According to the client, his boss is "a real pain in the rear." What does the client mean by "pain in the rear"? What specifically does the boss do that the client finds irritating? It is important to document those events clearly. The statement can be rewritten as follows: "According to the client, he frequently becomes irritated at his boss at the glue factory. He elaborates that his boss frequently criticizes him when he takes a nap at work, demands that work be done on time, and threatens to fire the client when he comes to work under the influence of drugs. The client notes that his boss is 'a real pain in the rear.' " These statements shed more light on what is happening at work. Consider the following use of quotes from the client: The client describes her father as "odd, creepy, bizarre, a real nerd." Is it really clear how the father actually behaves? Does he suffer from a major mental disorder like schizophrenia? Or does he just like to watch old science fiction reruns and play fantasy games? It would be best to replace the quote with a clear description of father's behavior. Use quotations only after the facts have been objectively described. Quotations can add flavor to the facts, but do not describe them. Students who excessively rely on quotes should practice writing reports without any quotes. This challenges them to think about what the client is communicating and to ask for clarification and elaboration.

Jargon should also be avoided. It should never be used in an intake report (or in an interview session). Examples of jargon include: "The client demonstrated a *strong transference* reaction to the interviewer," "The client appears *fixated at the oral stage* of development," "The client has a *Type-A personality*," and "*Boundary issues* are prominent for the client." Therapists know what they mean by those terms, but someone else reading the report may not have that advantage. It is good practice to write the report so that it can be understood by someone without significant formal training in psychology (e.g., lawyers, disability evaluators, family members, the client). Jargon is typically vague and abstract and inhibits the flow of a well-written report.

Clients themselves sometimes use jargon or labels, especially those clients who are well educated and psychologically sophisticated. Even in these cases, jargon still has no place in the report. Ask clients to describe the behaviors that the label implies. A client explained rather emphatically at the beginning of an intake session that she was a "coda," evidently meaning a "co-dependent." Upon questioning, this client soon proceeded to describe many specific behaviors that led her to think of herself as a "coda." This information was documented in the report (e.g., "The client describes herself as unassertive, gullible, afraid to be alone, insecure, and dependent on others for self-esteem. She relates a long history of repetitive and destructive relationships with chemically dependent and abusive individuals whom she tries to help"). Some clients likewise use slang terms to describe themselves or others (e.g., "crazy," "nutty," "superhuman," "cool," "a worrywart," "has a bad attitude," "a loser"). These terms are also inappropriate in a professional report.

The intake report is focused on describing information elicited from the client. Therefore, self-disclosures or personal opinions are best left out (e.g.,

"I felt sad for the client when he discussed his painful childhood." "The client shouldn't be so bitter about her divorce because it probably was for the best, anyway."). Rather than include personal reflections in the report, the student therapists' feelings should be discussed during supervision, which can lead to a greater understanding of the client and themselves.

SECTIONS OF THE INTAKE REPORT

The following information is typically provided in a comprehensive intake report: client demographics and identifying data, referral source, informants, presenting problem (or chief complaint), history of the presenting problem (or history of current illness), other relevant history (or social history), mental status examination and client strengths, clinical formulation (or case conceptualization), psychiatric diagnosis, and treatment recommendations. Divided into these discrete sections, the final document is more organized and efficient. As each section is discussed, it may be helpful to consult the sample "Intake Evaluation" report presented at the end of this chapter (Appendix I). A checklist for writing up the intake report is also provided at the end of this chapter (Appendix II).

Title and Identifying Data

Typically, the name and address of the service agency or provider is listed at the top of the report. This is relatively unimportant if the report stays in this office's files, but it is necessary if the report is requested by an outside agency or other mental health worker. Many settings use letterhead stationery for this purpose. The title "Intake Evaluation" is also included below the address, as well as notification (printed or stamped) that the report itself is "Confidential." Next, identifying information is presented. The standard format includes the following data: full name of client, client gender, date of birth, age, level of education, name of examiner or interviewer, date(s) of examination, client employment status, and marital status. Think of these as minimally required demographics. Additional information sometimes includes ethnicity, nationality, primary language, and current medications. Most of this information can be found on the forms clients fill out prior to being interviewed. Make sure this information is complete before proceeding.

Referral Source

The referral source answers the question "Who sent the client?" Important facts prompting the assessment as well as specific referral questions should be noted. Common referral sources include family doctors or general practitioners, psychiatrists, crisis lines, local mental health or social services agencies (e.g., county mental health department, area agency on aging), probation officers, courts for mandated treatment, local therapists who cannot treat the client, clergy, employers, family members, friends, and teachers. Some clients are referred for follow-up therapy after discharge from a psychiatric hospital. Other clients are *self-referred*, which means they have decided for themselves that a mental health evaluation is warranted and no other agency, individual, or professional has specifically recommended treatment. The following are examples of write-ups: "The client was referred for a psychological assessment and possible counseling by David Joseph, MD, the client's local family doctor." "The client was self-referred for evaluation of depression and substance abuse." "The client was referred by Christy Farmer, MSW, a social worker at a local acute-term care nursing home, The Manors, for evaluation of nature and extent of psychiatric disability." "The client was referred by Daniel Heimlich from El Paso County Probation and Parole for psychological assessment and treatment planning after the client was found walking the streets naked, disoriented, and singing show tunes."

Informants

This section describes all sources of information used in the report. If the client and nobody else was interviewed, state that the client attended the session alone. In some cases, however, there may be multiple informants. For example, parents are often interviewed when they bring their children in for evaluation. Interviews with psychotic or demented clients are greatly facilitated by family members, spouses, or significant others who can provide valuable (and more reliable) information about the client's current and past functioning. Entire families may be interviewed during a family therapy evaluation. Also note if the client's previous chart or other records were reviewed.

Presenting Problem

The presenting problem (PP) refers to the client's current difficulties and is written in the report in terms of psychiatric symptoms. A clear and descriptive PP is a crucial aspect of the intake report. Indeed, if the PP is not clearly elicited in the interview and delineated in the write-up, the rest of the report will follow this faulty lead and remain offtrack. Unfortunately, the presenting problem (in terms of symptoms) is not always readily apparent. Besides symptoms, clients often express their problems in terms of patterns of maladjusted behavior (e.g., repeatedly fired from jobs), stressors (e.g., victim of a crime, divorce, friend moved away, lost business), or interpersonal conflicts.

More generally, clients typically present at intake either as *symptom* or *issue* focused. Clients with a symptom-focused presentation often list a litany of disturbing psychological and physical symptoms that they find distressing and from which they want relief. It is often easy to describe the PP for such clients. For example, a client brought in a typed, two-page list of symptoms for review. This action may also be diagnostically useful (e.g., it may be representative of an obsessive-compulsive personality disorder). Anxious or depressed clients typically see their symptoms as things to get rid of and can often describe some symptoms. For example, a depressed client may report "feeling blue" and having trouble eating, sleeping, and concentrating. The therapist should then inquire directly about other symptoms of depression (e.g., loss of interest in activities, low energy, psychomotor retardation or agitation, feelings of worthlessness) to flesh out all aspects of the problem or disorder experienced by the individual. Any additional symptoms become part of the formal PP write-up. Do not leave it up to the client to note all symptoms, because clients are not experts in psychopathology and often do not recognize some symptoms. In fact, individuals with schizophrenia or personality disorders may totally lack insight into their condition and therefore may be unaware that they suffer from an illness. Such individuals may clearly exhibit overt *signs* of the disorder (e.g., hallucinations and delusions in schizophrenia; flamboyant, seductive, and superficial behavior in histrionic personality disorder) but will not report them. It is the intake interviewer's job to identify and understand all psychiatric symptoms experienced by the client, whether or not the client actually recognizes such symptoms. Then, they should be listed in the PP in objective terms. Even with a symptom presentation, a therapist always wants to know why clients are seeking help now (as part of the PP picture).

Clients with an issue-focused presentation pose a different challenge. These individuals typically complain about what is going wrong in their lives or describe current problems or stressors with which they are struggling. One client, for example, complained that her main problem was that she caught her boyfriend with another woman and subsequently ended the relationship. Another client said the main difficulty was that he recently relocated to a new city and started graduate school. It is critical during the interview to ask clients to explore or describe how diverse current situations or stressors affect them. In this way, current symptoms can be elicited. For example, the previously mentioned woman revealed that as a result of the breakup she increased her alcohol consumption to the point of daily drinking; was feeling increasingly depressed, angry, lonely, and suicidal; and also experienced increased appetite, irritability, and lethargy. The neophyte graduate student said that due to the changes in his life he was experiencing intense anxiety, restlessness, poor concentration, difficulty falling asleep, ruminative thoughts, upset stomach, and diarrhea. These presenting problems should be reported in the write-up. Note that the environmental stressors are not actually the PP; rather, the PP refers to psychiatric symptoms. Therefore, stressful experiences like "being fired from a job," "diagnosed with cancer," and "parents' divorce" cannot be a PP. However, these stressors are valuable information, and they have their rightful place in the report.

Make sure to be comprehensive in listing symptoms. Some clients may suffer from more than one disorder, and all symptoms should be noted. Finally, all symptoms should be described as specifically as possible. Some dimensions of symptoms to note include frequency, duration, and intensity. For example, the symptom "sleep disturbance" is unclear. Do clients have trouble falling asleep, staying asleep, frequent nightmares, or do they wake up after their usual sleep but not feel rested? How many nights each week does it happen? Indeed, clear, behaviorally specific descriptions of symptoms make a report stand out.

History of Presenting Problem

This section generally includes three important components that help clarify and expand on the presenting problem already noted: onset, precipitants (stressors), and course. *Onset* refers to onset of the symptoms listed in the PP. Make sure to carefully assess when the symptoms began ("When did you first experience the symptoms of depression you have been telling me about?"), and also ask clients when they were free of all symptoms ("Up till what age were you free of any problems?"). Related to onset are *precipitants*, or *stressors*, that typically occur prior to the appearance or worsening of symptoms. Describe onset and precipitants clearly in the report to help the reader understand the context in which symptoms or distress have developed in the client's life. Some clients can provide lengthy descriptions of numerous life stressors, and all relevant details should be put in this section. If the client cannot identify any stressors, precipitants, or life changes, state so in the report. *Course* refers to the changes in the client's symptoms over time, preferably since the onset. Have the symptoms gotten better over time? Worse? Better for 3 months, then worse for the last 6 months? Has there been no change in the symptoms since they started? Whatever the facts, state them in the report. Here's a brief example of a description of onset, precipitants, and course: "The client relates that his depressive symptoms began around January 1997. According to the client, he lost his job in early December 1996, his wife filed for divorce 2 weeks later, and in early January 1997 his pet monkey was fatally wounded in a car accident. Since that time, his symptoms have gotten progressively worse up to the present evaluation (May 1997)." A full write-up would no doubt be considerably longer and more complex.

Other Relevant History

This section of the report includes information generated from the "social history" part of the interview (see chap. 5). This section provides a thorough overview of a client's life besides presenting complaint. This description of background information relevant to the present difficulties is critical because it helps place the clients and their problems within a context of general functioning. It is often helpful to describe where the client grew up, how many siblings were in the family, the birth order, school performance, and if there were any significant occurrences or problems (e.g., traumas, illnesses, disabilities, abuse) in early and middle childhood. Then, briefly comment on the client's functioning during adolescence.

The focus then turns to the adult years. The client's current functioning in many areas should be described. These areas include educational history, work history, dating or marital history, substance use history (drugs and alcohol), sexual history, interpersonal relationships with family and friends, legal and criminal history, medical problems, religion, current social life, and leisure activities. In addition, the client's history of mental health treatment (called the client's *psychiatric history*) should be clearly depicted. Dates of all previous mental health contacts, name of therapist or hospital, reasons for treatment, number of sessions, and reason for terminating treatment should be included. Such treatment history can greatly assist the clinician in reconstructing past diagnoses from other clinicians, identifying responses to certain types of intervention (e.g., cognitive therapy, medications), and confirming the current diagnosis. Similarly, always comment on any family history of mental illness, substance use, and suicide (called *family psychiatric history*). Clearly describe whether or not any family members have been diagnosed, treated, or hospitalized for psychiatric problems. Family history is important because many disorders have a familial component, and it can also speak to the environment in which the client was raised. Many counselors also make a statement in the report about any history of physical/sexual abuse, sexual assault, or intimate partner violence. If clients deny these experiences, state so in the write-up.

Mental Status Examination and Client Strengths

The Mental Status Examination (MSE) is often considered to be the cornerstone of a psychiatric evaluation, and this assessment focuses on the client's present functioning in the here and now. This information is often critical in assigning psychiatric diagnosis when combined with other parts of the intake evaluation such as presenting problem and psychiatric history. As such, the MSE should be carried out on all clients at intake. However, depth of the evaluation is often based on severity of the client's illness, with more disturbed persons requiring more comprehensive and formal testing of mental status. This section is devoted to a description of the information generated from the MSE part of the interview (see chap. 7). The report should include a statement about each variable assessed during the MSE. If the behavior or response was completely normal, then state this rather than omitting it.

Many MSE sections begin with a description of the client's demographics (age, gender, ethnicity of client), appearance, attire, grooming, hygiene, and eye contact. Provide enough information so that the reader can easily visualize the client's physical appearance at the interview. Definitely note anything unusual about the person (e.g., wore neck brace, malodorous, rashes on skin, fingernails bitten, 6 bows in hair stacked on top of each other). Also comment on the person's behavior during interview (e.g., fell asleep several times, hands tightly clasped, frequently cried, paced around the room, sucked thumb) and attitude toward interviewer (e.g., cooperative, suspicious, hostile, guarded, seductive, manipulative). If the client's attitude is labeled negatively, make sure to clearly describe the client behaviors that led to this inference. These vivid descriptions of appearance and behavior often give diagnostic cues. Next, describe the client's mood (e.g., euthymic, anxious, dysphoric, euphoric, irritable) and affect (e.g., broad, restricted, flat). Characterize the person's speech in terms of loudness, speed, and organization of thoughts (e.g., soft, loud; rapid, pressured, average rate; logical, coherent, goal directed, loose associations, circumstantial, tangential, word salad or senseless speech). Include comments about the person's orientation (to time, place, person, and situation), cognitive functions of attention, memory, and concentration, and provide a gross estimate of intelligence level. Discuss the reliability or quality of information obtained from the client. Is the person a good or poor historian? Make sure to include assessments of the client's judgment and insight (e.g., nil, poor, fair, good). In addition, always ask directly and comment in report about suicidal and homicidal ideation, plan, or intent; presence of delusions and hallucinations; and use of alcohol, drugs, and medications (list name, dosage, and prescribing doctor if possible). Finally, it is common to include strengths in the mental status write-up. This is important to balance out the report and focus on positives that exist with all clients. Some examples of client strengths include motivation for treatment, good verbal skills, ability to maintain employment, lives independently, good social support system, and no cognitive impairment.

Clinical Formulation

This section describes the therapist's theoretical analysis of the current case, addressing questions like "What has caused the person's present difficulties (symptoms) to develop?" and "What maintains those symptoms?" Based on theoretical orientation (e.g., psychodynamic, cognitive-behavioral, humanistic, family systems), a therapist can make some educated hypotheses about the etiology of the person's problems. Obviously, there is no definitive right or wrong way to conceptualize a case; it depends which theory is being applied. Student therapists who are having trouble with case formulation (and many beginning students do), should look to a supervisor for help in this area.

DSM–IV Diagnostic Impressions

This section provides a full diagnosis based on criteria for mental disorders listed in the *Diagnostic and Statistical Manual of Mental Disorders* (*DSM–IV*). *DSM–IV* includes a multiaxial system, which involves assessment of different domains of client functioning. There are five distinct axes in the *DSM–IV* system, and the report should include information on each one. Axis I refers to clinical disorders such as major depressive disorder, panic disorder, and alcohol abuse. Axis II includes personality disorders (e.g., borderline, paranoid, antisocial) and mental retardation. In the interview, always screen for lifelong maladjustment and lifelong recurrent coping deficits, which can alert the therapist that a personality disorder may be present. However, it often takes several sessions to formally diagnose these complex disorders. If the interviewee meets formal criteria for an Axis I or Axis II disorder, the therapist should write out the full name for each disorder (including severity ratings and specifiers, if applicable) and provide the official numeric diagnostic code stated in the *DSM–IV*. The diagnosis should be fully supported by symptoms listed in the presenting problem and history of the presenting problem sections. In cases of diagnostic uncertainty, note that the diagnosis is "provisional." According to the *DSM–IV*, this can be denoted by recording the word "(Provisional)" following the diagnosis.

Axis III includes general medical conditions. All medical problems relevant to the person's current functioning or potential management of the case should be recorded. It is acceptable to use the client's self-report in cases where there are no medical charts to verify, but it will be necessary to get the chart if the medical picture significantly influences presentation of current problems, case formulation, or treatment. Axis IV is for reporting of psychosocial and environmental problems. Note all stressors currently impacting the client. On Axis V, record judgments concerning the client's overall level of functioning. Use the Global Assessment of Functioning (GAF) Scale of the *DSM–IV*, which provides for rating on a scale that ranges from 0 to 100, with higher scores reflecting higher functioning. Consider the extent to which the person's symptoms have been interfering with school, work, family relationships, social life, and health. Typically, the client's current GAF score is provided, although this can be supplemented with GAF ratings for other times, such as at highest level in the past year or at admission to a psychiatric facility.

Tentative Treatment Goals and Recommendations

This final section is often the most important. Here, the therapist should clearly state any professional recommendations based on the full evaluation of the client. Possible recommendations include individual therapy, couples therapy, family therapy, group therapy, referral for personality, intelligence, and/or neuropsychological testing, referral for social work services, referral to medical professionals to rule out organic causes of psychiatric symptoms, referral to support or educational groups, consultation with psychiatrist for possible medication, hospitalization (for acutely suicidal, homicidal, or psychotic persons), another evaluation in 3 or 6 months to see if current functioning or impairment worsens, or no treatment indicated at present. If some form of psychotherapy is recommended, then the therapist should state the tentative goals of the therapy. These often are concordant with the presenting problem. For example, if the client presents with prominent symptoms of an eating disorder (e.g., low weight, refusal to eat food, distorted body image, dysphoric mood), some goals of therapy would be "increase weight, increase caloric intake, increase healthy eating behaviors, and reduce distortions in body image." For a depressed client who is unassertive and isolated, treatment goals may be to "reduce depression, increase assertive communication, and improve interpersonal skills." The client should always be involved in goal setting. Often, there will be a separate document describing treatment goals and objectives, called a treatment plan, that will be completed by the therapist and the client during the early phases of psychological intervention.

SUMMARY

Intake interviewing and report writing are important skills for the beginning therapist to practice and hone. This chapter has reviewed the purposes of the intake write-up and has provided tips to help produce well-written and thorough reports. The sections of the intake report were discussed, and tips for organization and professional writing were provided. Remember that the format and sample report presented here are not definitive models. Rather, students are encouraged to modify and adapt the information to meet their particular needs. Regardless of individual differences in style, a thorough evaluation and solid intake report are necessary components of a successful treatment.

ACKNOWLEDGMENTS

I would like to thank Cindy B. Kamilar, Frederick L. Coolidge, and Sara Honn Qualls for their helpful comments on earlier versions of this chapter. Thanks also to Philinda Smith Hutchings for excellent feedback on many reports. This chapter is dedicated to my students, because without their many drafts of reports, tough questions, innovations, and of course, innocent blunders, this chapter could not have been written.

SUGGESTED READINGS

Egan, G. (1994). *The skilled helper: A problem-management approach to helping* (5th ed.). Pacific Grove, CA: Brooks/Cole.

Evans, D. R., Hearn, M. T., Uhlemann, M. R., & Ivey, A. E. (1998). *Essential interviewing* (5th ed.). Pacific Grove, CA: Brooks/Cole.

Hersen, M., & Turner, S. M. (Eds.). (1994). *Diagnostic interviewing* (2nd ed.). New York: Plenum.

Morrison, J. (1995). *The first interview: Revised for* DSM–IV. New York: Guilford.

Othmer, E., & Othmer, S. C. (1994). *The clinical interview using* DSM–IV: *Vol. 1. Fundamentals.* Washington, DC: American Psychiatric Press.

Storr, A. (1990). *The art of psychotherapy* (2nd ed.). New York: Routledge.

Zaro, J. S., Barach, R., Nedelman, D. J., & Dreiblatt, I. S. (1994). *A guide for beginning psychotherapists.* Cambridge, MA: Cambridge University Press.

Zuckerman, E. L. (1995). *Clinician's thesaurus* (4th ed.). New York: Guilford.

APPENDIX I

Aardvark Counseling Center
291 Anteater Road
Colorado Springs, CO 80933

INTAKE EVALUATION

CONFIDENTIAL

Name: Evelyn Example   Examiner: Sue Student
Gender: Female   Date of Examination: 9/7/97
DOB: 3/22/40   Employment Status: Unemployed
Age: 57   Marital Status: Married
Level of Education: High School

Referral Source:

Ms. Example is a 57-year-old, married, White female referred to Aardvark Counseling Center by Dr. Ima Smart, her family general practitioner, for psychological assessment and therapy. The client states that she was referred after she had an uncontrollable crying spell in her physician's office and revealed thoughts of suicide to the physician.

Informants:

The client attended the session alone. However, records from a prior psychiatric hospitalization were brought by the client to the session and also reviewed for this report.

Presenting Problem:

The client reports that she is "depressed" and presents with the following symptoms: dysphoric mood, frequent crying, anhedonia, initial insomnia, overeating and weight gain, lethargy, poor concentration, and infrequent passive suicidal ideation. She also complains of increased social isolation and worry about the future. The client describes several physical problems including chronic arthritis, headaches, and occasional dizziness. She also states that she feels badly about herself and does not know why she is depressed.

History of Presenting Problem:

The client reports that she first experienced symptoms of depression in April 1990. She relates that at that time she and her husband moved from California to Colorado because of business opportunities for her husband. She states that she missed her children who lived near her in California and became increasingly isolated. She notes that her depressive symptoms worsened over the next year, and in May 1991, she was hospitalized for 5 days at St. Luke's Hospital due to severe depression and suicidal thoughts. She reportedly was prescribed Paxil (60 mg daily), but notes that she stopped taking the medication soon after discharge due to side effects. She states that in June 1991 she received follow-up individual therapy with local psychologist, Dr. Heather Jones. The client relates that her symptoms slowly remitted and she ended therapy in September 1991. That treatment is described by the client as cognitive-behavioral in nature. She reports that for the following several years she experienced few symptoms until about age 53 (1993). Since that time, the client reports chronic and debilitating depressive episodes lasting several months at a time. These episodes include all the symptoms noted previously. The current episode reportedly began in January 1997 after conflict with her husband greatly intensified. She also relates that at that time her cat died and her son was diagnosed with bone cancer. She relates that she has not sought treatment since her brief therapy in 1991. The client denies ever experiencing symptoms of mania.

Other Relevant History:

Ms. Example grew up in Sunnyside, California, a rural farm town. She is unaware of any complications during her birth or postnatal difficulties. All developmental milestones were reached without delay. She describes a happy childhood working on the family farm. She is the youngest in a sibship of three. She states that she maintains regular contact with her two sisters who both live in California, but does not feel close to either. She has two children who live together in California. She states that she is very close to her daughter (age 34), son (age 31), and two grandchildren, but is unable to see them very often due to geographical separation. She states "I miss them all dearly." According to the client, her son was diagnosed with bone cancer in January 1997, and has a relatively poor prognosis for recovery. She states "He's doomed." Her father reportedly died in 1986, and her mother has lived with the client's children since that time. The client states that she is worried about her mother because she has not adjusted well to the death of her husband. The client reports that she worked for many years as a home health aide, but that in February 1993 she lost her job when the agency went out of business and has not worked since then. The client notes that both of her parents have a history of depression, and her mother was briefly hospitalized in 1988 following a suicide attempt. She also suggests that her father had an undiagnosed alcohol problem. She states that she never got along with her father and did not like that he spent the family money on alcohol. Her relationship with her mother is generally characterized as warm and supportive, although not as close as when the client lived in California.

Ms. Example reports that she met her future husband at age 17, and married at age 18 (1958). Her husband reportedly works as manager of a local restaurant and bar. The client describes a stormy and conflictual relationship with her husband, with reported infidelity on his part. She states that initially the relationship was satisfactory, but that for the past 4 years they have frequently argued about diverse topics such as finances, children, and leisure activities. The client reports that her husband frequently gambles away his earnings, stays out overnight on a regular basis, and maintains romantic relationships with several female bartenders at his restaurant. She states "his cheating is so obvious it makes me sick." The client also states that her husband does not care about her but he becomes more responsive when her depression worsens. She denies a history of drug or alcohol abuse. Besides the history of recurrent depression in both parents, the client reports that one sister is a recovering alcoholic. She denies other significant family history of mental illness. She also denies a history of physical abuse, sexual abuse, or intimate partner violence.

Mental Status Examination and Client Strengths:

Ms. Example presented as a short, overweight, White female, who appeared older than her stated age. She was appropriately dressed in a skirt and blouse and appeared well-groomed with the exception of dirty fingernails. She initially appeared visibly anxious and described feeling dizzy during the early part of the interview. She attended the interview alone. The client demonstrated poor eye contact and appeared to be shy. Despite some shyness, she was cooperative throughout the interview and appeared to be an organized and reliable historian. She appeared to be of average intelligence. Her mood was dysphoric and affect broad. Her speech was logical, coherent, relevant, and goal directed. Recent memory and concentration were impaired, while remote memory was grossly intact. Judgment was fair, although insight into her problems was poor. She was oriented to time, place, and person, with no evidence of formal thought disturbance. She denied experiencing delusions or hallucinations. She admitted to current infrequent, passive suicidal ideation but denied current suicidal plan or intent. She further denied any homicidal ideation, plan, or intent. Her strengths include her supportive relationships with her children and mother, her stated desire for help, and previous positive response to therapy.

Clinical Formulation:

Ms. Example has suffered with bouts of depression for many years. Some episodes seem related to situational stresses, whereas others seem unrelated and may have a biological component. Her positive family history of depression, alcohol abuse, and suicidal behavior further indicates a biological basis. She also seems to have some difficulty with assertiveness and appropriate expression of feelings. The current episode appears to be related to increased conflict with her husband, the death of her pet, and illness in her son.

DSM–IV Diagnostic Impressions:

Axis I: 296.33 Major Depressive Disorder, Recurrent, Severe Without
            Psychotic Features (Provisional)
Axis II: Deferred
Axis III: Chronic arthritis, headaches, occasional dizziness, lethargy
Axis IV: Psychosocial stressors: unemployment, isolation, conflict with
            husband, death of pet, son diagnosed with serious illness
Axis V: Current GAF: 55
            Highest GAF past year: 75

Tentative Treatment Goals and Strategies:

It is recommended that the client be accepted for individual therapy on a priority basis, with the goals of reducing depression, reducing social isolation, and increasing assertive communication. Because she responded well in the past to a cognitive-behavioral approach, this method should be considered. Further, a referral for a psychiatric evaluation for consideration of antidepressant therapy is recommended. The client's level of suicidal thinking should be closely monitored and regularly reevaluated.

—Sue Student, BA   —Daniel Doctor, PhD
   Practicum Trainee   Practicum Supervisor

General considerations and conventions
1. Verb tenses consistent
2. Client name consistent
3. Formal name used
4. Document proofread

Professional writing
1. Statements regularly prefaced with qualifiers
2. Client statements translated into objective, behaviorally specific terms
3. Slang and colloquialisms replaced with objective, clinical terms
4. Specific details given when possible
5. Specific dates provided when possible
6. Quotes infrequently used
7. Quotes used only after the facts have been objectively described
8. No jargon in report
9. No self-disclosures in report

APPENDIX II
INTAKE REPORT CHECKLIST

SECTIONS OF THE REPORT

A. *Title and Identifying Data*
1. Name and address of service agency or provider on top
2. Labeled "Intake Evaluation"
3. Labeled "Confidential"
4. Complete identifying information provided

B. *Referral Source*
1. Referral source clearly stated
2. Important facts prompting the assessment noted
3. Specific referral questions noted

C. *Informants*
1. All sources of information noted

D. *Presenting Problem*
1. Presenting problem stated in terms of psychiatric symptoms
2. All psychiatric symptoms listed
3. Symptoms described as specifically as possible (frequency, duration, intensity)

E. *History of Presenting Problem*
1. Onset clearly stated
2. Precipitants or environmental stressors described
3. Course of disorders specified

(Table continues on next page)

F. *Other Relevant History*

1. Siblings and birth order reported
2. Early childhood, middle child-hood, and adolescence described
3. Adult history described:
   Educational history
   Work history
   Dating or marital history
   Substance use history
   Sexual history
   Interpersonal relationships with family and friends
   Current social life
   Legal and criminal history
   Medical problems
   Religion
   Leisure activities
4. Client's psychiatric history
5. Family psychiatric history
6. History of physical/sexual abuse, sexual assault, or intimate partner violence

G. *Mental Status Examination and Client Strengths*

1. Client demographics
2. Appearance, attire, grooming, hygiene
3. Eye contact
4. Behavior during interview
5. Attitude toward interviewer
6. Mood and affect
7. Speech and organization of thoughts
8. Orientation
9. Attention, memory, and concen-tration
10. Intelligence
11. Reliability of information
12. Judgment and insight
13. Suicidal and homicidal ideation, plan, and intent
14. Absence/presence of delusions and hallucinations
15. Use of alcohol, drugs, and medi-cations
16. Strengths

H. *Clinical Formulation*

1. Theoretical analysis of the current case provided
2. Hypotheses about the etiology of problems provided

I. *DSM–IV Diagnosis*

1. Five axes addressed
2. Full name for each Axis I and Axis II disorder provided
3. Official code numbers provided for each diagnosis
4. Diagnosis supported by symptoms in the presenting problem
5. On Axis III, general medical conditions noted
6. On Axis IV, psychosocial and environmental problems noted
7. On Axis V, current functioning noted on Global Assessment of Functioning (GAF) Scale

J. *Tentative Treatment Goals and Recommendations*

1. Professional recommendations stated
2. Tentative goals of treatment stated

9

Dealing With Defensiveness

Steven N. Gold
Nova Southeastern University

Learning to conduct an effective interview is essential to carrying out almost any form of clinical assessment or intervention. However, the unpredictability of the interviewing process can make mastery of this skill a challenging and, at times, even discouraging task. Each client introduces unique characteristics into the interview situation, which greatly limit the therapist's ability to control the direction of the interview. The most common complication is client defensiveness, which prevents the interview from unfolding predictably and straightforwardly. Therefore, an adequate understanding of defenses is essential for competency in interviewing. If interviewers do not understand defensiveness and how to effectively respond to it, the clinical interview is likely to be, at best, frustrating and, at worst, a pointless enterprise for both participants.

Clinical activities are most productive when there is a collaboration between practitioner and client. Defensive reactions can be easily misread by the clinician as a refusal or failure to take part in this cooperative effort. A therapist may wonder, "If clients really want help, then why are they so difficult, antagonistic, and evasive?" Such perceptions make it difficult to resist feeling irritated. Frequently, in these circumstances, therapists will become more confrontational and forceful in pressing for a straightforward response from the client. Almost invariably, this approach has the opposite effect and the situation grows increasingly unproductive.

UNDERSTANDING CLIENT DEFENSIVENESS

Therapists who are able to make sense of the client's defensiveness are more prepared to respond to it. At the very least, they may be able to limit the potentially disruptive consequences of such a reaction. In the best of circumstances, they may be able to manage it in such a way that it promotes therapeutic progress.

Identifying and Classifying Defensive Behaviors

Introductory texts on personality theory commonly include a classification system that catalogues types of defenses (repression, denial, projection, reaction formation, etc.). A familiarity with the varieties assists therapists in recognizing client defensiveness. Therapists who can recognize defensive reactions can effectively respond to them.

However, identifying the behavior and classifying the type of defensiveness is only part of the problem. Simply telling clients that they are "being defensive" is likely to compound the problem by eliciting more defensiveness. Clients may take it as an attack. Likewise, telling clients "You're in denial" or "You're projecting" is unproductive. These phrases may also be perceived as critical and insulting.

The Meaning of Defensiveness

Categorizing and labeling lends itself to the therapist assuming the position of an outside observer. The most constructive approach to defensiveness is to try to understand it from the client's experience and perspective. A useful starting place is to consider the meaning of defense not as a technical term in psychology, but in common, everyday usage. A defense is a protection. Clients who seem defensive can be understood to perceive themselves to be facing a threat or attack.

Clients' defensive behavior is an indication that they are feeling vulnerable and threatened. This can be difficult to accept, particularly for a student therapist. Therapists who focus on their intention to be helpful are more likely to become perplexed and impatient with the client's efforts at self-protection. Taking the client's vantage point increases the likelihood of being able to respond in a productive way. Begin by accepting that the client feels endangered, and then proceed by trying to appreciate why this might be the case.

Direct confrontation is unlikely to be effective because defenses are mobilized in response to a perceived threat. Clients react to it as criticism for employing forms of self-protection and as an attempt to remove them.

Explicitly challenging the client's defenses, therefore, is most likely to only increase efforts at self-protection.

Moreover, in its use as a psychological term, defensiveness often specifically refers to forms of self-protection that are triggered and operate automatically, outside of the person's conscious awareness. In these cases, clients are unaware that they are engaging in self-protection. Clients may view evoking self-protective maneuvers as unacceptable or unnecessary. Or perhaps the situation being faced is so disturbing that the perceived danger is too threatening and disruptive to acknowledge consciously. Under such circumstances, directly addressing the client's defensiveness will be confusing and anxiety provoking.

The Value of Self-Protection

The client's need for self-protection, nevertheless, may be perplexing to the interviewer. The purpose of the interview is to be helpful to the client. Why would the client feel endangered by a situation intended to provide assistance? Undeniably there are clinical situations in which clients have not fully chosen to participate, such as court-ordered or involuntary evaluation or intervention. In those circumstances it seems obvious why clients might feel threatened. Consider, however, the much more common situation in which clients have actively sought out counseling or therapy. It is particularly difficult to understand why someone voluntarily seeking help would feel a need for self-protection.

But imagine a hypothetical client at the other extreme—someone notably lacking in defensiveness. Picture a person who immediately, from the very first interview, reveals the most intimate, intense difficulties and shortcomings willingly and in detail, without conveying the slightest recognition of being in a vulnerable position. This is an individual who, rather than being at all guarded or self-protective, responds to any and all inquiries without any censoring and unhesitatingly accepts any feedback or recommendations offered by the interviewer.

This form of presentation, completely lacking in defensiveness, would probably arouse concern. After all, why should clients, who have not yet had the opportunity to get to know therapists—to determine whether they are understanding and responsive, can be trusted, or can be helpful—indiscriminately open up to them? If clients operate in a similar manner outside of therapy, there would be good reason to believe that they are extremely vulnerable to being manipulated and taken advantage of by other people.

This extreme example highlights a crucial point: Some measure of defensiveness and self-protection is both expected and desirable. Life is often complicated, demanding, and stressful. Managing interpersonal relationships is frequently a challenging and convoluted enterprise, especially with unfamiliar people. Some degree of caution and self-protection is a useful and even necessary component of effectively dealing with day-to-day pressures and interpersonal interactions in the real world. In many instances, precisely because the business of managing daily life is so complex and taxing, it is useful that these safeguards be mobilized rapidly and spontaneously, without having to be filtered through conscious processing. From this perspective, client defensiveness becomes much easier to comprehend.

COMMON REASONS FOR CLIENT DEFENSIVENESS

In addition to the general value of and need for self-protection in day-to-day life, there are numerous reasons why clients experience pulls to protect themselves that are specific to the interview situation. It would be impossible to catalogue all of these reasons. To better understand client defensiveness, however, it is useful to understand some of the more common motivations for self-protection in the interview.

The Stigma of Seeking Help

Many people who seek counseling or psychotherapy do so months or even years after the difficulties first began. This itself can be seen as a manifestation of defensiveness. Receiving professional help constitutes an acknowledgment that there are problems, that it has been impossible to resolve them, and they are severe enough to warrant the attention of someone with special training and skills. The stigma of having psychological difficulties leads many people to conclude that having problems requiring outside assistance is a shameful sign of weakness. Moreover, a cherished value in society dictates that people should rely on themselves and resolve their own difficulties, or, failing that, be able to turn to friends or family members for assistance in solving problems. For many people, in other words, the very fact of seeking counseling or therapy is seen as an admission of a failure that constitutes a serious threat to their self-esteem.

A related concern is clients who believe they do not deserve professional help. Some clients have had life experiences that have led them to feel very comfortable giving to and assisting others, but awkward and insecure receiving help from others. Clients with this background tend to minimize the seriousness of their difficulties. They may wonder aloud to the interviewer if their problems are severe enough to require professional attention. Particularly when it is clear to the interviewer that the problems are substantial, these clients may reveal feeling that they are not worthy of caring, concern, and assistance. The attention and interest of the interviewer challenges this belief about themselves, thereby creating confusion and anxiety.

The Threat of Betrayal

Many clients seek help for problems caused or compounded by adverse circumstances and painful life experiences. In many instances, these misfortunes center around interpersonal relationships in which the client experienced mistreatment or hurtful interactions with others. This client comes for help in a particularly vulnerable position. How can clients trust that the therapist will not betray them as others seem to have in the past? Obviously, clients cannot know this, at least not without having time to observe therapists and develop an appraisal of how safe it is to rely on them. Once again, it is reasonable from this vantage point that clients will employ a certain degree of defensiveness. Attempting to maintain protection against being hurt or betrayed by the therapist, at least until a certain level of trust can be established, is understandable. However, clients often find it difficult to acknowledge harboring mistrust toward the therapist who is assisting them.

The Threat of Change

Another threat is the uncertainty created by the prospect of change. As bad as a problem may be, it is familiar and known. Despite being disturbing and disruptive, clients often experience it as part of who they are. The possibility of being without it, therefore, carries with it the concern that life, and even feelings and behavior, will be unpredictably and unsettlingly different.

Change is also threatening because it usually requires substantially altering a viewpoint. Most individuals are strongly invested in the way they see things. To a large extent, their self-concept is anchored in subscribing to particular beliefs and perspectives. In other words, people define themselves in part in terms of their convictions. Taking the risk of altering the way they see and think about things can be confusing and anxiety provoking because it calls into question the very definition of who people are and endangers the security that comes with a sense of certainty that things are as they believe them to be.

The Threat of Relinquishing a Solution

Clients are sometimes defensive because problems themselves serve as forms of self-protection. Clients may employ a problem as a solution to whatever difficult circumstances exist at that time. Recognizing that clients' problems sometimes also represent solutions and therefore serve a purpose raises another conundrum. Resolving the problem may simultaneously represent to the client losing a valued solution.

For example, some people are mistreated as children—they are beaten, yelled at, and criticized—and find it difficult to express, or in some instances, even experience emotions. These individuals learned that if they displayed intense feelings—particularly anger or sadness—this would often lead to being screamed at or hit. To solve the "problem" of having to cope with growing up in these circumstances, and to reduce the frequency with which they were battered or criticized, they developed the *ability* to control their feelings. Whereas this was an effective and perhaps even necessary solution at the time, the inability to express emotions in the present prevents others from knowing and being able to respond to their feelings. This is likely to cause interpersonal misunderstandings and to create considerable personal frustration. But, at the same time, this ability shielded them from extremely painful mistreatment. A therapist's attempts to "help" these clients express feelings more clearly and effectively, therefore, are likely on some level to be experienced as efforts at removing a valuable form of protection. It is understandable, from this perspective, why clients might react defensively to such "assistance."

The Threat of Acknowledging Responsibility for a Problem

People can only change those things over which they have control, which may seem obvious. However, some people go into counseling only to end up blaming their difficulties on others and refusing to take responsibility for overcoming their problems. Having gained insight into the past experiences leading to their difficulties, they now feel powerless over changing their present circumstances. They reason that if situations in the past created their problems, then they have no hope of resolving their present difficulties.

Many of the problems that people bring to a therapist are not of their own making. Initially, at least, they arose in response to faulty learning or unfortunate, overwhelming circumstances. In most cases, therefore, the origins of clients' current difficulties may have been entirely outside their control, and therefore were not their responsibility.

Some clients find it difficult to acknowledge responsibility for overcoming their difficulties. They have difficulty understanding that even if they were not to blame for creating their own problems, only they have the capacity to resolve them. Consequently, clients may defensively deny having the power to correct the problems that brought them to therapy. They confuse responsibility in the sense of having the ability to respond with being at fault.

CONSTRUCTIVE RESPONSES TO CLIENT DEFENSIVENESS

So how can therapists effectively deal with defensive reactions in the clinical interview? According to the central premise presented here, in order to be productive, therapist responses to defensive reactions must be guided by the ability to make sense of them from the client's point of view. This process is guided by the idea that clients engage in defensive behavior when they perceive the existence of a threat or danger. Once a hypothesis about the reasons for the defensive reaction has been formulated, it provides a rationale from which the therapist can construct an effective response.

The process of dealing with defensiveness in the clinical interview is presented here in a series of steps. However, remember that rigidly executing the full range of steps is neither practical nor desirable in many situations. There is nothing magical or sacred about the steps described here, or the order in which they appear. They are, rather, a teaching device to organize the material and make it easier to understand. In actual practice, some steps may be skipped, blended together, carried out in a different order, and so on, depending on what judgment dictates in that particular instance.

Prevention of Defensiveness

Beginning therapists are often puzzled when clients feel threatened by the very process designed to assist them. Recall, as discussed in the previous section, that, for many clients, the clinical interview is an inherently threatening situation. Help-seeking situations implicitly carry the threat of stigmatization, betrayal, change, assuming responsibility, or other "dangers."

Therapists who recognize these threatening qualities can prevent many defensive reactions by creating an atmosphere that reduces the likelihood of clients feeling vulnerable and in need of self-protection. It is a common temptation, however, to deny or minimize this aspect. Therapists' attempts to reassure the client with direct statements such as "There is nothing to be afraid of," "You can trust me," or "Things can only get better" are likely to have the exact opposite effect. For many clients such denials further convince them of their need for self-protection from the counselor. They may conclude that the therapist is naive, foolish, a liar, or simply incapable of understanding their concerns.

Acknowledging that the situation is threatening to the client is somewhat more likely to be successful. Statements such as "I know this is difficult" or "People don't come to trust someone overnight" can be somewhat comforting. They let clients know that the therapist recognizes and appreciates the dangers of the situation. Knowing the counselor understands can help some clients to feel validated, reassured, and safer. However, for other clients, acknowledgment can be threatening in its own way. Some clients reason that if therapists know their vulnerable areas, then therapists have the power to use those vulnerabilities against them. Thus, before making direct statements about perceived threats, therapists should consider how clients are likely to react. This means asking, based on what is known about this client's personality, the circumstances that brought this individual to counseling, and the nature of the problem, how will this person react to this statement?

When therapists are uncertain about a response, it is best to avoid direct statements about potential threats, whether they take the form of denial or affirmation of danger.

In most instances, therapists should be mindful of the potentially threatening qualities of the clinical interview and to take anticipatory action to minimize the likelihood that the client will feel endangered. Traditionally, defensiveness has been thought of as an intrapsychic process, something that originates and occurs within the individual. In contrast, it is useful to conceptualize defensiveness from an interpersonal, interactive point of view. It is true that certain people have a greater tendency to react defensively than others. Similarly, particular situations are more likely to elicit defensiveness than others. However, the quality of interaction between therapist and client can have considerable influence on the probability that defensiveness will actually arise. Each of the following four strategies facilitates a quality of interpersonal relations to minimize the likelihood that clients will feel threatened and, consequently, defensive.

Do Not Move Prematurely Into a Goal-Directed Stance. Little can be accomplished in a clinical interview if therapists are not goal directed. They must be clear about the purpose of the interview and have some plan for achieving that goal. Therapists are ultimately responsible for monitoring and ensuring that steps are being taken to attain the goals established for the interview.

However, it can be counterproductive to become too invested in a goal-directed stance from the outset of the interview. Whether an interview is being conducted as part of an assessment or for treatment purposes, it is important for therapists to avoid immediately focusing single-mindedly on "getting down to business." Particularly in an initial interview, therapists should remember that clients do not know them and may not even be entirely clear about the purpose or format of the interview. Taking a few minutes to address these issues at the outset is likely to pay off immeasurably in the long run. If clients feel more comfortable, there is likely to be a much more collaborative and less defensive interchange between therapist and client. This, in turn, will result in a more productive and efficient use of the time allocated for the interview.

In most instances, the approach will vary depending on whether it is an assessment interview or a part of a course of therapy. This is primarily because, in most cases, clients make the decision themselves to seek therapy, but were referred by a third party (e.g., a social worker, physician, attorney, or teacher) for assessment. Therefore, it is especially important in an assessment interview to ask clients upfront about why they think they need the evaluation. In this way, therapists can correct misconceptions that may create unnecessary apprehensiveness and evasiveness on the part of the client. This also implicitly conveys that the therapist is attentive to clients' concerns and is interested in treating them as informed and active participants in the assessment process. Perhaps, most important, by opening the interview with this discussion, clients have a chance to ease into the interview process and develop some familiarity with the therapist's interpersonal style and intentions.

In an initial treatment interview the client should be allowed to make the transition into the therapeutic process and to develop some sense of comfort with the counselor. It is usually more desirable for clients to take a more active role in shaping the direction of the therapy interview. Consequently, therapists should avoid setting a precedent or expectation for clients that their role in the therapy interview is to passively respond to questions. If therapists decide to use direct questioning to help put the client at ease at the outset of the interview, then it is especially important to "shift gears" when making the transition from rapport building to exploring the problem.

Consider, for example, an instance in which an interviewer chooses to help a client feel at ease by asking direct, informational questions (e.g., "Did you have any trouble finding the office?," "Who referred you to me?," or "Have you ever been in counseling before?"). If the counselor then immediately moves into the more therapeutic portion of the interview by asking further direct, specific questions (e.g., "What is your problem?," "When did it start?," etc.), then the client is likely to answer each question, stop, and wait for the next question to be asked. Instead, it is often more useful to begin exploring the problem by asking very general, open-ended, or indirect questions (e.g., "What do you want to talk about today?," "Tell me about yourself," or "Why don't you fill me in about your situation?").

This approach has several advantages. It subtly communicates to clients that they are expected to take some responsibility for the direction of the interview. It also is likely to minimize defensiveness in many clients, because the open-ended and permissive aspects of this approach give them some measure of control over what is discussed, in how much detail, and at what point in time. For many clients, the more power they are given in governing the therapeutic process, the less threatened they feel, the more willing they are to open up and work collaboratively with the counselor, and the less defensive they are likely to be.

However, no one approach is effective for all clients. Some clients will feel more threatened and guarded when presented with general, open-ended questions. In order to feel more comfortable they need the clarity and direction provided by more specific, closed-ended questions at the outset of the interview. Once they feel more at ease, then they can tolerate the ambiguity of more general, open-ended questions.

Continually Monitor the Quality of the Interaction and Relationship With the Client. Establishing rapport, and helping the client to feel at ease rather than threatened, is not something that can be accomplished once and

for all at the outset of the assessment interview or therapy process. Throughout the course of assessment or treatment, therapists must be attentive to the quality of their interactions and relationship with the client. If they become too immersed in being goal directed at the expense of the client's comfort level and of maintaining a collaborative relationship, then there is an increased risk that the client will feel threatened.

A great deal of defensiveness can be avoided through regular monitoring of the client's level of security and the quality of the therapist–client relationship. It may be especially useful in an ongoing course of therapy for the therapist to assess the client's degree of comfort at the beginning of each interview. When the therapist senses that the client is feeling apprehensive and threatened, this is often a sign that defensive reactions are likely to follow. A therapist who is responsive to this uneasiness can use the mechanisms discussed later in the section on responding to defensive reactions.

Recognize the Legitimacy of Perceived Threats. Therapists must be responsive to perceived threats although they may seem groundless. It can be difficult to see things from the clients' perspective and appreciate their vulnerability. But, the more the therapists can empathize with a client's perception of danger, the more effective they are likely to be in helping. For this reason, it is usually not helpful, and perhaps harmful, to try to deny clients their feelings. Instead, making a purposeful effort to appreciate the legitimacy of their perceptions from their point of view will aid therapists in responding to clients' concerns in such a way as to make them feel understood, respected, and, ultimately, safe. When clients feel confident that therapists empathize with and are willing to validate their perceived dangers, they feel less of a need to protect themselves from therapists or the interview process.

Anticipate Potential Threats. An invaluable strategy for preventing defensive reactions is for therapists to anticipate aspects of and points in the assessment or therapy process that are likely to be perceived as threatening to a particular client. With this knowledge, therapists can develop a plan to avoid the development of a defensive response. And the client's general propensity to become defensive is likely to diminish with the realization that the therapist is committed to helping maintain a sense of safety and security. Clients will feel less of a need to be guarded, wary, and self-protective.

Before approaching a threatening target area, it is helpful to first introduce a related topic. As that topic is being discussed, the therapist has the opportunity to observe the client's level of discomfort and evasion. If the client does not appear unduly distressed, then the interview can proceed to another topic more closely related to the target area. In this manner, the therapist can maneuver progressively closer to the target area, simultaneously attending to the client's level of discomfort and avoidance. If at any point the client seems to grow excessively agitated, uneasy, or elusive, then the therapist can elect to postpone raising the target topic.

Another useful approach is to explicitly suggest that the issue not be discussed unless the client feels ready to. This often makes self-protection unnecessary. It makes it clear that the therapist considers it the client's decision whether or not to proceed. It also conveys that the client is in control of the direction and pace of therapy.

Responding to Defensive Reactions

The likelihood of defensive reactions can be greatly reduced with the afore-mentioned measures. However, these can not always completely eliminate the problem. Therapists therefore, must be prepared for defensiveness and know how to respond to it. The following are possible responses.

Do Nothing. In many instances, the more effective initial response may be to do nothing, or, in other words, to take a "wait and see" approach. There are several reasons for adopting this strategy. Frequently, the therapist's first impulse is to feel annoyed or irritated in response to client defensiveness. If these feelings show, then the sense of threat that triggered the defensive reaction, and consequently the defensiveness itself, are likely to increase. On the other hand, maintaining a calm and supportive interpersonal stance may be sufficient to dispel the whole problem. Often the most useful aspects of identifying and understanding client defensiveness is that it alerts the therapist to the value of not reacting or intervening. The following example illustrates this point:

> A very bright and articulate woman entered therapy due to depression caused by the loss of a loved one. Several sessions into counseling, in the midst of talking about her depression, she "interrupted" herself, abruptly changing the subject and stating, "This fat [she was markedly overweight] is a protection, you know." She then immediately resumed discussing her depression. When she had finished what she was saying, her therapist asked her what she had meant by the remark about her weight. She replied nonchalantly that she had no idea and immediately returned to the topic of her depression.
>
> A few sessions later, there was a similar incident. In the midst of discussing another topic, she suddenly asked the therapist if he had seen the magazine cover depicting a celebrity who had revealed that she had been sexually molested as a child. "Do you think the same thing could have happened to me?," she asked. "I don't know," the counselor replied, upon which she immediately resumed what she had been saying before she interrupted herself.
>
> Over the next few months, the same pattern of events recurred every few sessions. The client would interrupt herself with a remark off the topic she had

been discussing. On those occasions when the therapist would ask her what she meant by the remark, she would reply "I have no idea," and return to what she had been saying previously.

As these incidents accumulated, the remarks made by the client increasingly seemed to suggest that she had been the victim of sexual abuse as a child. However, the therapist made a purposeful decision not to propose this to her, assuming that if this was the case, and she was prepared to recognize it, she would do so on her own. Finally, after a number of these incidents had occurred, the client herself began to suspect that she had experienced and blocked out childhood sexual abuse. "Do you think that's possible?" she asked the therapist. "I don't know, what do you think?," he replied. At that point she began to address the issue directly, gradually retrieving a number of memories of childhood sexual abuse.

Considerably later in treatment, the counselor asked her, "What would have happened if in one of our initial meetings I had asked you if you had ever been sexually abused as a child?" "Why," she responded, "the same thing that happened when any therapist I saw before got anywhere near that area. Although I did not know about the abuse consciously, I was aware of it on some level. When they got anywhere near that subject, I would panic inside, and immediately leave treatment."

Align With the Protective Function.   When therapists conclude that the situation calls for more active intervention, it is important that they find a way to respond in a way that aligns with the protective function of the defensive reaction. This can be done, for example, by overtly encouraging clients to slow down or postpone confronting the threatening material until they are ready to do so. This is often extremely effective. It has the advantages of simultaneously acknowledging the threat, affirming its legitimacy, validating and supporting the impulse to be self-protective, and endorsing the value of addressing the threatening material. However, shifting the issue from whether to confront the threat to when is most reasonable to do so because it permits the client to postpone confronting the threat while affirming the importance of addressing it eventually. Consider this example:

A man told his therapist in the first session of therapy that he was experiencing serious and very disturbing problems. He stated that he desperately wanted help with them. However, having said that much, he then began to explain in an agonized tone of voice that as much as he wanted to resolve his problems, he did not feel comfortable telling the therapist about them.

After a brief silence, during which the client appeared extremely distressed, the therapist replied that she could certainly understand his hesitancy. They had just met, and it was not reasonable to expect that he would feel sufficiently comfortable with her to discuss such sensitive matters. She told him that they could always return to that topic some other time, and asked him what else he would like to talk about. Another brief silence passed, and the client replied, "Oh heck, I might as well go ahead and tell you what's troubling me," and proceeded to do so. From there on in, the therapy continued without any major episodes of defensiveness. The man was able, in fact, to resolve his problems within a few sessions.

This illustrates an additional component of effective responses to defensiveness: offering the client choice. A common component of the experience of threat is the perception that the choices or options are limited (i.e., being cornered or trapped). A response that offers more options or choices than clients had recognized will help remove the feeling of being trapped and thereby lower their defensiveness.

Discuss the Defensive Behavior Directly. There are instances in which direct discussion of defensive behavior is appropriate. Often this is referred to as "confrontation" of the defenses. The adversarial connotation provides an indication of why this strategy is frequently ineffective. Challenging or assailing behaviors aimed at self-protection can only be expected to result in an increased sense of threat and a resulting increase in defensiveness. A key element in the effective application of direct discussion of defensive reactions is timing. A direct approach is most likely to be effective after the defensive reaction has been allowed to develop fully. Resisting the temptation to challenge or attempt to dismantle the client's defenses prematurely implicitly conveys to the client that the interview situation is safe and secure. Clients are likely to be reassured that the therapist appreciates the value of defensiveness and therefore can be trusted. Usually, at that point, clients are in a position to acknowledge and relinquish the defensive behavior. For example,

A woman came into therapy to address a series of extremely violent assaults throughout her childhood, the emotional effects of which continued to have a debilitating impact on her functioning as an adult. After making substantial progress and experiencing considerable relief in the first several months of therapy, she repeatedly forgot about and failed to appear for her appointments. In each instance she would apologize and reschedule, providing a plausible excuse. Her therapist made a point of avoiding suggesting to her that these incidents were defensive in nature, accepting her excuses without questioning them.

Once this sequence of events had occurred a number of times, the therapist remarked to the client, "There certainly have been a good number of times when you forgot about your appointment. What do you make of that?" Without any further prompting, the client replied, "I guess I'm relying on the old pattern I've always used in the past to deal with difficulties. Instead of recognizing and dealing with problems before they get out of hand, I pretend they're not there and let them grow so big that I can't ignore them anymore." Not only was she able to let go of defensively forgetting her therapy appointments, but she was able to recognize and modify a pervasive pattern of behavior that had been adversely affecting many areas of her life until that time.

SUMMARY

Defensiveness indicates an effort to maintain self-protection in response to a perceived threat. It is easy for therapists to become irritated by defensive reactions, seeing them as obstacles to accomplishing the aims of the interview. However, it is essential for them to appreciate that the capacity for self-protection is a desirable and essential component of effective functioning in a complex, stressful society. The likelihood of developing defensive reactions is greatly reduced when therapists are aware of the potentially threatening aspects of the interview situation, appreciate the legitimacy of self-protection, and establish and maintain a supportive and nonthreatening relationship with the client. When defensive reactions do occur, effective intervention is guided by understanding the nature and source of the threat perceived by the client. Resisting the temptation to react prematurely to client defensiveness, encouraging clients to maintain self-protection for the time being while suggesting that eventually it will no longer be needed, and offering choices to clients to counteract the misperception that they are trapped or endangered are effective strategies for reducing defensiveness.

SUGGESTED READINGS

Benjamin, L. S. (1995). Good defenses make good neighbors. In H. R. Conte & R. Plutchik (Eds.), *Ego defenses: Theory and measurement* (pp. 53–78). New York: Wiley.
    Presents an interpersonal model for understanding defenses that emphasizes their adaptive function.
Lankton, S. R., & Lankton, C. H. (1983). *The answer within: A clinical framework of Ericksonian hypnotherapy.* New York: Brunner/Mazel.
    Chapter 3, "Principles of Treatment: The Attitudinal Framework," provides a useful perspective for appreciating the value of self-protection from the client's point of view.
Linehan, M. M. (1993). *Cognitive-behavioral treatment of borderline personality disorder.* New York: Guilford.
    Chapter 4, "Overview of Treatment: Targets, Strategies, and Assumptions in a Nutshell," presents a conceptual framework and series of strategies that are especially effective in handling defensiveness in clients who are difficult to manage.
Teyber, E. (1997). *Interpersonal process in psychotherapy: A relational approach* (3rd ed.). Pacific Grove, CA: Brooks/Cole.
    Chapter 3, "Honoring the Client's Resistance," discusses how client defensiveness manifests itself and how the counselor can effectively respond at various points in therapy.
Vaillant, G. E. (1992). The clinical management of immature defenses in the treatment of individuals with personality disorders. In G. E. Vaillant (Ed.), *Ego mechanisms of defense: A guide for clinicians and researchers* (pp. 59–86). Washington, DC: American Psychiatric Press.
    This article discusses, from a psychoanalytic perspective, how to manage the developmentally primitive defenses of clients with personality disorders.

10

Dealing With the Overtalkative Client

William I. Dorfman
Nova Southeastern University

Typically, novice therapists approach the initial interview fearing that the session will be filled with long silences, unanswered questions, one-word replies, and premature termination. Having begun to master the skills of effective listening, empathic reflections, and probative inquiry, the enthusiastic new therapist looks forward to working with the client who is spontaneous, can explore feelings and conflicts freely, and is willing to report difficulties and relevant history with minimal prompting. These clients are ideal; they seem able to take responsibility for the interview process and reduce the therapist's anxiety about saying and doing "the right thing." They can maintain a nondirective role, listen and respond attentively, and leave the session with a feeling that something was accomplished. Therapists are not forced to structure the interview or be responsible solely for its content when the client does most of the talking.

In contrast, overtalkative clients can be very difficult to interview and pose real challenges to the most skilled clinicians. Overtalkativeness should not be confused with the response style of the "ideal" client, who engages with the therapist in a collaborative and reciprocal interpersonal process. They may alternatively listen, respond to questions, and spontaneously share information with the goals of self-exploration, assessment of the problem, and formulation of a treatment plan. When interviewing an overtalkative client, however, the new therapist's initial relief in playing a less directive role turns to anxiety and frustration when they cannot interrupt the client to ask a question. They feel overwhelmed by the volume of information, begin to feel the press of time, and recognize how little information has been covered. Efforts to redirect the client's attention to another area are met with resistance, increased volume of speech, more irrelevant information, or even anger at the counselor "for not being interested." Although some of the information may be relevant, much important information is obscured, intentionally or unintentionally, by this client. The therapist feels frustrated, overwhelmed, and frequently out of control of the interview process.

This chapter reviews the variety of forms that overtalkativeness can take, the manner in which it presents in several psychopathological disorders; how to use the overtalkative behavior to understand the motivation and defensive operations of the client, and finally, techniques that are helpful in interviewing these difficult clients.

DIMENSIONS OF OVERTALKATIVENESS

In general terms, the overtalkative client is one whose rate, flow, and quantity of speech is so excessive that it disrupts the purpose of the interview session. Overtalkativeness can prevent therapists from asking questions and from understanding the nature of the client's real problem and concerns. Ultimately, it can prevent therapists from exerting the necessary control over the structure and pace of the interview. Through excessive talking, clients can consciously or unconsciously avoid uncomfortable topics or feelings, steer the clinician away from painful areas, and generally reduce their own discomfort about being interviewed.

Clinicians gain valuable knowledge about their clients when they understand the variety of motives that can drive overtalking. Overtalkativeness can have diagnostic significance and assume a variety of forms within a clinical interview. When therapists understand the motivational and diagnostic implications of this behavior, they develop important clues into the client's difficulties. Furthermore, such insight often leads to effective techniques designed to manage or even eliminate the client's need to engage in excessive and disruptive overtalking.

SPECIFIC FORMS OF OVERTALKING

The overtalkative client may manifest this problem in a variety of forms of thinking and speech, described clinically as circumstantiality, tangentiality, rambling speech, pressured speech, flight of ideas, and volubility. Some of these disturbances are common to most people and represent idiosyncrasies in speaking style or are a reflection of anxiety and discomfort in certain situations. Others are very pathological and occur only in the most psychologically impaired clients.

Circumstantiality

Circumstantial speech is indirect and delayed in getting to the point. The circumstantial client eventually gets to the desired goal, but is sidetracked by many unnecessary details and parenthetical remarks. Circumstantiality is recognizable in normal individuals and most people can name a friend whose storytelling is endless and filled with facts, ideas, and sidelights that do not seem to be related to the story. Circumstantiality is common in very overtalkative, manic clients who enrich their responses with many irrelevant details, often only loosely connected to the points being made. It is also very characteristic of obsessive-compulsive clients who need to insure that nothing is omitted from their answers, lest the interviewer misunderstand them. The obsessive's flood of speech often provides much data but no real information. Therapists often become bored. They must remember that obsessive clients are trying to avoid real emotional experience, and such overtalkativeness serves this purpose. The following is an example:

Interviewer: When did your panic attacks begin?

Client: Just thinking about them scares me. I remember my wife telling me a long time ago I shouldn't be so afraid. When we first got married I remember she called me "fearless" because I would try anything. I never was afraid. In fact, I remember going skydiving one year and I wasn't phased a bit. My friends kidded me that I was a little crazy for doing it. Panic . . . I never felt panic. I did have a very good friend who was pretty nervous. He and I would pal around together, and I would reassure him about his stress. But me, never! That is, until about 3 years ago when my father died. That's when the attacks began.

Tangentiality

Clients who manifest tangentiality also introduce irrelevant content and detail into their responses but are unable to "get to the point." They seem to abandon their original purpose or goal for some peripheral ideas and never return to the original point. Tangentiality associated with overtalkativeness often results in thoughts that sound disorganized, illogical, and even incoherent. Although some tangential thinking can be observed in normal individuals, when it results in loose associations and disorganization, it is indicative of serious thinking disturbances (e.g., schizophrenia or other psychotic disorders). Here is an example:

> *Interviewer:* What do you do during the day to keep yourself busy?
>
> *Client:* My mind is busy all the time. I think about why they are bothering me. The mailman rang my doorbell but he left no mail. That wasn't fair. I called the post office and they hung up on me.
>
> *Interviewer:* What do think is the meaning of this?
>
> *Client:* The telephone company may be responsible for the static on the line after all. I wasn't sure at first but when the phone broke I knew. My stove has been acting up and I'm disgusted with all these people who claim to help you but don't come through.

Rambling Speech

Clients who ramble move from one set of ideas and sentences to another set of ideas without any real connection or goal. Each group of sentences is interconnected but not associated with the next interconnected group. This type of overtalkativeness results in incoherence and speech that is difficult to follow. It is often seen in clients with serious cognitive impairments, like those found in delirium and several types of substance intoxication. Here is an example:

> *Interviewer:* Why did your family doctor refer you to me?
>
> *Client:* It should be obvious. I thought you were the expert. Can't you give me something for the headache? Pills make me feel . . . wait a minute. Have you seen my keys? Hold on a minute, I'm getting mixed up with all this confusion. Put this . . . what time is it anyway? I thought I brought my watch. Can I see that magazine? I like to read. . . . Did my wife come in yet?

Pressured Speech

Pressured speech is characterized by its very rapid speed, increased quantity, and the difficulty or impossibility of interrupting it. Interviewers dealing with clients with this "push of speech" are unable to "get a word in edgewise" and experience difficulty in derailing the flow of the client's thoughts. The client ignores the attempted interruptions, speaks faster or louder, and continues to "push" forward toward an uncertain goal. Pressured speech is seen frequently in anxious and obsessive-compulsive clients, but is most indicative of manic disorders. Consider the following example:

Interviewer: What brings you here today?

Client: Well actually it's my brother. He and I can't seem to get along with one another . . . he fights with me . . . I know he is nervous and all . . . and the doctor told me to be tolerant, but I get nervous too . . . and Doc, I'm nervous now . . .

Interviewer: Could you tell . . .

Client: . . . about being here because I don't know you. Excuse me for interrupting, but you need to understand how nerve racking he can be . . . sometimes I feel like killing him when he won't listen and this happens often, especially when I say no . . .

Interviewer: Killing is a strong . . .

Client: . . . to him, but something has got to be done right now, Doc . . . you understand don't you?

Interviewer: You're very scared that . . .

Client: I sure hope you do because I can't take it any longer. . . .

Flight of Ideas

Flight of ideas involves rapid, continuous talk or, sometimes, plays on words with constant shifting from one idea to the next. In contrast to other forms of overtalkativeness that can be incoherent (e.g., tangentiality and rambling speech), the ideas typically are connected and often the therapist can follow and understand them. Flight of ideas is frequently the result of distractibility in manic individuals. Clients will respond to a therapist's question and, triggered by a word in the response, precipitously move to a new train of thought. The therapist's ability to follow the client's ideas is in sharp contrast to the difficulty in understanding the more disorganized and illogical schizophrenic client. Flight of ideas often occurs along with pressured speech, and these can be difficult to distinguish from one another. Here is an example:

Interviewer: How are you sleeping at night?

Client: Why would I sleep at night? Would you be able to sleep with all my work to do? I whistle while I work and I'm damn happy to do it all. Sounds a little like "haul," which is how I move stuff around. I can't slow down . . . or slow up if you know what I mean. My wife accuses me of being nasty, not

mean, but nasty. I'm "happy" and not "dopey" . . . do you
like Snow White Doctor? . . . I feel . . .

Interviewer: Sounds to me like your mood is . . .

Client: I'm moody, yes. And musical too. . . . Moody Blues is my
favorite group. . . . I love music and I'm thinking about
buying a new stereo when I have the time . . .

Interviewer: Are you feeling irritable these days?

Client: No, I'm busy as a bee . . . a bee in a tree . . . Why all these
questions? I'm in a hurry and I have to go, and not go slow
. . . Is that all?

Volubility

Volubility or more precisely, *logorrhea*, is very copious but linear, logical,
and coherent speech. It is the clinician's way of describing a client who simply
talks too much! It best describes the very benign client whose overtalkativeness is judged to be counterproductive and difficult to manage. Anxious
clients, in general, might display this garden variety of overtalkativeness
when they are interviewed.

UNDERSTANDING THE CLINICAL AND DIAGNOSTIC
SIGNIFICANCE OF OVERTALKATIVENESS

Overtalkativeness can have important diagnostic value when therapists understand the variety of forms it can take. Each form or manifestation of this
behavior can point to specific diagnostic entities and inform clinical decisions
around managing and treating these problems. Earlier, it was pointed out
that pressured speech and flight of ideas, for instance, may point to a manic
disorder, whereas circumstantiality is often associated with very obsessive
clients. In many cases, overtalkative behaviors associated with these specific
disorders are difficult to eliminate through interviewing skills alone. Often,
they are symptoms of serious emotional disorders and are eliminated only
after extensive treatment. Sometimes, they represent stable, intractable
speech characteristics sometimes indicative of personality disturbances and
are thus unlikely to change. In many cases, however, overtalkativeness in its
less pathological forms can serve as a clue to the interviewer in understanding
what is happening with the client during the process of the interview. That
is, this behavior can assist the therapist in detecting client resistance and
defensiveness, areas causing anxiety and distress, and topics that are consciously and unconsciously very important to the client. Armed with this

information, skillful clinicians can empathically and insightfully intervene to deal with these critical issues and even eliminate the need for the volubility.

The single most common motivation for overtalkativeness is anxiety. Fearfulness, confusion, and impairments in concentration and attention frequently combine with increased rate and pressure of speech to define overtalkativeness in an anxious client. Silences and the ambiguity they promote are not well tolerated by the anxious client who tries to fill every minute with words. In this way, clients seem to reduce the possibility of losing even more control over the environment while they discharge much of their emotional and physical tension verbally. Responding effectively is critical if the therapist wants to establish good rapport, put the client at ease, and elicit clear, relevant, and useful information in the interview session.

Volubility often varies within a single interview and over the course of several sessions. Therapists must listen closely to how clients respond to certain topic areas or questions that have been posed and compare the manner of speech to the general baseline that has been established. Highly emotionally charged areas that create much conflict and pain will often result in resistance and defensiveness in the form of overtalkativeness. In the following example, when the client is questioned about his criminal history, he suddenly changes his speech from clipped, short answers to very circumstantial, irrelevant, but copious speech geared exclusively toward avoiding a difficult area and taking control of the interview. The client may or may not be aware of his motivation or underlying discomfort:

Interviewer: Tell me why you were referred by your boss.

Client: Guess he thought I needed help.

Interviewer: What kind of help did he have in mind?

Client: Counseling, I guess.

Interviewer: What help do you feel you need?

Client: Hard to say.

Interviewer: Have you ever had any difficulties before?

Client: No.

Interviewer: Have you ever had psychological help?

Client: No.

Interviewer: Ever been in trouble with the law?

Client: Listen, what are all these questions about. I do have some hassles at work. I get lousy pay and my benefits haven't kicked in yet. Yeah, I'm worried about medical benefits because my wife is pregnant and we have no money. I do need some help in handling all this stress. I have headaches, too, Doc. Can you help me get rid of these headaches? I take aspirin but my stomach is real sensitive to them. I am glad the boss sent me over here. Can you help me? My schedule is busy but I'll make arrangements to come.

Thus, overtalkativeness can be a strategy to avoid and obscure important feelings and information rather than attempt to engage in productive discussion. Therapists must be vigilant to this ruse and not be led away from the client's real problems, drowning in a sea of interesting, but irrelevant, information.

In other cases, an increase in the rate and quantity of speech may signal the true importance of the material being discussed. Clients who have responded passively with little or no elaboration may suddenly become highly descriptive and talkative when presented with a particular question or topic area. At times only experience and a finely tuned therapeutic ear will be able to differentiate relevant from irrelevant speech. Sometimes the interviewer will be helpful simply by acknowledging the increased quantity of speech and reflecting the possibility of discomfort and anxiety in the client. In this way, the therapist ignores the content of the interchange and focuses on the process that motivates it. The awareness that is created in the client may be sufficient to reduce defensiveness and allow exploration of the problems. Reassurance, support, and genuine understanding go a long way in reducing the anxiety that can motivate volubility. The overtalkative behavior thus serves the therapist as a clinical marker for problem areas that need to be examined and dealt with rather than a hurdle to be eliminated or skirted. Strategies for accomplishing the latter are discussed later.

MANAGING THE OVERTALKATIVE CLIENT

Severe psychopathology, like schizophrenia and mania, result in circumstantial, tangential, and pressured speech, and variants of overtalkativeness characterize many personality styles, including obsessive-compulsive and histrionic personality disorders. A client's defensiveness or clinical anxiety can also contribute to the problem and serve to alert the therapist to the importance of the topics discussed. Overtalkative behavior is frequently not the sole creation of the client, however, but the result of collaboration with the unwitting interviewer. That is, the client's copious speech, detailed descriptions, and elaborations are reinforced by the interviewing style of the clinician, who asks open-ended questions, nods continuously, and fails to structure the interview or be directive. The interviewer basically holds the door open for the client to enter! Regardless of the source of the problem, several techniques may assist the interviewer in focusing the client in a way that enhances productivity of the interview.

Reinforcing Overtalkativeness

Open-ended questioning, nonverbal prompts, and even note taking serve to reinforce client overtalkativeness. Therapists learn to listen effectively and encourage their clients to express their concerns freely and openly. Skills that facilitate such self-exploration and self-disclosure with most clients backfire with the overtalkative client.

Open-ended questions allow clients a wide latitude in responding and the opportunity to interpret the meaning of the inquiry based on their unique perceptions. Generally, open-ended, more ambiguous questions stimulate increased verbal productivity in clients. This nondirective approach provides overtalkative clients with the perfect venue for their meanderings. In dealing with overtalkative clients, therapists should ask more closed-ended questions that provide clear direction and focus for client responses. Focusing prematurely, however, may result in missing important information that clients might share spontaneously. Give them the opportunity to respond initially to open-ended inquiries until it is clear that such an approach is counterproductive and does not yield the sought-after information. Here is an example:

Interviewer: What was it like for you growing up?

Client: It was hell. My parents were merciless. My brother and sister got all the kindness. School was difficult, but my grades were pretty good. I did have a great social life . . . parties in high school were fun. I was outgoing, but I was always uptight around guys . . .

Interviewer: I'd like to know a bit more about your relationship with your parents. Were they ever abusive to you?

Client: They treated me like dirt. Mean? They were terrible. I ran away four times before I was 15 years old.

Interviewer: Did your parents physically abuse you?

Client: Yes. [*crying*]

Interviewer: Tell me specifically what they did to you.

Active listening involves both verbal and nonverbal components. Therapists learn to communicate their attentiveness by nodding their head, maintaining good eye contact, leaning toward the client, and maintaining an interested facial expression. Even note taking communicates to the client that what they are saying is important and encourages them to continue. In effect, the therapist is saying, "Please tell me more; this is important enough to write down." When interviewing highly voluble clients, these otherwise effective skills increase the likelihood that the interview will become unproductive. According to learning theory, behaviors followed by positive consequences increase in frequency in the future. Frequent head nodding, note taking, and other nonverbal cues may insure that the overtalkative client will continue to talk excessively about content areas to which the eager counselor is so actively attending. Absence of reinforcement alone will help to discourage the overtalkative client and, in learning theory terms, "extinguish" such inappropriate talking. This is not to suggest that therapists should be inattentive to their clients. However, they should utilize their skills judiciously in maximizing productivity in an interview, tailoring their approach to each patient and interview topic.

Structuring the Interview

A directive, highly structured interview generally provides the therapist with more control over the ramblings of the overtalkative client. The skillful therapist can vary the degree of structure along a continuum of minimal to virtually authoritarian intervention based on the client's response to the increase in structure.

Initially, in response to a client's mildly circumstantial or tangential speech, the interviewer might simply redirect the client back to the original topic of discussion. For example:

Interviewer: Can you tell me how your job is going?

Client: Getting through the day is torture. I have no energy, I cry all the time. My wife is getting tired of hearing me up in the middle of the night. I can't sleep. I just feel worthless. Food doesn't even taste the same. I stopped playing softball, which I used to love. I just don't give a damn. When I'm with friends they think I don't care.

Interviewer: Uh-Um. And your job? How are you performing?

If the overtalkativeness continues, a more direct question may assist in refocusing the client's thinking or derailing this pressured speech. In some cases, the therapist may need to make a very specific request that clients stay on a particular topic. Here is an example of a counselor imposing increasing structure in response to an overtalkative patient who is alleged to have been abusive to his family during a manic episode:

Interviewer: Can you tell me how you are getting along with your friends and family? [*open-ended question with mild structure*]

Client: They love me. Everyone comes to me for advice and I just don't have time to give it to them. . . . They get irritated. My wife is beautiful, though, and we have been married for 25 wonderful years. We met in Las Vegas and did we win big when we were there! Reminds me; can I use your phone? I need to make reservations in Reno for next week. Time is running out and I need to run. . . .

Interviewer: Are you having conflict with your wife these days? [*closed-ended question*]

Client: These days everyone has conflict. I was reading in the paper that the police are out in force this weekend. I plan on joining the reserve force. I need to use my judo . . . I'm a black belt. . . .

Interviewer: John, have you been fighting with your wife recently? [*closed-ended question*]

Client: Yes, but she didn't understand that I had to withdraw my money from the bank to take to Reno. Blackjack requires a big bankroll. I'm on a roll and I'm going to the pole. I'm going to win big . . . then it's time to buy the new business. . . .

Interviewer: In the time we have left, John, I want you to tell me about how you have been treating your wife and daughter. [*highly structured command*] The social service worker reported that you physically abused both your wife and daughter. Is that true? [*closed-ended question*]

In some cases, it may be helpful to address the process rather than the content of the client's interview behavior. The next example addresses the possible motivation for the client's overtalkativeness rather than simply trying to manage it. In these instances the client's underlying conflicts are addressed. The following client is a 28-year-old, single male who presents with complaints of anxiety and loneliness:

Interviewer: How has your mood been lately?

Client: I've been a bit down.

Interviewer: How do you mean?

Client: I have no interest in things. I feel bummed out.

Interviewer: How are you sleeping?

Client: Fine. And my appetite is good. I don't feel really that depressed. Just lonely.

Interviewer: Tell me about your social life.

Client: I go out to eat a lot and to the movies. I love cinema, especially art films. I wrote a movie review column for the college newspaper and loved it. By the way, have you seen the latest Spielberg movie? I recently ordered the new cable movie channel and I can't tear myself away from it. When I'm not watching movies I read. Mystery novels are my favorite. I keep three books going at the same time. . . .

Interviewer: Do you date much?

Client: Uh . . . sometimes I go out with friends. Not that often. Everyone is busy working and trying to make a living. The economy is bad. The market is unstable. I try to save money but it is real difficult to make ends meet. I work at a local department store in the men's department. I do like to sell clothes. You should see my closet . . . packed! In fact, I thought about building some new shelves, just to store my shoes. . . .

Interviewer: Bill, whenever I ask you about your relationships with others, you get way off the topic. This seems like a very disturbing issue for you. What are you struggling with?

Increasing structure to the point of stopping a client in midsentence, interrupting their response in order to ask a specific question, or commenting on their avoidance of some topic can be quite jarring to the client and risky for the therapist. Therapists often fear that they will offend clients with this directive style; clients may feel that the interviewer does not understand the importance of their feelings and concerns. Therapists can minimize the impact of such interventions by introducing their redirective interventions with empathic statements. In this way, they acknowledge the importance of what the client is discussing as well as reflect an understanding of clients' emotional experience. This approach moderates the impact of more aggressive structuring, yet allows the therapist to maintain the focus of the interview with the overtalkative client. Here is an example:

Interviewer: Mrs. Jones, have you ever seen a counselor or psychologist before?

Client: I've seen everyone and no one can cure this pain in my head. Doctor, it hurts real bad and I can't work. I've tried to get disability but they turned me down. How can I live on my savings? My friends don't help me . . . well I do have one friend who likes me. We go to bingo when the pain isn't too bad. My kids are sure no help. My son is an alcoholic and . . .

> *Interviewer:* [*cuts client off*] It sounds to me like you are truly over-
> whelmed with problems and you're really hurting. I want to
> cover each one of these issues a bit later, but right now could
> you tell me if you have ever received psychological treatment?

Eliminating subtly reinforcing interview behavior like open-ended inquiries, nonverbal prompts, and note taking, along with increasing interview
structure should be effective with most highly talkative clients. Those with
significant psychopathology, including manic episodes, severe obsessional
disorders, and substance intoxication, often may be unable to respond to these
strategies. In these cases, therapists are advised to employ the interventions as
best they can and utilize the behavior as a helpful diagnostic sign.

PUTTING IT ALL TOGETHER

The following is a transcript of a 68-year-old male client who was referred
for outpatient evaluation by his wife of 42 years. She insisted that he seek
help after she noticed significant personality changes that had developed
since the loss of their only son in a boating accident 6 months before. She
reported that her husband had become quite anxious and irritable, had lost
interest in his golf, and avoided all their friends. He rarely mentioned their
son and was very resistant to coming to a professional for help. She warned
that her husband was very adept at avoiding his problems and appeared
outwardly to be a very affable fellow. Notice in the transcript how the
therapist deals with the client's circumstantial speech, his pressured quality,
and his attempts to avoid confronting his emotional suffering through voluble
speech. The therapist attempts to give the client free rein initially, but adds
increasing structure and redirection when the client does not respond pro-
ductively to the questions:

> *Interviewer:* Mr. Allen, what brings you to see me today? [*open-ended
> question*]
>
> *Client:* That's a good question, Doc! You probably should ask my
> wife.
>
> *Interviewer:* What would your wife say? [*open-ended question*]
>
> *Client:* She worries too much . . . but she's a great gal. We've been
> married 42 years and what a wonderful life we've had. Sure
> we've had our tough times, but we've gotten through them.
> We met when I was in the service and when I first saw her
> I knew I would marry her. . . .

Interviewer: [*interrupting*] You must care about her very much. [*empathic response*] I'd like you, though, to help me understand what has been going on in your life recently. [*redirects client to the reason for referral with another open-ended question*]

Client: Like I said, she worries too much. I just gave up golf and she got all upset about it. Golf is a tough game and I'm getting too old for all the aggravation. I've been playing for years with my friends. It's too hot on most days in the summer and I can't take the heat. I wish those carts were air conditioned . . . what an invention that . . .

Interviewer: [*interrupting*] Have you been feeling . . .

Client: [*with pressured quality*] . . . would be. Excuse me, Doc, but anyway she's worrying for nothing. I'm doing okay.

Interviewer: Mr. Allen, have you been feeling depressed or down lately? [*closed-ended question*]

Client: Sure, I've been a little down in the dumps . . . but . . .

Interviewer: Tell me about those feelings. [*reinforces relevant response with direct request*]

Client: That's all. I've had some stress in my life recently, but I'm doing okay. Everyone has problems, but we've got to deal with them. Look at me Doc! Do I look in such bad shape? By the way I bet you treat a lot of folks much worse than I. I think I'm wasting your time.

Interviewer: It seems very difficult for you to answer my questions directly. [*focuses on the process of resistance*] I'm wondering what it is that is so painful to talk about? [*open-ended question that attempts to gently focus the client*]

Client: Like I said, I've had stress recently. My son passed away and that's real hard to deal with. But life goes on, I guess. I know I'll snap out of this and my wife will be more content with me. I can be quite a bear, you know. Never was I an easy guy to deal with . . . but she has been terrific . . . we planned a vacation a few months ago but . . .

Interviewer: [*cuts client off*] It must be devastating for a father to lose his son. [*empathic response*] You seem to be doing your best to avoid facing his loss. Right now, Mr. Allen, I need to know how serious your depression has become. [*redirecting the focus of the response*] How have your sleep and appetite been? [*closed-ended, qualitative question*]

Client: [*crying*] I hurt so much . . . I can't sleep; I have nightmares . . .

Interviewer: And your appetite? [*redirecting with a closed-ended question*]

Client: I have no desire to eat. I have no desire to do anything. You can't help me. You can't bring my son back. I don't care anymore. . . .

Interviewer: Have you felt like hurting yourself? [*closed-ended question*]

Client: Nothing matters. I told my wife that we have been punished for something and I don't know what. We have been good people. We lived a moral life, went to church. We have been good to people . . . [*sobbing*] so what, it's all for nothing now. . . .

Interviewer: Mr. Allen, have you thought about killing yourself as a way to end your terrible grief? [*redirect focus with closed-ended question*]

Client: Sometimes. But I doubt if I would do it. I'm a coward. My wife has always said I was a chicken. I remember when I was in the service . . .

Interviewer: [*interrupting*] Have you considered how you might kill yourself? [*redirecting to topic of suicide with open-ended question*]

Client: Never thought of a way . . . no, never.

SUMMARY

Dealing with overtalkative clients can be one of the most troublesome issues for both new and experienced counselors. It is a common concern raised in the supervision of therapists and one that inevitably produces frustration, resentment, and anxiety in the most well-intentioned therapist who is unable to gain control of the interview. This chapter has reviewed the major clinical presentations of overtalkativeness, including circumstantiality, tangentiality, rambling speech, pressured speech, flight of ideas, and volubility. The diagnostic significance of overtalkativeness was explored and specific presentations in several psychopathological disorders were described. Finally, the following strategies for managing the overtalkative client were presented:

1. Avoid open-ended questions, nonverbal reinforcement like head nodding, and excessive note taking.
2. Refocus client discussion with direct, specific questions.

3. Address the motivation for clients' overtalkativeness rather than the content of their speech.
4. Use empathic statements along with refocusing questions to "take the edge off" very directive interventions that may appear aggressive or discounting to clients.
5. Increase the use of closed-ended questions.

Understanding the motivations for clients' overtalkativeness and utilizing more directive, highly structured interviewing skills to cope with this problem will result in a much more satisfying and productive interview for both clients and therapists.

SUGGESTED READINGS

Egan, G. (1994). *The skilled helper* (5th ed.). Pacific Grove, CA: Brooks/Cole.

Hersen, M., & Turner, S. M. (Eds.). (1994). *Diagnostic interviewing* (2nd ed.). New York: Plenum.

Leon, R. L. (1982). *Psychiatric interviewing: A primer.* New York: Elsevier/North-Holland.

MacKinnon, R. A., & Michels, R. (1971). *The psychiatric interview in clinical practice.* Philadelphia: Saunders.

Othmer, E., & Othmer, S. C. (1994). *The clinical interview using* DSM–IV: *Vol. 1. Fundamentals.* Washington, DC: American Psychiatric Press.

Pope, B. (1979). *The mental health interview: Research and application.* Elmsford, NY: Pergamon.

Shea, S. C. (1988). *Psychiatric interviewing: The art of understanding.* Philadelphia: Saunders.

11

Ending the Interview

Eric F. Wagner
Nova Southeastern University

Jon D. Kassel
Shannon I. Jackson
University of Florida

The first clinical interview is a dynamic, interpersonal process. At its core is a human relationship. A universal description of the process is as impossible as it is impractical. Nonetheless, this chapter attempts to provide a pragmatic overview of what is involved in *ending* the first interview. The list of issues addressed is by no means exhaustive; nor are the suggestions intended to be absolute prescriptions. The goal is simply to introduce some of the more critical elements of the closing phase. The changing needs of the client and therapist will determine to what extent the suggestions are applicable and the manner in which they are followed.

The initial interview may be conceived of as consisting of three consecutive, temporally distinctive phases: the opening phase; the main body, or data-gathering phase; and the closing phase. Progression from the main body to the closing phase is essentially a transition from information gathering to clarification, analysis, synthesis, and feedback. Although this chapter focuses on the closing phase, it also acknowledges the importance of the transition between phases. It identifies and describes a number of issues related to ending the first therapeutic interview, including: professional and human agendas in the therapeutic relationship; precedent setting; the importance of client education; the transition from the main body to the closing phase; the provision of summary information; the need to address diagnosis, prognosis, and treatment; consultation and referral; the need to set time limits; and special considerations. Where appropriate, case examples and/or therapist scripts are included. It concludes with a summary of essential closing skills and suggested additional readings.

THE THERAPEUTIC RELATIONSHIP: PROFESSIONAL AND HUMAN AGENDAS

As already mentioned, the relationship between a client and a therapist, at its most fundamental level, is like any other human relationship. Factors such as mutual courtesy, respect, warmth, and understanding are essential, regardless of whether those involved are two neighbors or a client and a therapist. Of course, the client–therapist relationship, by definition, is a professional arrangement whereby the therapist is contracted by clients to aid them in addressing their presenting complaint. The professional aspects of the client–therapist relationship (e.g., confidentiality, payment contract, etc.) are important and necessary conditions, but the human aspects of the therapeutic relationship are what make it work. The alliance formed between a client and a therapist—a productive, open, and trusting relationship—is the single most necessary prerequisite for effective psychotherapy.

The best first interviews are those that resemble natural first meetings. As with any other meeting between a client and a professional, there is the *explicit*, or professional, agenda and the *implicit*, or human, agenda. The therapist's explicit agenda for the first therapy interview typically includes educating clients about the nature of the therapy profession, learning what clients expect from the relationship, learning about clients and their presenting complaint, addressing issues related to time and cost of assessment and psychotherapy, ensuring that necessary housekeeping tasks are performed (e.g., filling out forms, providing information about available services), and establishing the therapeutic contract. The implicit agenda for the first interview is to connect with the client so that a therapeutic alliance begins to form.

It is important to recognize that therapists and clients may have their own separate agendas. It is important for therapists to acknowledge and work toward understanding the client's agenda. Clients' agendas may be viewed as complementary to those of the therapist. Clients also have a human agenda and typically wish to connect with the therapist; however, they also have concerns that are more personally relevant, more pressing, and often more emotionally arousing than those of the therapist. Clients usually wish to convey the presenting complaint accurately, provide all of the necessary information, gain the therapist's approval or reassurance, obtain a diagnosis and prognosis, and learn about treatment options.

The following brief interaction reflects some of the agenda-related issues already noted:

Therapist: What I'm hearing from you is that you feel misunderstood, that nobody in your life seems to know the "real" you, and that you feel quite lonely as a result.

Client: Well, I guess. But it's not like I'm a loser or anything. I just wish that my parents and girlfriend would *listen* to me more. Nobody wants to hear what *I* think.

Therapist: That does sound like a very lonely place to be. You know, I often tell my clients that one way to think of therapy is as a luxury of sorts, a place where you can speak your mind, share your feelings, and hopefully feel understood. And for some people this is the only place where they feel safe doing that. Just so you understand, one of my goals for us is to get to know you better as a person and to gain an understanding of precisely what you're going through. I guess the idea is that you can take what you learn about yourself in here and use it to help you feel better outside of this office.

Client: Do you really think that can happen?

Therapist: To be perfectly honest, yes, I do. I've worked with many clients like yourself, who are sad or depressed and who feel misunderstood. I know it might feel a bit scary or overwhelming at times, but if you're ready to work hard I think that you'll really benefit from therapy.

Connecting with the client and developing a mutual understanding can be a powerful motivator. It can instill a sense of reassurance and hope that forms the very foundation for successful therapy.

SETTING PRECEDENTS

The first interview sets the precedent for subsequent sessions. Conclusion of the initial interview has important implications for whether or not clients will show up for the next session and what they may expect from subsequent sessions. One of the best ways for therapists to avoid beginning poorly is to end the first session well. Ending on a productive note ensures that the work accomplished during the first session is not undone. This influences the emerging therapeutic alliance. Clients' enthusiasm for both therapy and the therapist can be gravely damaged if the session ends on a sour note. According to the recency effect, the final (or most recent) item from a list of items is the item best remembered. Applied to the initial interview, the final few moments of the initial session are those clients typically best remember.

During the first session, the client develops beliefs about therapy and the therapist. At the close of the first session, it is important to set a pattern for the interview that is as comfortable as possible for both therapist and client. The manner in which the first interview ends has a "domino effect" because it directly influences clients' expectations about future sessions.

THE IMPORTANCE OF CLIENT EDUCATION

A good ending depends largely on if the client has been educated about how the first interview will be conducted. Thus, the therapist's professional agenda should always include giving the client instructions regarding the goals of the interview, and the length of the interview. This helps clients pace themselves throughout the session and prepare for the end of the interview.

Once entering the closing phase, therapists should field any unanswered client questions. This is a critical, but often overlooked, aspect of ending the interview. Correspondingly, the therapist should acknowledge that therapy is a "two-way street," in which clients are encouraged to evaluate—and share in the early course of therapy—the match between themselves and the therapist. It is perfectly acceptable for clients to decide that they would like to pursue therapy elsewhere, and the therapist should allow for this possibility. Finally, therapists should give clients a business card with their name, office phone number, and the time and date of the next appointment. Such a gesture is reassuring and enhances the likelihood that clients will return for a second session. The following scenario illustrates one way in which these issues can be addressed at the first session's end:

Therapist: Well, I see that we're almost out of time. We've covered a lot today, and I want to thank you for sharing as openly as you have. I'm wondering if you have any questions about therapy that we haven't yet addressed.

Client: Well, how long do you think this is going to take, and what if I don't like it?

Therapist: Those are certainly reasonable questions. How about if we go about it like this. I often tell my clients that the first several sessions really serve the purpose of allowing you to "tell your story," so to speak, so that I gain as clear an understanding as possible of your concerns. At the same time, you should use this time to evaluate how useful therapy may be for you. Now, some of what we do in here will be hard work, and you should think about whether you're ready for it. But you should also evaluate whether I am a person you would like to work with on your concerns. Why don't we agree that

> after three sessions, we'll both take stock of where we're at, discuss things, and plan accordingly? Does that sound reasonable?
>
> *Client:* Well, sure.
>
> *Therapist:* Good. Let's plan to meet again at this same time next week. Here's my card, on which I've written the date and time of our next appointment. I'll look forward to seeing you then.

This kind of interaction fosters a sense of collaboration and openness. Therapists should continue to "consult" with clients throughout the course of therapy, eliciting questions, concerns, and even testimonials concerning how they feel the process is going.

THE TRANSITION FROM THE MAIN BODY
TO THE CLOSING PHASE

Making the transition from the information-gathering phase to the closing phase of the interview requires good judgment about when the transition should occur, and poise in accomplishing that transition. Overextension may occur when therapists attempt to gather additional information, neglect to attend to the time, or because the client does not seem ready or willing to bring the session to a close. It is the therapist's task to pace the client, if necessary, by signaling that the interview is drawing to a close. Abrupt attempts to move into the closing phase may leave the client feeling disjointed, confused, and rejected. The therapist who appears calm, unhurried, and concerned for the client is the most successful in transitioning to the closing phase. Here is an example of a therapist's transition to the closing phase:

> *Therapist:* We've covered a lot about what brought you in today to see me, and you've probably got a lot more you could tell me. But we've only got about 10 minutes left, and I want to spend that time reviewing what we've discussed. I think I'm beginning to understand your most pressing concerns, and I want to make sure I've gotten the basics of what you've told me so far . . .

PROVIDING SUMMARY INFORMATION

The closing phase often begins with a recapitulation of diagnostic data. Clarification of ambiguous statements, discrepancies, or omissions is often required before the therapist can provide a summary. The best summary is succinct, concise, and stated in language the client can understand. The therapist should strive to give the client the essential information without elaborate or unnecessary details. In addition, it is best to modulate feedback based on the client's presentation. For instance, age, cultural background, intelligence, and personality factors may influence the extent to which a client can understand and utilize information. Some clients, particularly young children, find that analogies and examples increase their understanding of concepts. More intelligent clients, on the other hand, may solicit more elaborate explanations. Most clients tend to be offended by affectation, and will respond much better to a discussion that is direct and honest and shows respect for their intelligence. Finally, the therapist should allow plenty of time for the summary, so the client can fully absorb the information and ask for clarification when necessary.

Throughout the summary, the therapist should remain attuned to the client's response to ensure that the explanation is accurate, understood, and acceptable to the client. Some clients do not ask questions and do not indicate that they have not understood something for fear of appearing ignorant or impolite. Thus, after summarizing the main points of the session and areas of uncertainty, the therapist needs to make sure the client has comprehended the summary. Often, simply asking "Did you understand?" may prove unproductive because many clients simply reply "Yes." Therapists should make additional queries if they suspect that important elements of the summary may not have been understood. The goal here is to address any misunderstandings and correct any inaccuracies in the summary. Ultimately, it is critical that clients and therapists come to a mutually constructed understanding of the clients' issues. Otherwise, it is unlikely that therapy can progress.

In addition, queries regarding the client's feelings may be advisable at this stage. Often, as the client's "story" is constructed and retold, certain questions and emotions are evoked. Some questions reflect the client's concerns about the helpfulness of psychotherapy, the possibility of receiving a diagnosis, and even the extent to which the therapist likes the client. Emotional reactions may include fear, anxiety, or despondency. Eliciting the client's emotional response allows the therapist an opportunity to counter negative emotions and to provide support. In addition, if the client expresses fear or anxiety that is disproportionate to the situation, these unrealistic responses can be addressed.

It is not uncommon for clients to exhibit the "good patient" syndrome: that is, they uncritically accept everything the therapist says. These clients make no demands, express no fear, ask no questions, and act as if the therapist has already skillfully resolved their presenting complaints. This reaction may reflect denial, a desire to please the therapist, or a paradoxical fear reaction. Thus, ongoing appraisal of the client's verbal and nonverbal responses during the feedback portion of the interview is essential. Helping clients to make realistic appraisals of their situations and develop constructive ways of dealing with their issues is fundamental to psychotherapy and integral in providing a summary of the first session.

ADDRESSING DIAGNOSIS, PROGNOSIS, AND TREATMENT

Many clients approach the therapist–client relationship expecting answers to their questions during the initial interview. This natural propensity is reinforced by experiences with other health professionals who usually provide some type of diagnosis and a recommended treatment course. Skilled therapists provide this information to the extent possible, but also inform clients if and why they cannot provide a diagnosis and a treatment recommendation at the close of the first session. Diagnoses are dependent both on the data collected and its organization. The information gathered during the main body of the interview should be complete, coherent, and accurate. Ensuring that these conditions are met usually requires additional assessment.

The presentation of a tentative diagnosis is an important consideration. A diagnosis usually elicits emotional responses and creates expectations in clients. A simple, concrete presentation using examples and specifically referencing the client's presenting concerns and symptoms is recommended. In addition, it may be helpful to briefly discuss etiology and prevalence rates of specific disorders.

Of course, if a diagnosis is conferred, then the therapist may wish to discuss treatment options. If treatment alternatives are discussed, the client is best served by a thorough explanation of the treatment procedures and explanations of potential risks and benefits associated with each treatment so that an informed decision can be made. Realistic, concrete treatment goals facilitate progress and enable easy assessment. Furthermore, it is sometimes helpful to differentiate short-term from long-term goals to ensure that clients remain optimistic yet realistic about what and how quickly changes will occur.

Sometimes, homework assignments are given during the interval between the initial interview and the following session. This practice serves multiple purposes, including allowing the client to work on issues independently, fostering a sense of self-reliance for the client, gathering additional information for the therapist, providing the client insight into the nature of his difficulties, and facilitating client engagement in the therapeutic process outside the confines of the therapy session.

As part of the discussion of diagnosis, prognosis, and treatment, it may be possible to provide a provisionary estimate of the time necessary to complete therapy. This should be done whenever possible to ensure that both client and therapist remain oriented to the ultimate goal of therapy—addressing clients' concerns to their satisfaction. It may also be necessary to discuss third-party payment options paying specific attention to imposed limits on the number of sessions. Often, providing the client with expectations about how long therapy can or should last facilitates therapeutic progress and eases the inevitable termination issues associated with ending therapy.

Once treatment goals and plans have been established, it may be helpful to assess the client's intentions to comply with the therapist's recommendations and follow the treatment plan. Indeed, if clients do not comply with the treatment plan, in many respects, the interview has failed. It is helpful to consider some of the reasons clients may return for a second session and comply with therapists' recommendations. These reasons encompass beliefs about therapy (e.g., the client feels that something has been accomplished during the interview, or the client believes that therapy can be helpful) and beliefs about the therapist (e.g., the client trusts the therapist, or the client feels comfortable with the therapist). Therapists can assess these beliefs by asking for feedback about their performance (e.g., "So what do you think about how things have gone today?"). This conveys empathy and concern for the client, and allows therapists to evaluate the client's comfort level in the relationship. A client with positive evaluations is more likely to comply with or participate in the treatment plan. The closing phase of the interview is an opportunity for therapists to enhance these positive beliefs and to counter negative beliefs.

Some clients may ask for a prognostic statement (e.g., Is there hope?, Am I crazy?), and, in such cases, reassurance is often necessary. This may involve restating the necessity for following through with therapists' recommendations. However, reassurance should not be mistaken for a promise. Conservatively phrased reassurance can ease anxiety, but remember that an unequivocal prognosis is often impossible during the first interview. Finally, therapists need to remain open to the possibility that some clients may not need psychotherapy or exhibit any true psychopathology. One of the worst mistakes that a novice therapist can make is to find disturbances where they do not exist.

In sum, effective therapists end the session in a way that allows clients to feel like their concerns have been understood. Moreover, they leave a client with a sense of what needs to be done next and, whenever possible, optimism about the ultimate outcome if recommendations are followed. They should also summarize what has been discussed in the session and offer support and encouragement.

CONSULTATION AND REFERRAL

Effective psychotherapy requires that the therapist's expertise is commensurate with the client's needs. Many therapists "specialize" in one or more areas. Ethically, therapists' ability to assess their competence and ability to assist a client is essential. If therapists decide to consult another professional, then the client should be informed of this decision, the reasons for the consultation, the information that will be given to the consulting professional, and the information expected to come from the consulting professional (see chap. 12). If a visit to a consultant is recommended, therapists should specify the duration and number of visits necessary. Some clients may have a variety of concerns or fears related to a referral. Thus, leave enough time to adequately discuss these concerns at the end of the session.

The following exchange is an example of how the therapist can broach the issue of outside referral. Note that the client is quite capable intellectually, but has become convinced that she is "stupid" and reports that cognitive difficulties (e.g., poor memory) are significantly interfering with her day-to-day life:

Therapist: Let me try and briefly summarize what you've shared with me today. You've been feeling pretty depressed and anxious for some time now, particularly since the accident you suffered at work about 5 years ago. You're still struggling with accepting the physical limitations imposed upon you by the shoulder injury. At the same time, you've shared that you have always felt "stupid," that you are forgetful, absent-minded, and have trouble following through on plans. You mentioned that one of your fears is that you may have Alzheimer's disease or maybe even attention deficit disorder. Does what I've said sound correct?

Client: Yes, I think you've got it. If I weren't so scatterbrained, I could cope with my pain and other problems. I'm just so stupid, I can't stand it!

Therapist: Let me run this idea by you. I think it might be really helpful if you underwent a full neuropsychological evaluation. This would allow us to see if, indeed, you really do have some sort of memory or attentional problem. Also, we could get a good sense of your overall intelligence, too. Now, I don't do those kinds of exams myself. But I know of an excellent psychologist, Dr. Johnson, who could provide this service to you. The testing would probably take several hours and you could do it at Dr. Johnson's office.

Referrals, such as the previous one, are commonplace in clinical practice. In this particular example, findings revealed no significant impairment in cognitive functioning, which allowed the subsequent therapy to address the client's "real" issues regarding chronic low self-esteem and pain management.

SETTING TIME LIMITS

Defining the length of a clinical session constitutes an explicit therapeutic boundary. It is recommended that the initial session begin with a brief introduction on how psychological evaluation and psychotherapy work, and that part of this introduction be devoted to the length of sessions. Concluding sessions on time is important, because deviations from the agreed on time limit can cloud therapeutic boundaries and invite misunderstanding and unnecessary complexity to the therapeutic relationship. Hence, the therapist should be cautioned that straying from the time boundary by shortening or lengthening the session may alter the client's perception of the therapist and of the therapist–client relationship, which may in turn diminish the effectiveness of subsequent encounters. Lengthening the session can be particularly problematic because it calls into question the therapist's integrity and professionalism. This may set the stage for future transgressions by implicitly conveying the notion that the therapist is unable or unwilling to adhere to the previously established conditions of psychotherapy and, perhaps, that the client ultimately has control over those conditions. From a more pragmatic perspective (i.e., the professional agenda), setting such time limits helps ensure that the therapist successfully makes it through a busy day of meeting with clients.

On rare occasions, in cases of emergency, it may be necessary to extend the session beyond its normal time limits (e.g., client suicidality or suspected physical or sexual abuse). Fortunately, the vast majority of sessions do not involve emergencies, and thus, it is recommended that time limits be observed in all but the most dire of circumstances.

Ending on time is important, but it is also critical for it to end with both the therapist and the client feeling comfortable. It is unwise and unhelpful to cut clients off too abruptly, even if they are about to go beyond the time limit. Therapists should anticipate the end of the session by beginning to bring the session to a close at least 10 minutes before the scheduled end. It is helpful to use statements such as, "We have only a few minutes left of our time together, so some of what you are talking about may have to wait until we meet again. Let's see if I've got the main points, though," or "Our time is almost up and there are a few things I need to clarify with you before you leave today." When the session really does end, conclude with a statement such as, "There's no more time left. I really want to hear more about what you've been telling me, so let's plan to pick up next time where we left off today."

A critical therapist task, therefore, is to keep track of time. Therapists should have a clock in the office, in a place where they can glance at it easily without turning their head. Some therapists choose a large wall clock, but a desk clock can work similarly well. Relying on a wristwatch for session timekeeping is not recommended. Therapists who attempt to glance at a wristwatch run the risk of alienating the client. Arrange the office so that keeping track of time is a natural and simple process.

SPECIAL CONSIDERATIONS

Thus far, the chapter has presented a model of closing the interview that applies to most cases. This section addresses a variety of special circumstances that may arise.

Evaluation Versus Treatment Session

Sometimes a formal assessment, or evaluation, session precedes a client's formal entry into therapy and may (or may not) be conducted by someone other than the therapist. During an assessment session, self-report questionnaires (assessing areas like personality attributes, symptoms of depression and anxiety, substance abuse, etc.) and/or intellectual tests are often administered with the goal of helping to clarify client symptoms and to provide initial data toward making a diagnosis. In fact, a session devoted to such psychological testing is usually warranted and highly informative.

However, the first clinical interview is usually conducted without any previous evaluation session. As such, several important implications arise. If during the closing phase of the first clinical interview, therapists express the belief that further testing would be helpful to gain a better understanding of clients and their underlying issues, then no formal diagnosis could be given until such testing had taken place. Therapists must express this condition to the client, as well as normalize and explain the subsequent testing phase. Indeed, some clients may be put off by psychological questionnaires, wondering about their importance and relevance to therapy. Skilled therapists can explain that psychological assessment is simply a process to gather information that will be used to further their understanding of the client as a person. The following is an example of such an interaction:

> *Therapist:* I see that we only have a little time left. So let me share some of my thoughts with you, based on what you've told me today. Clearly, you have been feeling overwhelmed lately. It also sounds like you've been having difficulty concentrating, trouble sleeping, decreased appetite, and feelings of sadness. Does what I've said seem to capture it pretty well?
>
> *Client:* Ya, I guess. But I still can't figure out why I'm feeling this way? Do you think I'm crazy?

Therapist: No, I don't think you're crazy, but clearly there's something that's bothering you and significantly interfering with your life. And I'm afraid that at this point in time, I'm not exactly sure what's at the root of your problems either. I think it might be helpful, though, to have you come in next week and complete some questionnaires. These questionnaires will ask you about aspects of your personality, how you generally cope with things, and about your moods. I think that your answers could prove really helpful in helping us both get a better idea of what's going on with you. How does that sound?

Client: I don't know. Who's going to read these things? And what are they going to tell you about me that you don't already know? And what if I fail the test?

Therapist: First of all, no one will see them other than myself. Also, there are no right or wrong answers. You simply answer the questions as honestly as you can. And I really think that psychological questionnaires like we're talking about can be quite helpful in pointing out problem areas that aren't easily expressed verbally.

The first clinical interview sometimes occurs subsequent to a formal testing session. In this instance, it is important to share the findings of the evaluation with the client. Thus, as the therapy hour enters the closing phase, this represents an excellent opportunity for therapists to integrate the data from the testing session with their observations during the initial interview. For example, the therapist might express "Well, why don't I take a few minutes now to share with you the findings from the questionnaires you completed last week? If you have any questions about what I'm saying or about the tests themselves, please feel free to ask me. I think that the information from the tests coupled with what you've shared with me today gives me a pretty good sense of your concerns."

MANDATED CLIENTS

It is becoming increasingly common for therapists to treat clients mandated by the legal system. Similarly, some clients are coerced by some other party (e.g., a spouse or family member) to seek help for problems they may not feel they really have. Clearly, the factor that differentiates these clients from others is their level of motivation. The extent to which a client wants, or is motivated, to engage in therapy therefore becomes a critical factor in the therapeutic process and relationship. Whether addressed in the opening, body, or closing phase of therapy, the motivation level of the mandated client must be addressed and acknowledged. Simply stated, the therapist must acknowledge via reflection that the client is ambivalent about participation in therapy. The next step is to provide understanding and reassurance of the client's position. For example, consider a 31-year-old male, who was mandated to seek therapy for problems stemming from substance abuse:

Therapist: Okay, let's see if I understand what you've said. You admit that you drink too much on occasion and that your use of cocaine has created some financial and legal problems for you. At the same time, however, you don't believe that you really have a problem with alcohol or drugs, and that you can handle these issues yourself. Does that essentially sound right?

Client: Damn right. I don't need you or anybody else telling me what to do. I'm my own man. I can handle these problems myself. And they're not problems anyway.

Therapist: Alright. So it sounds like you resent being here. You're feeling like others are trying to control you. And maybe you're right, to a certain extent. After all, the court said you have to undergo therapy or face possible jail time. But given the circumstances as they are, is it possible for you to become open to the possibility, as remote as it might seem to you right now, that therapy could be helpful to you?

Client: Well, I guess I don't have much choice. I'll come, but I don't really want to. What the hell do I have to lose?

Even if nothing else was achieved in the previous example, the therapist expressed an understanding of the client's position, and in doing so elicited from the client a commitment (albeit a begrudgingly offered one) to come back. Clearly, issues of resistance and ambivalence are inherent among mandated clients and are a continuing issue throughout the course of therapy. Addressing them upfront, at the close of the first interview, can make the difference in whether or not the client returns at all.

CHILDREN AND MINORS

Closing the first interview with a child or adolescent client involves specialized skills. A skilled clinician will gear the closing phase of the session to the developmental level of the child, using words and explanations that can be understood by the child. In some cases, children may have difficulty with the end of a session, especially if some attachment to the therapist has been formed during the session. Reassurance from the therapist is often helpful at such junctions, and should include statements about how much the therapist enjoyed meeting and spending time with the child. In most cases, the parents or guardians of the child will be present during the closing phase of the session. Here, follow the guidelines outlined previously about how to close a session. Perhaps the best way to view this situation is to think of the child and his parents as the clients, and to attend to the needs of both parties in closing the initial session.

PHYSICAL CONTACT

The issue of physical contact—even as apparently benign as a handshake—between therapists and their clients has long been a subject of debate and controversy within the field. For example, the first interview is winding to a close. Everything has gone relatively well, the next session has been scheduled, and the therapist stands up to see the client out. At this point, the client extends a hand outward while expressing thanks, and awaits a handshake in return. What is the appropriate response? Though it is beyond the scope of this chapter to fully address this issue, it is perfectly appropriate for a therapist to shake the client's hand. In fact, to do otherwise would likely be construed as rejection and, hence, could negatively impact the therapeutic relationship—particularly during the first therapy interview. A handshake essentially represents a gesture of thanks, appreciation, and closure, and, as such, should be reciprocated.

Of course, the issue of physical contact at the end of a therapy session becomes more complex when, for example, clients extend their arms in anticipation of a hug. Here, the boundaries become more diffuse, and it is recommended that, particularly with respect to the first clinical interview, the hug not be reciprocated. An example speaks to this issue. A therapist conducted an initial interview with a woman diagnosed with Dependent Personality Disorder. At the session's close, she moved forward, in the "hug position." In this instance, the therapist chose to not reciprocate, based on the facts that this was the first session, and this woman's presenting problems were rooted in her difficulty in establishing healthy physical and emotional boundaries. Hence, in this instance, the therapist simply offered a hand for a handshake, which the client accepted. Of course, a hug initiated by a client at the conclusion of a series of therapy sessions may seem appropriate and relatively benign.

SUMMARY

Some of the more critical elements of the closing phase of the interview process have been discussed. A therapist who carefully considers each of the issues discussed will be better able to help clients. The following is a list and brief synopsis of the most important aspects of ending the interview:

First interviews should resemble natural first meetings between two individuals. However, it is important to remember that the therapeutic encounter is a professional meeting. Hence, there is both an explicit, or professional, agenda and an implicit, or human, agenda in every therapy session.

The first interview sets the precedent for subsequent sessions and has important implications for clients' expectations about and commitment to subsequent sessions. Ending the first session well is especially important to setting a good precedent for the remainder of therapy.

Client education is vital to the success of therapy. Clients should be informed of what the goals are for the initial interview and how long the interview will last. Moreover, an overview of the nature of psychological evaluation and psychotherapy should be provided by the therapist.

Ending a session involves transitioning from the main body to the closing phase of the interview. From the clinician, this requires good judgment about when the transition should occur and poise in accomplishing the transition.

Ending the first interview should always include a verbal summary of the session. The best summary is succinct, concise, and stated in language appropriate to the client. During the summary, clients should be encouraged to ask questions, and therapists should be open and honest in their responses.

Clients often expect some type of diagnosis, prognosis, and recommended treatment course by the end of the first interview. This expectation should be met by the therapist whenever possible. However, the therapist should not provide this kind of information prematurely, and may choose to wait until a subsequent meeting to discuss such issues. If so, the therapist should explain to the client the reasons for this postponement.

Referral for consultation is commonplace following an initial interview. In cases of consultation, the client should be fully informed of the reasons for and the processes involved in pursuing consultation.

Sessions should end on time. Only in cases of emergency should this boundary be violated.

SUGGESTED READINGS

Choca, J. (1996). *Manual for clinical psychology trainees*. New York: Brunner/Mazel.

Enelow, A. (1979). *Interviewing and patient care*. New York: Oxford University Press.

Johnson, W. R. (1981). Basic interviewing skills (pp. 83–128). In C. E. Walker (Ed.), *Clinical Practice of Psychology*. Elmsford, NY: Pergamon.

Kottler, J. A. (1991). *The compleat therapist*. San Francisco: Jossey-Bass.

Morsund, J. (1993). *The process of counseling and therapy*. Englewood Cliffs, NJ: Prentice-Hall.

12

Knowing When to Refer

William J. Burns
Clio V. Hatziyannakis
Nova Southeastern University

A well-stated referral sets the diagnostic process into motion. A poor referral may sidetrack the diagnostic process and result in inadequately planned treatment. The referring professional must provide sufficient information for a good beginning.

There are many reasons why a therapist decides to refer a client to another professional. Most frequently, the therapist does not have the expertise in the area required to treat a particular client. Or, the therapist may not have an opening for a new client. Whatever the reason, the referring therapist is faced with a series of questions about the referral process. This chapter addresses the issues of when to refer, how to refer, and to whom a referral should be assigned.

THE INTAKE PROCESS

When prospective clients visit a mental health center, they are usually assigned to an intake worker (see chap. 8). The intake interviewer obtains a history of the client's problem and investigates the client's needs. Although these interviews may follow various formats, a highly structured one is recommended. It must adequately screen the complex life circumstances typical of client's with psychiatric emergencies and routine mental health problems.

The intake evaluation is a brief report that includes a summary of the client's problem and contains some history of factors related to the development of the problem. The purpose of the intake is twofold: to establish a diagnostic impression and to recommend an appropriate referral.

The Diagnostic Phase

The following is an example of one format for an intake evaluation. The content of the evaluation is described as it applies to the referral made by the intake worker.

Presenting Problem. A clear statement of the client's symptoms, complaints, and reasons for seeking mental health services are needed for a complete referral statement. This assessment should include an estimate of the duration, frequency, and intensity of the symptoms and their effect on the client's functioning. Some sample questions might be:

How much has the disorder disrupted your work?

How many times per day do you feel anxious?

When an interviewer is called on to make decisions about an emergency referral, this information will be important. For instance, the interviewer must determine whether or not the client has indicated if there is a life-threatening problem (to self or others). If so, the intake worker must immediately consider referring the client to a hospital.

History of the Illness. It is important to obtain information about the development and course of the client's problem: prior episodes, previous treatment (effective and ineffective), periods of remission, and the effect of the illness on client's functioning. Such information can help decide on the appropriate referral. Some sample questions are:

When did this problem first begin?

What else was happening at that time?

Have you received treatment for this illness?

What helped most and what was not helpful?

Medical History/Prior Treatment. Medical illnesses/diseases have an effect on the psychological functioning of an individual, and vice versa (see chap. 6). An assessment of medical history should include past/current illnesses, hospitalizations, past/current medications, and treatment received for the illness. This information will aid the intake worker to make a referral to a medical professional, or a neuropsychologist. Sample questions include:

Have you had any significant medical problems?

Do you have medical problems that continue to bother you at the present time?

What type of treatment have you had for these problems?

Have you had any head injuries, car accidents, headaches, brain X rays, or brain problems?

Have you been diagnosed with epilepsy, a tumor, HIV, or heart or vascular problems, such as stroke?

Drug Use History. A thorough drug history is important to determine how the substance use is contributing to the client's problems (see chap. 6). If a client has a history or problem with prescription or illegal drugs, then that is likely to have an effect on the decision regarding the referral. For instance, an emergency decision may be made for hospital admission for detoxification. Sample questions might include:

Do you consider your drug use to be a problem?

Do you want to be helped to stop using?

What happened the last time you stopped?

Has your use of this drug interfered with your functioning at work/ school/home?

Clients who take psychotropic medication at the time of intake need to be assessed for the type of medications they are using. Referral to a professional with special expertise in the treatment of substance use disorders should always be considered when the client has received a diagnosis of addiction or dependence.

Mental Status Examination. The mental status evaluation alerts the intake worker to the presence of a rapidly deteriorating or stable-but-severe condition in which mental functioning has been significantly compromised (see chap. 7). The presence of prominent deficits on a mental status exam may be an indication of the need to refer the client for a comprehensive neuropsychological or neurological exam.

An example of a widely used mental status examination, which might be used during intake, is the Mini Mental State Exam (MMSE) (Folstein, Folstein, & McHugh, 1975), which is a brief assessment of disturbances in mood, perception, thought, and memory. The MMSE aids in establishing a diagnosis. It assesses the following areas: appearance, behavior, speech, orientation, mood, affect, flow and content of thought processes, perceptual disturbances, attention, concentration, memory, intelligence, impulse control, judgment, and insight.

Family History. Information regarding the client's family of origin and current family should be assessed for any aspects impacting on the client's current functioning. Areas to explore may include: ages of family members; cultural, ethnic, and religious background; client's relationship with family members; quality of marital relationships; where family members live in relation to the client; family medical history; family history of mental illness; family substance abuse history; and childhood memories. Information about the support provided by the family, as well as those factors that may interfere with client functioning (e.g., alcoholic spouse) are necessary for decision making concerning referral. Questions such as the following may be helpful:

Tell me about your parents. (i.e., Describe your mother; describe your father.)

How did your life at home as a child affect your present life?

What is your present relationship like with your siblings? parents?

Has anyone in your family had symptoms similar to the symptoms you are now experiencing?

Social History. The client's relationship with others is the focus of this section (see chap. 5). Client's peer relationships, marital history, group membership, and participation in social activities should be included. Problems in forming and maintaining good social relations have been found to be closely related to problems in mental health. It is a common practice for psychodiagnosticians to refer clients to therapists who have expertise in social skills training and social problem solving. Sample questions that may help to uncover problems in social functioning are as follows:

In what activities or groups do you participate?

Tell me about your friendships.

How is your relationship with your spouse?

Tell me about your dating history.

Educational History. Information about clients' highest level of academic achievement and overall performance in school activities is helpful in estimating their general cognitive functioning. When the intake worker suspects problems with learning, a detailed history of schooling experiences may be appropriate, including the type of school attended, area of study, favorite and least favorite subjects, grade failures, regular/special classes, lapse in education, and type of educational programs. If such problems are a part of the client's complaint/symptom cluster, a referral may be made to an educational specialist (e.g., reading tutor) or to a learning disability specialist (e.g., child neuropsychologist) for a thorough diagnostic evaluation.

Occupational History. Occupational history affords a look at the client's ability to apply intelligence and skill to a particular task. Failure in occupation is often a part of the history of a client with psychopathology because of the demand for consistent daily efficiency and successful social interaction with employer and fellow employees. Therefore, occupational problems may be a result of personal problems, or may be due to the inabilty of the client to sustain work and social relationships over a long period of time. An assessment should be made of the client's current occupation, work history, and relationship with coworkers. Some questions might include:

How long have you been at your current job?

What prior employments have you had?

Why did you change jobs?

How do you like your work?

What type of work would you like to do?

Do you take pride in doing your job well?

Referral may be made to a therapist with expertise in social skills training or personal problems. Educational counselors, who have expertise in occupational guidance, may be the most appropriate referral when the problem concerns a mismatch between job and personality.

Legal History. In some cases, the referral may come from a court, judge, or lawyer, wherein a referral problem has already been stated (e.g., What are treatment recommendations for this client's substance use disorder?). The task of the intake worker in such a case may be very limited (e.g., find a detoxification unit). However, problems involving the law, legal charges or arrests, and past/current lawsuits may call for extensive diagnostic assessments. Therefore, referral to neuropsychologists or forensic specialists may be required. Questions that may be asked of such clients are:

How often have you been arrested?

Have you ever had your license suspended/revoked?

What lawsuits are currently pending?

How does your lifestyle bring you into conflict with the law?

Diagnosis. A referral is often made for the purpose of obtaining or confirming a diagnosis. Intake workers may wish to give their initial diagnostic impression, despite the brevity of their evaluation. In such a case it is appropriate for the intake worker to clearly state that the diagnostic impression is tentative, and has not been made on the basis of a complete evaluation. The criteria used in making a tentative diagnosis should be clearly delineated, and the report should include a statement about the necessity for further assessment in order to confirm or disconfirm the diagnosis.

If criteria have been met for a diagnosis listed in *DSM–IV*, then that diagnostic code should be given along with a list of the criteria used to make this diagnosis. All five axes of the *DSM–IV* diagnosis should be given if the information is available:

AXIS I: Clinical Conditions or Other Conditions

AXIS II: Personality Disorders and Mental Retardation

AXIS III: General Medical Conditions

AXIS IV: Psychosocial and Environmental Problems

AXIS V: Global Assessment of Functioning

Referral for Diagnostic Consultation. After completion of the intake, the client is often referred to a specialist for a full battery of tests in order to confirm or disconfirm the impressions of the intake worker. If a treatment recommendation has been made in the process of these consultations or referrals, then the client is moved to the treatment phase.

The Treatment Referral Phase

After the diagnostic phase of the intake is completed, it is customary for the intake worker to estimate the treatment needs of the client. Immediate and long-term treatment goals may be discussed in order to feel out the client's motivation for entering treatment. Such a discussion with the client should be directed toward alleviating the symptoms and improving the client's daily functioning. Goals are most helpful when they are specific and behaviorally defined. Recommendations are made regarding treatment modality, frequency of sessions, and duration of treatment.

Sometimes clients do not keep their appointment with the referral and do not follow-up to reschedule another appointment. One way to prevent dropouts is to conduct a thorough intake where the client's needs are accurately assessed. A second strategy is to avoid making a referral for treatment in which the client has no interest, or a treatment that has already ended in failure before. Prior to making a choice about a referral, a clinician should ask about successes and failures in past interventions. Clients who do not feel supported, or who do not believe the treatment will be successful, are not likely to follow through with the treatment referral. Therefore, this process may enhance the motivation of the client to keep the referral appointment with the therapist, because it may increase the client's certitude about the process of therapy and reduce fear of the unknown.

A sample intake report is presented in Appendix I (also, see chap. 8).

MAKING THE REFERRAL

Knowledge About Referral Sites

After completing the intake interview, therapists are expected to make referrals or recommendations. This would be difficult for a therapist who is ignorant of the appropriate referral resources. Although it is not essential for therapists to know the professional to whom the referral is made, such personal knowledge would be beneficial. It is essential that the therapist be familar with the credentials of the professional to whom the referral is made. There are many published sources of credential information. For psychologists, there is the *National Register of Health Service Providers in Psychology*. Regional health provider information is often published for professionals to use in the referral process. For example, in Broward County, Florida, the Mental Health Association has the publication *Connections: A Guide to Mental Health and Support Services*, which lists all available mental health institutional referral sites in Broward County.

In addition, some communities have referral services to assist clinicians in finding the appropriate professional. However, be aware that these services are financially supported by the professionals on their list.

When the question is about the treatment that would be most beneficial for the client at this time, a variety of assistance is available. Prescriptive treatment manuals are now available in libraries and bookstores. Case conceptualization courses are offered in most clinical psychology graduate programs to train professionals in the process of treatment formulation. Mental health facilities often have a staff member who can advise clinicians about making appropriate referrals. Individuals or facilities who take referrals are often the best resource for answering questions about how to make a referral. However, procedures may differ from individual to individual and site to site.

When to Make a Referral

A referral is made when the therapist conducting the interview or session does not have the expertise to help the client with a particular problem. A referral may be necessary to either help the client deal with a primary complaint (e.g., referring a client with severe headaches to a neurologist), or it may be used to address a secondary situation that has resulted from the primary complaint (e.g., a client having difficulty at work or at school).

There are several reasons for making a referral to another professional:

1. The first, and most common, reason is the need for special expertise. The professional who conducted the intake does not have the skill to do the necessary evaluation (e.g., physician referring to a psychologist). Another example would be a mental health worker who does the intake, but is not trained to perform a comprehensive battery of tests, and consequently refers 100% of clients to someone else.

2. A referral may be necessary if there is no room on the professional's schedule for another client. In other words, the referral is made in order to assure the client a timely evaluation. The intake professional has the required skill to continue with the case, but would have to place the client on a waiting list.

3. The intake professional may wish to have a second opinion from a colleague (e.g., psychologist referring to another psychologist). With such a consult the referring professional maintains primary responsibility for clients, and refers them for a diagnostic evaluation to obtain recommendations. In this case, the consulting professional evaluates the client and then sends a report with the client back to the referring professional.

4. There may be an emergency, such as suicidal or homicidal intent. A hospital or holding facility is commonly used to protect these clients from themselves or to protect others.

5. A referral may be done at the request of the client. For instance, the client may prefer a therapist of the opposite gender.

6. When treatment progress has not been made, the therapist may wish to offer referral to another therapist.

7. When unresolvable conflict develops between client and professional, a referral may need to be made in the best interest of the client.

How to Make a Referral

Making a referral entails direct communication with the professional. This is done through a telephone call and should be followed with a letter, either by mail or fax, to the party to which the referral is being made. The letter should contain identifying information regarding the client being referred, the referral question, and relevant client history.

How to Receive a Referral

When a referral is received, the recipient makes a decision about its appropriateness and should respond to the person making the referral. If the referral is inappropriate, then the receiver has the responsibility to refer the client to yet another professional and to notify the referrer.

The law prohibits any rebate, bonus, or renumeration for receiving or referring a client. For example, Chapter 490 of the Florida Statutes clearly states that giving a fee in return for a referral is called a kickback, or fee-splitting, and is illegal. When kickbacks occur, clients are typically unaware of the fee arrangement. This practice is also unethical because it may interfere with providing an appropriate referral. Hence, a client may be easily exploited. For example, a referral should be made in the best interest of the client or when clinically necessary, not for monetary gain. Other ways of finding referral sources include making connections with social workers who have been trained in making referrals, contacting state/community mental health services, and using sources from the telephone book.

Sample Written Referral Letter and Response

A sample referral letter and a letter of acceptance of a referral are found in Appendix II.

SPECIAL TYPES OF REFERRALS

Emergency Situations

Violent Clients. Among the most difficult clients are those who are violent or homicidal. Violent clients, who are a danger to themselves and to others, require special strategies to ensure the safety of all concerned. Intake workers may request that another professional be present at the intake.

Assessment of the immediate potential for harm to self and others is the top priority. Direct inquiry should be made about the client's violent intentions and impulses. Therapists must evaluate whether the client has a plan and the means to carry out the plan. Indirect methods may also be used to determine the intensity of hostile feelings and anger. However, intake workers should be prepared to terminate the interview if clients indicate they are going to act out their impulses (e.g., "I feel that I am going to hit someone"), or give indirect indications that they are unable to control their feelings. The intaker worker must decide what action to take. If the client is likely to become aggressive or violent, then action should be taken to have the client hospitalized immediately. This involves an involuntary commitment (e.g., in Florida this is called the "Baker Act"). Typically, the police are contacted and medical personnel are notified. A medical psychiatric unit is the proper place for these clients because personnel there are prepared to control aggression and then conduct a thorough diagnostic assessment.

There is also a responsibility to protect others who may be in danger. Although confidentiality is crucial to the client–therapist relationship, there are situations where it is necessary to breach confidentiality. For example, breaking confidentiality would be warranted if a specific threat had been made against a particular person. The decision in the well-known case, *Tarasoff v. Regents of the University of California* (1976), specifies that it is the duty of therapists to protect a third party if there is specific knowledge of danger to that person.

The intake worker should routinely ask every client about past violent behavior because past behavior is one of the best predictors for future behavior. If the client is against hospitalization but does exhibit violent behavior, the intake worker should ask the client to sign a contract, contact and warn significant others with the client's permission, make a referral to a therapist indicating the need for prompt attention and frequent sessions, and recommend therapy focusing on anger management strategies. If there is any uncertainty about how to proceed, consult with a colleague before the client leaves the office. Finally, the clinician should document what has been done, including a rationale for the actions taken.

Suicidal Clients. Researchers have found that mental illness is often present in individuals who have exhibited suicidal behavior, so it is important for intake workers to be aware of the signs of suicidal behavior, to know how to assess for suicidality, and to know how to proceed with a suicidal client. Although suicidal behavior has been found in people from many different backgrounds with a variety of traits, certain demographic characteristics have been found to be more highly correlated with suicidal clients. The following factors have been found to be related to a higher risk of suicidal behavior:

1. Major psychiatric illness (i.e., affective disorders, psychosis, border-line personality disorder)
2. Male gender
3. Caucasian ethnicity
4. Recent psychiatric hospitalization
5. Elderly and adolescents
6. Alcoholism or other substance abuse
7. Marital status: widowed or divorced
8. Previous suicide attempt(s)
9. Unemployed or retired
10. Serious physical illness
11. Recent personal, financial, social loss
12. Living alone (loss of social support)
13. Verbal expression of suicide
14. Aggression

Attempts should be made to predict future suicidal behavior. A clinician can assess for suicidal risk by administering an assessment measure. See the suggested readings at the end of the chapter for articles containing self-report measures for assessing the possibility of suicidal intent.

Suicidal ideation and suicidal intent should be a standard part of the initial session with the client. Asking about suicide does not put the idea of suicide into the person's head. In fact, clients may be relieved that someone has brought up the subject for discussion. They may have wanted to talk about suicidal feelings but felt uncomfortable about bringing it up. If a decision is made that the client is not safe to return home, then the police must be contacted to escort the client to an appropriate facility. Clients need to be escorted because they may try to kill themselves before reaching the facility. If there is no emergency, then they should be referred to a therapist who will begin treatment as soon as possible. Intake workers must be familiar with the code and standards of each state for the referral of special patients. Appendix III presents a vignette concerning the problem of referring suicidal adolescents for treatment.

Nonemergency Special Types of Referral

Chronically Ill Clients. Chronic illnesses include diagnoses such as schizophrenia, bipolar disorders, anorexia, and bulimia. When gathering information during intake, it is important to supplement the information obtained from the client with other sources of information. These other sources may include family members, friends, past chart information (i.e., regarding treatment interventions, hospitalizations), and prior therapists. Due to the extreme sensitivity often observed in these clients, it is necessary for the intake worker to establish a relationship that is genuine and non-judgmental. Because interpersonal relationships are often anxiety provoking for the chronically ill, especially in individuals with psychotic disorders, pay extra attention to these clients to make them as comfortable as possible.

Individuals with AIDS are clients with chronic illness. They may be referred for individual therapy to focus on dealing with deterioration in cognitive functioning, rejection from others, and issues of death. Support groups that are often sponsored by community hospitals are another beneficial referral source. Depending on the stage of the AIDS illness, a referral to hospice may be necessary.

Substance-Related Referrals. Clients who are substance abusers may be referred for individual therapy, to support groups, such as Alcoholics Anonymous (AA) and Narcotics Anonymous (NA), and to other substance abuse programs. If a client is abusing drugs at the time of the interview, hospitalization for detoxification may be needed prior to treatment. Hospitalization would also be necessary if the client becomes suicidal and/or severely depressed.

Referrals Involving Cognitive Impairment. When clients complain about loss of a cognitive ability (such as intelligence or memory) or of deterioration in prior ability, then a referral would be made to a neuropsychologist or neurologist. A medical evaluation should be considered when there is a question about a possible disease process or where there is a question about medication. Causes of cognitive impairment include tumor, head injury, infection, ingestion of toxic substances, hypertension, stroke, epilepsy, and vitamin deficiency.

Some clients may be referred for an evaluation of competence. Competency may be decided following an interview and the administration of selected psychological tests. Competence assessment may be necessary for court proceedings or to assess clients' ability to care for themselves. This type of evaluation would be conducted by a forensic psychologist. Typically, referrals for competency assessment are requested by lawyers, physicians, client's relatives, or community workers.

Referrals and the Law: Mandated Referrals. In certain situations, the person seeking treatment is there involuntarily at the request of others (e.g., a judge, lawyer, probation officer, or child protection agency). These cases are difficult because clients may be uncooperative and resistant to treatment. When treating these clients it is important to be aware of the effect that the referral agency (i.e., court) has on the treatment. Therefore, educating the referring source on the structure of therapy, therapeutic expectations, and on the process of rehabilitation is essential. One of the most difficult aspects of mandated referrals is preventing the referral source from interfering with the treatment process. Successful therapy with mandated referrals requires an active rather than passive therapy style.

SUMMARY

The primary purpose for making a referral is to help the client receive the best assessment and find the most beneficial treatment possible for the client's presenting problem. The referring professional must rapidly assess the complexity of a client's problem, integrate the salient details of the intake evaluation, and refer the client to the most qualified professional. Knowing when to refer a client to another professional is a skill based on the intake worker's experience and training in the identification and classification of psychological disorders. Knowing how to refer requires an understanding of the specific types of intervention that would be most appropriate for the identified problem and the procedure or format for referral that is customary in the local region. Knowing which site or professional to chose is based on information about availability, cost, and quality of care provided by clinical sites and professionals who use those types of intervention.

However, all three aspects of the referral process—knowing when, to whom, and how to refer—need to be carried out in a synchronous fashion, because the skill with which each aspect is carried out may depend on expertise in all three components. The quality care given by psychodiagnostic and treatment professionals determines, to a great extent, the outcome of a psychological disorder. But, the first step is always to refer clients to the appropriate source for intervention. In this respect, the referring professional starts clients on the road to recovery.

SELECTED READINGS

Anastasato, J., & Zito, P. (Eds.). (1996) *Connections: A guide to mental health and support services of Broward County.* Lauderhill, FL: Mental Health Association of Broward County, Inc.

Council for the National Register of Health Service Providers in Psychology (1994). *National register of health service providers in psychology* (12th ed.). Washington, DC: Council for the National Register of Health Service Providers in Psychology.

Department of Health and Rehabilitative Services. (1988) *Comprehensive directory of state-supported alcohol, drug abuse and mental health community services.* Tallahassee, FL: State of Florida.

Folstein, M. F., Folstein, S. E., & McHugh, P. R. (1975). Mini-mental state. *Journal of Psychiatric Research, 12,* 189–198.

Jenkins, S. C., Gibbs, T. P., & Szymanski, S. R. (1990). *A pocket reference for psychiatrists.* Washington, DC: American Psychiatric Press.

APPENDIX I:
SAMPLE INTAKE EVALUATION

Name: Linda Morano   *Examiner:* Sam Johnson, Ph.D.
Age: 27   *DOB:* 08/12/65   *Sex:* Female
Date of Examination: 06/10/95   *Level of Education:* Some College
Marital Status: Married   *Employment Status:* Unemployed

Presenting Problem:

Client is a 28-year-old, White, married female who comes to the Community
Mental Health Clinic with complaints of hearing voices, thought broadcasting, and feeling that others are controlling and following her. She has been
experiencing these symptoms every day for the past 6 months. During this
period of time, she has exhibited violent behavior toward her husband and
has had suicidal ideation. She also states that she feels depressed, and is
experiencing early morning awakening, a poor appetite, anhedonia, and
problems with memory and concentration.

History of Current Illness:

Mrs. Morano first began hearing voices and feeling that others were following her and controlling her mind in February 1993 while working as
a stenographer. She felt that someone from the courthouse was responsible
for putting thoughts into her mind and wanting to hurt her. She went to
see a psychiatrist, Dr. Gonzalez, who prescribed Risperdol (2 mg. bid).
Mrs. Morano stated that she did not take her medication as prescribed
because she was "uncomfortable about putting chemicals into her body."
However, she admits to taking 3 pills and stated that her symptoms subsided after 1 month.
    These symptoms returned in February 1995, but although she stated that
this time her symptoms were more severe, she was unable to take any
medication due to being in her third month of pregnancy. She reported that
since February 1995 she has been hearing voices that criticize her behavior
and lecture her, receiving messages that are being transmitted through the
television and radio into her mind, having "strange dreams," and feeling
that people know private things about her life and are doing things purposely
against her. In addition, she stated that she has been having difficulty with
her memory and concentration and has been feeling depressed. She has made
two suicidal gestures, one 4 months ago and one 2 months ago. Her first
suicidal gesture consisted of taking between 3 and 8 Tylenol pills; the second
gesture was putting a knife to her wrists, threatening that she was going to

cut herself. She has also attempted to stab her husband on two separate occasions 4 months ago with a knife because he would not listen to her.

Other Relevant History:

Mrs. Morano states that her parents live in the nearby area and she has contact with them daily. Although she states that she has a close relationship with her parents, she describes them as being very controlling and overprotective. She reported that as a child she wanted to spend time with friends and have a part-time job but her parents forbade her, preferring that she stay home. Mrs. Morano stated that she thinks her parents kept her in a "bubble" because their first daughter died at age 15 years, prior to her own birth. Client's mother became pregnant with the client at age 40.

As a child, Mrs. Morano recalls having difficulty leaving home to begin school, and although she never enjoyed school, she became an A student. However, when she entered the ninth grade, she had to change schools and became very rebellious. She began to receive mostly Bs on her report card and this angered her parents, so they would punish her for her failure by grounding her. Mrs. Morano completed high school and then attended a community college for 5 years. She was two courses short of completing her associate's degree.

Mrs. Morano first married at age 18, stating that she just wanted to get out of her home to attain some freedom. However, after 1½ months of marriage, she divorced this man because she was uncomfortable with the living accommodations that he provided and felt they did not have much in common due to their age difference (i.e., he was 18 years older). After her divorce, she returned to her parents' house to live. At age 21, she married a second time. She stated that due to differences in their religious beliefs, she divorced this man after 3 months. Mrs. Morano married for the third time in January 1992 and has been married for over 3 years. She and her husband have 2 children, a 3-year-old son, and a 10-day-old daughter. Mrs. Morano expressed that she and her husband argue often, but she wants to try to improve their relationship.

Mrs. Morano's husband is from South America and came to the United States 5 years ago. He is working three jobs in order to support the family and is employed as a mechanic and a gas station attendant. He has joined the U.S. Army and will be leaving in July for basic training. He will be away for at least 1 year.

Mrs. Morano does not socialize much with members outside of her family. She states that she attended church regularly in the past and had several friends at church but she is feeling angry with them and, therefore, has stopped attending. She had one close friend but has been suspicious of her and feels this woman may be responsible for trying to control her mind.

Mrs. Morano used to socialize with her brother, age 45, and his wife but because he works for the U.S. government she is also suspicious of him.

Client has worked several jobs as a stenographer. She reported that she does not stay very long at one job (i.e., a few months) due to problems getting along with the other employees. In the past, when she was employed, she worked part-time. The last time she worked was in August 1993. One job that she stated she did enjoy was when she was 17 years old and worked full-time in a Christian bookstore.

Mrs. Morano stated that she is in good medical health. She delivered a baby girl 10 days ago and both are doing well. Two years ago, Mrs. Morano was in a car accident and was hospitalized for 1 week with a collapsed lung and a punctured liver. She denies any problems at this time. She denies using drugs or alcohol.

Mental Status Examination and Client Strengths:

Mrs. Morano arrived to the session neatly groomed and dressed. She appeared to be her stated age. She was guarded and seemed uncomfortable; therefore, rapport was difficult to establish. Eye contact was good. Client was alert and oriented to all three spheres. Speech was soft but coherent. Gait and psychomotor speed were slow and posture was stiff. Memory and concentration were fair. She appeared to be of at least average intelligence. Thinking was obsessive. Affect was appropriate to content and mood was depressed. Suicidal and homicidal ideation were denied at present but she reported having suicidal ideation and gestures in the past. She also has had homicidal ideation in the past toward her husband. She admits to auditory hallucinations and paranoid delusions. Insight and judgment were poor. Client's strengths include her intelligence, verbal ability, and good hygiene and self-care.

Clinical Formulation:

Client's constant overprotection by her parents and their desire to control all aspects of her life have resulted in Mrs. Morano feeling angry and depressed. She has difficulty coping with these emotions and will turn to fantasy to escape. Her auditory hallucinations are critical and demanding due to her negative self-concept, feelings of worthlessness, and guilt for attempting to separate from her parents. Because she was overprotected, she has not developed appropriate coping skills to deal with stressful situations. In addition, her feelings of vulnerability and fear of rejection seem to have contributed to the development of her symptoms.

Diagnostic Impressions:

AXIS I   295.40 Schizophreniform Disorder
AXIS II   R/O Dependency Personality Disorder
AXIS III   None
AXIS IV   Psychosocial and Environmental Problems: birth of a baby, husband joining the army, unemployment, inadequate finances
AXIS V   Global Assessment of Functioning:
       Current: 25
       Highest Level in the Past Year: 60

Tentative Treatment Goals and Strategies:

Individual therapy is recommended twice per week with Dr. Johnson as her therapist. Goals include eliminating hallucinations and delusions, improving her interpersonal relationships, increasing her level of independence, and decreasing her level of depression. Therapy will be used to attain these goals by focusing on her affect and exploring her relationship with her parents and significant others. Mrs. Morano will also be referred for a psychiatric evaluation.

Signature (Name, Degree, & Title)

**APPENDIX II:
SAMPLE REFERRAL LETTER AND
SAMPLE LETTER OF REFERRAL RESPONSE**

June 10, 1995

Dear Dr. Smith:

I would like to refer one of my clients, Linda Morano, to you for a psychiatric evaluation. She is a 27-year-old, White, married female who has been complaining of hearing voices, thought broadcasting, paranoia, and depression. She has been experiencing these symptoms for the past 6 months. She has never been hospitalized but has been previously treated with Risperdal in February 1994 for similar symptoms. During her present episode she was unable to take medications due to her pregnancy, but she delivered 2 months ago.

Sincerely,
Sally Johnson, Ph.D.

The Response Letter:

June 17, 1995

Dear Dr. Johnson:

Thank you for the referral. I saw Linda Morano on June 16th for a psychiatric evaluation and she will continue treatment with me. I gave her a prescription for Risperdal 2mg. tid. She is scheduled to see me again in 2 weeks.

APPENDIX III:
VIGNETTE OF A SUICIDAL ADOLESCENT

A 15-year-old, Hispanic female who was in county custody came to the clinic with her county case worker. On entering the clinic, the county case worker informed the therapist that the client expressed suicidal ideation. Because this client was new to the clinic, consent forms needed to be completed prior to the session. At this time, it was realized that the county worker forgot to bring the information that indicated custody. According to Florida state law, consent from the parent (i.e., person in custody) must be attained prior to engaging in therapy with a minor. So, what does one do when appropriate paperwork is not complete and a crisis situation exists? Well, Florida state law allows therapists to conduct a maximum of two sessions with a minor, without consent, if a crisis exists.

During the session, the client stated that she was thinking about killing herself because nothing in her life was going right and she could see no way out. She stated that she had attempted suicide 2 years earlier by taking 3 to 4 aspirins. She did not have a plan and stated that even if she wanted to kill herself her foster mother or boyfriend were always with her. Religion and her relationship with her boyfriend were used as ways to deter her from killing herself. After careful assessment, it was decided that it was not necessary to hospitalize her. Her foster mother was telephoned and told that her daughter must be supervised at all times. The client was given a contract to sign stating that she agreed to return for the next session. The client returned for the next session and continued in therapy to work on her depression and anger.

13

Identifying Targets for Treatment

Warren W. Tryon
Fordham University

Psychotherapy is a process-oriented, time-unlimited relationship between therapist and client. This process emphasizes *transference*, or feelings the client has toward the therapist that stem from significant others in their life, and *countertransference*, or reciprocal feelings the client elicits in the therapist. Comments made by the client during therapy are periodically interpreted in terms of conflicts and defense mechanisms used to cope with these conflicts. Treatment targets are not explicitly defined. The client wants to feel better and the therapist wants the client to improve. This mutual understanding is generally not further refined. If pressed, therapists may indicate that their goal is personality reconstruction. What constitutes such a reformation remains unspecified. Other therapists specify shoring up psychological defenses but little further specification is given. Many therapists resist specifying particular treatment targets on the basis that this equates therapeutic success with symptom reduction, which is not necessarily a good thing. There is some concern over symptom substitution—meaning that if particular improvements were engineered in one area of a client's life, then new problems would emerge in other areas because basic underlying problems have not been resolved. These problems can be stated theoretically but are not easily defined in terms of specific treatment targets. Other therapists resist focusing on specific treatment targets on the basis that the client may take a "flight into health" as a defensive maneuver to terminate therapist inquiry into conflictual material. Again, therapeutic objectives are framed in more general theoretical, rather than specific practical, terms.

Behavioral therapists introduced the idea of treatment targets after identifying particular changes that were planned to occur as a result of specific interventions. Therapeutic intervention to achieve these results also became specific to the point that much of it could be reported in the methods section of a research report. Recent changes in mental health service delivery reinforce the desirability of and need for specific treatment targets in addition to empirically validated treatments for achieving these specific objectives. Consequently, therapists of different theoretical persuasions are now much more sympathetic to the idea of identifying specific treatment targets and evaluating treatment in terms of goal attainment. This chapter hopes to facilitate identification of specific treatment goals.

Therapists cannot treat clients who do not make or keep subsequent appointments. In other words, the therapist's first goal is to keep clients coming in long enough to implement assessment and intervention. The discussion begins with the initial session, clients' motivation for therapy, and the importance of engaging clients to the point where they will return for subsequent sessions. The focus is on the initial dropout problem and what can be done to engage clients to remain in therapy. An important part of the engagement process is rapid identification and specification of treatment targets (perhaps as early as the end of the first session and preferably by the end of the third session).

Clients should participate fully in the treatment process. Some clients have clear treatment goals and even distinct preferences for a certain type of treatment. Other clients have clear treatment goals but are open to various treatment methods. Still other clients are unclear about what they want from therapy but are more certain about the type of therapy they feel they need. These clients often have a preference for psychodynamic approaches. Finally, there are clients who are unclear about treatment goals and who have no firm views or expectations as to the type of treatment.

Therapists should be alert to and accepting of the possibility of clients changing their treatment targets. Clients may choose the initial treatment target to evaluate how the therapist behaves in session rather than because it is an important, personally relevant topic. These clients focus on new treatment targets in subsequent sessions without explanation, trusting that the therapist will follow their lead. A fraction of this group becomes problematic when clients either continue to change treatment targets or develop a long list of targets with similar priority.

Couple- and family-identified treatment targets are an extension of client-identified treatment targets. The main thing to remember is that all participants should share equally in identifying and selecting treatment targets so that they also share a commitment to reach these objectives. Therapist-identified treatment targets are discussed as a last resort. Even in these cases a consulting role is emphasized, whereby the therapist suggests rather than dictates targets and then engages discussion prior to selecting and committing to these ends. Specific treatment targets should be outlined with sufficient clarity to meet the need for fully informed consent.

The issue of modification versus cure is discussed and is found to depend on therapeutic orientation. Sometimes treatment targets involve new behaviors that clients must continue to perform to maintain the desired effects. Relationship problems are a good example because they can be modified but not cured. There will never come a time when a relationship will remain rewarding without cultivation by both parties.

THE INITIAL SESSION

People who seek professional assistance for psychological and/or behavioral problems often have a lengthy history of attempting to cope with their problem on their own or with the aid of family and friends. Their partial, or lack of, success allows matters to continue to worsen until they precipitate or a crisis develops that drives them to seek professional assistance. The cost, inconvenience, and admission to themselves and others (usually family members) that help is needed usually delays the decision to seek professional help. It becomes a last resort. In short, clients often enter therapy in mild to severe crisis. For many clients, this time of crisis provides the greatest motivation for change. Because they will work hard for change, it is also the time of greatest opportunity for the therapist to effectively intervene.

Therapists should capitalize on this heightened client motivation to focus on treatment targets and begin treatment. It would not be wise to conduct one or more intake interviews followed by a team meeting the following week (to discuss case assignment) followed by one or more history-taking sessions in the next couple of weekly sessions. Such a leisurely approach assumes that the client's motivation for therapy is both constant and enduring. Although this may be the case with a few clients, most—especially most lower SES and minority clients—are unlikely to meet these expectations. A leisurely intake process is also costly and increasingly cannot be justified in today's managed-care mental health market.

People believe and behave as they do largely based on their prior experience. When plans work out, people are encouraged and are more hopeful and confident that they will be able to control their future. This promotes a positive self-concept and good psychological adjustment. When repeated efforts have failed or fallen seriously below expectations, people often become discouraged, lose confidence, and may even become depressed and/or anxious over a future they perceive to be both troublesome and out of control.

Confidence is a key element of successful therapy. Clients with confidence in the therapist are more apt to believe and carry out difficult therapeutic suggestions that call for new and unfamiliar behaviors, for confronting unpleasant issues, or for tolerating unpleasant emotions. A positive referral may help institute this confidence. A therapist who handles the initial session in an empathetic, understanding, and confident manner preserves, and hopefully augments, this confidence. However, the most compelling evidence for the clients are the consequences of therapeutic recommendations. It is therefore paramount to select a treatment target and begin a course of treatment designed to maximize positive outcomes in the first session, if at all possible. A comprehensive list of treatment targets is not necessary during the first session. But, identifying an initial treatment goal with enthusiastic endorsement from the client is the most important (i.e., best) place to start.

Therapists who delay in identifying one or more treatment targets run the risk that clients will become frustrated and drop out. On the other hand, jumping too quickly toward a treatment target is also unwise because it may misdirect treatment, undermine the client's confidence, and precipitate termination. These factors must be balanced in every clinical situation. Treatment can almost always begin somewhere during the first three sessions. If a single treatment target cannot be identified by the end of the first session, it would be appropriate to say something like: "I have learned a lot about you today but need to know more before I formulate a treatment plan. This may take one or two more sessions but by then I should be able to tell you how treatment will proceed." Clients are reassured by the three-session assessment limit. It is a reasonable compromise between their motivation to finally do something and the therapist's need to understand the complexity of the clinical situation before acting.

It is advisable to have the same therapist handle both intake and treatment. Going through an intake interview with one clinician and beginning treatment with another is unnecessarily frustrating to the client and may erode a client's patience with therapy. Important personal information can be obtained by having the client fill out a personal data sheet on the day of first visit or prior to the time of the initial appointment. If necessary, the client can stay after the first appointment to complete a form. Computer-administered structured interviews for *Diagnostic and Statistical Manual* (*DSM*) diagnostic purposes, as well as objective personality tests and other measures (such as Continuous Performance Tests to evaluate attention deficits) are also currently available. As mentioned earlier, it is unfortunate when record keeping and routine history taking dominate or fully occupy the first session (or worse, first couple of sessions). Extensive historical data are often unnecessary at the beginning of treatment and often can be explored as the need arises. Deferring as much routine information gathering as feasible reinforces the importance of time spent with the therapist. Having therapists perform what clients often perceive as routine clerical tasks delays and dilutes clients' primary motivations for seeking treatment—to finally do something about their problem.

CLIENT-IDENTIFIED TREATMENT TARGETS

There is much current discussion about cultural sensitivity. There is concern that therapists may misunderstand and therefore misdiagnose what are normal practices in other cultures as signs of mental disease. Imposing alien and unwanted values on clients in the name of psychotherapy may augment problems clients have in their relationships with their spouse, parents, and other family members. Most of these problems can be avoided through active client participation in target identification and by seeking information from them about how their culture views various behaviors.

According to Carl Rogers (1992), therapists should always practice a good "bedside manner" while interviewing. First, they should pay close attention to clients when they speak so that it is obvious that clients have their undivided attention. Eye contact should be made as often as the client will permit. Therapists should nod frequently to indicate that they follow what is being said. They should also restate what is said so that clients know that they really do understand. Something like the following is appropriate:

"Correct me if I am wrong, but I understand you to say that _____."

"Does this mean that you feel like _____?"

"Are you saying that you want _____?"

The first statement expressly invites clients to correct thoughts, feelings, and behaviors that therapists attribute to them and/or to others. Such language makes the therapist the student and the client the teacher. Not only does this relationship facilitate client expression, but it also empowers clients with an authority that will subsequently help them to complete therapeutic requests and homework.

The second two comments are in question form. It is always best to use the question form because questions imply information seeking and invite new corrective information. A therapist's declarative statements can appear to be closed, authoritative interpretations that leave the client only two possibilities: accept or resist. Resistance is often the more frequent choice, especially when the content is sexual or aggressive. This transforms the interview from a cooperative information-seeking enterprise into an unproductive competitive debate.

Client Presentation

Clients should be encouraged to present their point of view right from the beginning. A good way to begin would be to ask clients to begin talking in one of the following ways: "What brings you here?", or "What seems to be the matter?" This short invitation to speak serves at least two important functions. First, it gives clients a chance to express or vent feelings and to present whatever ideas they have prepared. Some have much to say; others have very little. Clients may be very emotional during their presentation or calm and detached. Their remarks may seem measured or quite extreme. Presence of a thought disorder, pressured speech, and other manifestations of serious clinical disorder can be revealed. The way the client organizes the presentation of the complaint is informative. Often, the very first statement of the problem is the most revealing. Subsequent clarification can obscure as much as enlighten.

It is important to accept clients' perspective and work with them using this formulation as a starting point. If the therapist-identified treatment target differs from the client-identified treatment target, then therapists should by all means begin treatment using the client's agenda. This increases cooperation and avoids resistance, which is almost always a sign of therapy gone wrong (a breach in the client–therapist relationship, working alliance).

Clients can and do change treatment targets. This sometimes occurs as early as the second session. This may mean clients do not feel sufficiently at ease to fully reveal their problem and desires for treatment at the beginning of therapy. Psychological and behavioral problems are private and personal. People are often reluctant to fully share these feelings and attitudes. Consequently, they sometimes introduce a "sample" problem to test the therapist's response to determine if they really want to open up to this person. Clients do not announce the end of a trial period and the beginning of the real agenda. This would be embarrassing and the transition may be somewhat unclear to them as well. Put otherwise, clients are not always honest with themselves about the reasons for seeking treatment and are therefore not always able to inform the therapist about why they are there or what they want out of treatment.

Changes in client priorities are most obvious at the start of each session. Observe whether clients continue where they left off with last week's theme or whether they begin with an entirely new theme. Let the client structure up to the first half of the session. Treat the second session as if it were a new first session. However, if new content has been introduced, then the therapist can bring this to the client's attention to seek advice about how to best interpret these events. Consider a female client who talks about agoraphobia during her first session and about her relationship with her husband during the second session: "Today I heard you talk about the problems you have been having with your husband and their effect on your marriage. Last week you mainly talked about the anxiety you feel while walking and driving. We can work on one or the other or both of these problems depending upon where you would like to start." The client may select the relationship problem and continue with it consistently across subsequent therapy sessions, which boosts confidence that this is the "core issue." Or, the client may explain that her relationship with her husband exacerbates her agoraphobia. For example, "I find that I am much more anxious about leaving the house after my husband and I have an argument. I see our relationship as part of my anxiety problem."

Cultural Values and Priorities

All clients should be given the opportunity to disclose their values and priorities before selecting treatment targets. This is especially true for clients of a different cultural background, sexual preference, religious heritage, or other important demographic variable. Some cultures emphasize obligation to family and community over personal well-being. Treatment targets designed to enhance self-esteem through assertiveness training may not be in the clients' best long-term interest because movement toward such goals may set the occasion for argument and bad feelings among family members. If, however, the client wishes to break with family traditions and fully understands the consequences of making self-esteem and assertiveness treatment goals, then therapists must be certain that this is the client's choice and not what they have chosen for the client.

Similar issues arise with regard to treatment targets for gay and lesbian clients. Their goal may be to preserve and enhance their relationship with their companions and to feel better about their lifestyle. Religious convictions may also influence treatment targets.

Therapists may not always condone or be comfortable with client-formulated treatment targets. For example, many therapists would have a problem with finding new and better ways to subjugate women and children to male advantage. Others may not be able to assist gay and lesbian couples in good faith. In these instances, referral to another therapist is the best option.

Client Selection

All treatment decisions should be made by clients because they must live with the consequences of what is and is not done. Therapists should maintain the position of consultant and/or coach, pointing out the advantages and disadvantages of various treatment goals and methods for attaining them.

Clients who actively participate in selecting treatment targets and treatment options are more likely to comply with therapeutic recommendations. Clients need to feel that intermediate treatment goals are their own personal goals. They must feel confident that they can correctly perform any assigned homework and that such efforts are meaningful and reasonable therapeutic efforts.

After about 40% of the first session has passed (usually 20 minutes), therapists should focus the client on treatment targets by asking something like, "If I had a magic wand and could grant you three wishes regarding treatment outcome, what would they be?" Clients differ in the focus and practicality of their answers. Sometimes clients also know what type of therapy they want. Perhaps they have read about recent successes of one approach or another and believe they can benefit from its use. Their conviction that this approach will be helpful is a valuable source of motivation that an appropriately trained therapist should preserve and work with. A referral is in order if the therapist is not well qualified to use the chosen approach. Clients will likely resist trying something else and their motivation to pursue alternative courses of action would probably not be as strong.

Still other clients come in because it is required. For example, the court may require that a person seek counseling. Although therapeutic goals may be identified, do not presume positive motivation for realizing them. The motivation is probably to avoid further court-imposed sanctions or to limit the duration of existing sanctions (i.e., the time until they may visit their child or the time until they can regain custody). Their therapeutic goal is to lay low, make nice, and get a good recommendation. In other cases, spouses may require their mate to participate in therapy prior to consenting to divorce. In the latter case, the man usually accompanies his wife to placate her rather than to work on their relationship. Effective treatment goals usually cannot be identified in these cases.

The therapist's objective is to help clients express each of their treatment targets in behavioral terms. If clients say they want to be less afraid, then therapists should ask them what new behaviors they want to engage in that they presently do not practice. If they wish to have an improved relationship with someone, then therapists should ask how this person now treats them and how that differs with desired reality. If clients choose greater self-confidence, then ask what new behaviors they see themselves doing or how their present behavior changes if their wish comes true. When clients claim that they are uncertain of how their wishes translate into new behavior by themselves and others, therapists should work with them and offer hypothetical possibilities stimulating the clients' thoughts on these matters. For example, therapists could raise the issue of assertion by suggesting a particular instance of assertive behavior, such as: "Would you be more likely to ask for a raise?," or "Would you be more likely to say I don't like Chinese food, could we go to an Italian restaurant?"

Clients seeking professional assistance with psychological and/or behavioral problems may or may not have a clear idea of their treatment goals prior to the first visit. The decision to consult a psychologist is often precipitated by a crisis resulting in an intolerable situation. The primary motivation for seeking professional help is relief from the precipitating crisis.

Hence, the client's initial presentation is likely to be dominated by strong affect and a concern with whether the therapist can really help.

It is important to give clients maximum freedom in presenting complaints because the choice of what to talk about first and how to describe the issues reveals their perspective. For example, clients who primarily describe their feelings and the feelings of others are construing the problem at hand as mainly one of affect. Clients who primarily describe the behavior of other people as the problem are framing the problem in terms of controlling other people. Some clients identify the problem in terms of something wrong with themselves, whereas others identify the problem in terms of what is wrong with other people and how poorly they have been treated. In short, therapists must begin where clients are, and this requires understanding the initial perspective regarding the problem for which they are seeking help.

If clients cannot formulate a treatment target because they lack sufficient self-information, then it is advisable to assign self-observation homework and discuss the results during the next session. Clients can keep a diary based on either critical incident recording or time sampling. In *critical incident recording*, clients wait for a target event to occur and then record certain information about it. The event may be a thought, feeling, or behavior, or something another person said or did to them. Notes about the circumstances that preceded the target event and the consequences that followed should be recorded. The *time sampling procedure* requires that clients ask themselves a list of questions, say, every hour. These questions might include, How do I feel right now? or Am I depressed, anxious, insecure? These self-observation episodes disrupt ongoing behavior for the purpose of examining what is going on at that moment.

COUPLE-IDENTIFIED TREATMENT TARGETS

Couples therapy means two clients with equal influence in establishing treatment targets. Unequal roles and communication problems can lead to situations where one member of the couple, often the man, is inclined to exert more than half interest in establishing treatment targets. Or, the man may completely withdraw during the session leaving the entire question of treatment target selection to the woman. This sets the occasion for him to complain about the appropriateness of treatment target selection when his noncompliance brings little change. Therefore, it is paramount to insure that all treatment targets are endorsed by both persons after mutual discussion.

Sometimes couples are much more clear about the negative feelings they have for each other than they are about the behavioral bases for these emotions. Obtaining a naturalistic behavioral sample using unobtrusive home tape recordings by mutual consent is often very useful. This can be done by purchasing an omnidirectional microphone and plugging it into a portable tape recorder. The microphone is placed in a central location, such as where meals are taken or where conversations occur most frequently. A 120-minute tape is used and the tape recorder is allowed to play until either the tape reaches its end and needs to be turned over or an event is captured. This procedure is continued until at least one event illustrative of the referral problem is recorded. A new tape is inserted after the first event is recorded to prevent taping over this information.

The tape recorded event can be thought of as containing three parts: events leading up to the event, the event itself, and resolution of the event. Home tape recordings allow therapists to go back in time and review who said what leading up to the incident in question. The results of this review may have direct bearing on treatment target selection. If Party A is found to say things that increase the probability that Party B will get angry, then treatment should target A's behavior in addition to B's behavior. How the couple resolves unpleasant events is also important, partly because what is said and done at this time is an antecedent to the onset of the next event and may constitute a setting event for the next occurrence of the referral complaint.

The tapes can be put to at least three clinical uses. First, by listening to their own tapes a day or two after the incident when feelings have subsided, couples can better "observe" themselves because they are in a listening rather than behaving mode. Couples can often better understand each other when reviewing an objective record of prior events, because the tape focuses conversation on who said what to whom rather than on allegations of who said what to whom. Memory is a subjective and reconstructive process that is not especially accurate when dealing with emotionally charged and personally sensitive material. The taped record is readily accepted as evidence of what happened. Couples can be encouraged to select treatment targets on the basis of their review of one or more taped incidents.

Second, these tapes can be mailed to therapists, who can listen and form their own impressions about what treatment targets are appropriate. Clinicians can discern important reciprocal influences that clients may think are relatively unimportant and therefore not otherwise report during sessions. It also allows the therapist to better evaluate how much distortion of events is created by each party.

Third, the couple and the therapist can jointly listen to these tapes during their session. This can be done before or after the couple and the therapist have separately reviewed the tape. In both cases, the therapist should elicit both parties' perspectives on the taped interactions and what treatment targets seem most worthwhile.

Courtship involves clients being attentive to the needs and interests of their partner, doing things of mutual interest, and sometimes doing things for their partner just because they know it will be appreciated. These behaviors of monitoring what the other person wants and providing rich schedules of positive reinforcement for a wide variety of actions can, and often do, diminish over time. Couples in distress are often characterized by low levels of these behaviors, which result in one of several consequences. Some couples drift apart and assume separate lives. Other couples become openly critical of actions and events they once either approved of or condoned. In both cases, a lack of control develops where the desires of one person no longer serve to reinforce the behavior of the other. In this case, the general treatment target is to reinstate control. Behavioral contracting is an excellent method for reestablishing mutual influence, but it requires selecting specific treatment targets— particular behaviors that each will carry out for the other. The choice of these specific treatment targets should emerge from joint discussion and not be imposed by one or the other member of the couple or by the therapist.

FAMILY-IDENTIFIED TREATMENT TARGETS

Families entail three or more clients, all of whom should participate in selecting treatment targets. Because family members have their own unique perspective about events, the possibility of many conflicting accounts of events increases rapidly with family size. Home tape recording can be especially informative under these conditions. It is important to obtain informed consent of all family members to tape conversations at communal times (e.g., meals).

Home tape recordings facilitate treatment target selection in three ways. Family members can listen to themselves several days after the event to better appreciate how they behave toward each other. Second, therapists can listen to these tapes to form their own opinion about treatment targets based on primary evidence rather than on multiple self-reports. Third, the family and therapist can jointly listen to these tapes in session and discuss treatment targets.

Families are extensions of couples when it comes to reciprocal influence, except that the possible combinations of reciprocal influence increase rapidly with family size. Behavioral contracting is a good method of reestablishing reciprocal influence that requires all family members to participate in selection of specific treatment targets.

THERAPIST-IDENTIFIED TREATMENT TARGETS

Not all clients, couples, and families can clearly articulate their responses for seeking professional assistance. Some people know that they feel poorly and are dissatisfied with their lives but have only a vague or no idea about why they feel the way they do. Hence, they rely on the therapist to select treatment targets. This inclination to look to the professional is understandable given the experience most people have with physicians, who diagnose the disorder and select the treatment targets. Therapists may suggest treatment targets for discussion but should not unilaterally select treatment targets, because such actions can set the occasion for subsequent resistance to and noncompliance with therapeutic recommendations. Clients should always fully participate in selecting and actively endorse treatment targets, because they have to live with the consequences of therapy.

The ultimate treatment goal is usually to remediate the problem that brought the client to therapy. This goal can be approached in at least two ways. The first approach is based on a causal understanding of the etiology of the client's problem. Treatment goals are then defined in these terms. Psychoanalytic theorists emphasize early emotional experience and the formation of psychological defenses. Hence, treatment goals entail formation of a transference neurosis and working through resistance to more appropriate and less destructive psychological defenses. This can include recollection of early memories and interpreting them so that they fit into a more benign and satisfactory life view. Cognitive therapists implicate illogical self-statements, such as those that use the word "must": "I must be loved" or "I must get this job." Treatment goals from this perspective entail more adaptive self-statements and more logical thinking. Behavioral therapists emphasize interpersonal interactions and reinforcement contingencies; they are concerned with the consequences of actions, including the consequences of inaction. Treatment goals are often expressed in terms of changing the consequences associated with the behavior of self and others. Behavioral contracts may be used to structure these changes, thereby reducing conflict and renormalizing relationships. Psychopharmacologists construe the client's problems in terms of neurotransmitter excesses or deficiencies and therefore identify a medication regimen as the treatment target. This global approach to identifying treatment targets focuses the discussion on the field of abnormal psychology with the requirement of choosing one or another etiology. Interviewing recommendations follow accordingly. Therapists interview to identify what theory considers to be etiologically pertinent information; treatment goals are framed within the context of that assessment. Entire books have been written from this perspective and their content cannot be summarized here.

The etiological orientation to identifying treatment targets leads to classifying some approaches as symptomatic and others as curative. It has often been alleged that behavioral treatment goals are *symptomatic* because they do not address underlying causal issues. This view assumes that etiology of the client's disorder is as psychoanalytic theorists hypothesize. If the cause of a client's depression is actually due to helplessness at work or in important relationships, meaning that the behavioral etiology is correct, then psychoanalytic treatment goals would be "symptom" oriented and behavioral treatment would be *curative*. In short, treatment goals that correctly reflect actual etiology address the underlying causes and treatment goals based on all other theoretical positions constitute symptomatic approaches. Because there is no way to know for certain what the etiology of any particular problem is for a specific person, there is no way to determine which treatment goals are curative and which are symptom oriented. But this is an unproductive way to approach the problem at hand.

The second approach is based on the assumption that the way out of a problem is not necessarily the inverse of the way into the problem. This approach maintains that it is not necessary to understand etiology in order to remediate a problem. For example, if lost in a forest, there are more ways back to civilization than by retracing one's steps into the woods. Genetic and developmental factors may have created disabilities that can be effectively treated by nongenetic and nondevelopmental methods. An example is phenylketonuria (PKU), a genetic disorder where the congenital absence of phenylalanine hydroxylase means that the individual cannot properly metabolize phenylalanine, resulting in the accumulation of toxins, resulting in neural degeneration and mental retardation. A beneficial treatment target is to restrict the diet to substances low in phenylalanine given that currently a genetic deficit cannot be normalized. Rehabilitation psychologists also reflect this perspective. Their treatment goals are not to reverse the physical damage that caused the current disability. Rather, the emphasis is on maximizing existing abilities. Haynes and O'Brien (1990) argued for selecting as targets those behaviors that are likely to make the greatest improvement in the client's problem.

SPECIFICITY

Varying opinion exists about degree of specificity required when identifying targets for treatment. Some professionals are content with diffuse global generic conceptions of treatment targets, whereas others may formalize treatment targets in terms of a written statement, or contract, signed by both parties. The principle of fully informed consent requires reasonable specificity before clients can be expected to understand what they are consenting to. It is recommended that therapists be as descriptive and concise as possible about treatment goals to minimize misunderstanding.

ENGAGEMENT

All therapists must engage clients in the therapeutic process. Because therapists cannot help people who do not attend therapy sessions, engagement is the first treatment target. The only exception to this rule is where psychological tests are interpreted or a referral is made. It is naive to believe that all, or even most, clients are motivated to maintain long-term therapeutic relationships. Approximately half do not return for a second therapy session. Approximately half of those returning for a second therapy session do not return for a third. Hence, only about one quarter of clients, on average, return for a third session. Further attrition at a reduced rate can be expected. This phenomenon has traditionally been interpreted as *early premature termination*. However, I have observed that individuals cannot terminate what never began in the first place (Tryon, 1990). I reinterpreted this issue in terms of *engagement* and indicated that it is the therapist's responsibility to engage the client. I calculated an engagement quotient (EQ) by dividing the number of clients coming back for a second session by the total number of clients seen for a first session. Student trainees in a college counseling center taking referrals on the basis of mutual free time without prescreening by a professional averaged approximately 43% versus an average 60% EQ for the professional staff. One might recalculate EQ on the basis of clients coming for a fourth session meaning that they have passed the critical three-session point.

Dealing with problems of immediate concern to the clients, communicating an understanding of the client's perspective about the problem, and educating clients about their problems and treatment possibilities for their amelioration facilitate engagement. In addition, being able to identify the third session as the point where assessment will be sufficient to establish a treatment plan provides clients with an initial "package" they can accept (i.e., an initial agreement regarding their participation). Depending on the initial treatment plan, therapists need to be able to communicate its possible therapeutic benefits without making unwarranted promises that, in addition to being unethical, may well lead to disappointment and the conviction that all therapists are a waste of time, money, and effort. However, reasonable hope must be extended to further engage the client.

Some clients are so desperate for help that they practically engage themselves and will return to see all but the most inept and offensive therapist. Some may be truly satisfied with a single crisis management session and feel no need to return for further assistance. Others may only reluctantly attend a first session and require a highly skilled therapist to engage them in a second session. Still other clients may attend sessions regularly because they are court mandated to do so but are otherwise extremely resistant. Then there are the spouses of motivated clients who attend sessions only to placate their spouse but otherwise have little or no personal motivation for therapy.

CHANGE VERSUS CURE

Experience with physicians leads clients to expect a cure, which implies that the causative agent is completely removed and the illness is terminated. With physical diseases, it is understood that reinfection can bring a return of the disease but that further treatment will result in another cure. Psychoanalytic therapies, on the other hand, offer the promise of cure by bringing unconscious drives and motives to light and under better ego regulation. Cognitive therapies offer cure in the form of altered cognitions that reform how clients process information and therefore how they think, feel, and act. Behavioral therapies are divided in terms of their orientation to cure. Systematic desensitization is based on the presumption that anxiety has not been deconditioned and, once this is accomplished, fear should not return unless reconditioning occurs. Operant therapies emphasize modification rather than cure. Behavior, both adaptive and maladaptive, is a function of its consequences. Like gardening, where one must take care to foster desired growth through proper water and fertilizer (reinforcers) and to pull the weeds that compete for these resources, therapeutic improvement will remain only so long as adaptive behaviors are reinforced at a considerably higher rate than maladaptive behaviors that hopefully are not reinforced at all. Relationships, like gardens, require continual care. Rarely will neglect have long-term positive consequences. Hence, treatment targets must incorporate an understanding of the necessary perpetual care to maintain treatment gains. The only promise of permanence is the extent to which the natural environment supports adaptive behavior. However, secondary gains for behaving sick indicate that environments do not always exclusively support rational, mature behavior. Therapeutic targets from the operant perspective should include an understanding of this reinforcement principle.

SUMMARY

All schools of psychotherapy articulate therapeutic goals in either general or specific terms. This chapter is concerned with establishing specific client-centered goals rather than with diffuse theoretical objectives such as enhancing personal integration or fostering identity. Our concern is with helping clients identify what they want from therapy so that we can better assist them in achieving these ends.

The initial session deserves special emphasis because approximately half of the clients that come for an initial appointment do not return for a second, and then approximately half of those that make and keep a second appointment fail to make and keep a third one. So, the universal first treatment target is client engagement. Rapid identification of treatment targets and initiating treatment in the first three sessions capitalizes on the heightened client motivation that usually accompanies referral. This consideration must be balanced against the possible problem of premature, incorrect, problem formulation and, therefore, misguided intervention. The therapist must not be so concerned about getting started with a treatment plan that they convey nervousness and anxiety to clients. A reasonable balance is required. One main point of this chapter is to warn against losing momentum by taking too long to identify treatment targets and initiate intervention.

Clients should be actively involved in treatment target identification to maximize their participation in and compliance with treatment recommendations because they will have to live with treatment results whether they are good or bad. Their active participation maximizes sensitivity to cultural, racial, and gender issues. When seeing couples and families, all participants should actively partake in treatment target selection for the same reasons. Should one party dominate treatment target selection, then other parties may not fully cooperate. When one person attempts to unduly influence treatment target selection the therapist should be aware that this behavior is probably part of the problem and, therefore, should respond accordingly. Therapists should not unilaterally select treatment targets.

Treatment target selection is not limited to the initial therapeutic stages but can, and frequently does, recur throughout treatment. Treatment targets may change early on as the client develops a good working alliance with the therapist and discloses more intimate concerns. Such changes should be accepted as long as the client soon focuses on one or even several targets. Treatment targets can also change after therapy has progressed and additional issues have surfaced. Sometimes initial goals turn out to be unrealistic and require modification.

Treatment targets provide a reference point for the client, therapist, and third-party payer to evaluate therapeutic effectiveness and the need for additional treatment. The former is determined by documenting progress toward the goal, whereas the latter is determined by extrapolating how much further off the goal is. Treatment targets provide a frame of reference for all concerned from intake to termination.

ACKNOWLEDGMENT

The author wishes to thank Georgiana Shick Tryon for reviewing this chapter and making helpful comments.

SUGGESTED READINGS

Barlow, D. H. (Ed.). (1993). *Clinical handbook of psychological disorders: A step-by-step treatment manual* (2nd ed.). New York: Guilford.

Comas-Diaz, L., & Griffith, E. E. H. (Eds.). (1988). *Clinical guidelines in cross cultural mental health.* New York: Wiley.

Haynes, S. N., & O'Brien, W. H. (1990). Functional analysis in behavior therapy. *Clinical Psychology Review, 10,* 649–668.

Hersen, M., & Turner, S. M. (Eds.). (1995). *Diagnostic interviewing* (2nd ed.). New York: Plenum.

Martin, G., & Pear, J. (1992). *Behavior modification: What it is and how to do it* (4th ed.). Englewood Cliffs, NJ: Prentice-Hall.

Rogers, C. R. (1992). The necessary and sufficient conditions of therapeutic personality change. *Journal of Consulting and Clinical Psychology, 60*, 827–832.

Tryon, G. S. (1985). The engagement quotient: One index of a basic counseling task. *Journal of College Student Personnel, 26*, 351–354.

Tryon, G. S. (1989). Study of variables related to client engagement using practicum trainees and experienced clinicians. *Psychotherapy, 26*, 54–61.

Tryon, G. S. (1990). Session depth and smoothness in relation to the concept of engagement in counseling. *Journal of Counseling Psychology, 37*, 248–253.

Tryon, W. W. (1996). Observing contingencies: Taxonomy and methods. *Clinical Psychology Review, 16*, 215–230.

Tryon, W. W. (in press). Behavioral observation. In M. Hersen & A. S. Bellack (Eds.), *Behavioral assessment: A practical handbook* (4th ed.). Boston: Allyn & Bacon.

Author Index

235

Subject Index

About the Editors

Michel Hersen received a doctorate in clinical psychology from the State University of New York at Buffalo and is currently Professor and Dean at the School of Professional Psychology, Pacific University. A Distinguished Practitioner in Psychology of the National Academies of Practice, he was the 14th president of the Association for the Advancement of Behavior Therapy. He is co-editor in chief of *Behavior Modification*; *Clinical Psychology Review*; the *Journal of Anxiety Disorders*; the *Journal of Developmental and Physical Disabilities*, and three other journals, as well as editor of *Progress in Behavior Modification*. He has been involved as author or editor in over 400 articles, chapters, and books, and serves as editor or co-editor of seven journals.

Vincent B. Van Hasselt received a doctorate in clinical psychology from the University of Pittsburgh and is Professor of Psychology and Director of the Interpersonal Violence Program at Nova Southeastern University. Co-editor of the *Journal of Family Violence, Aggression and Violent Behavior: A Review Journal*; and the *Journal of Child and Adolescent Substance Abuse*, he also recently co-edited the *Handbook of Family Violence*; *Behavior Therapy for Children and Adolescents: A Clinical Approach*; and the *Handbook of Psychological Approaches With Violent Offenders*. He has been involved as author or editor in over 150 articles, chapters, and books.